# TIBET

*Elisabeth Booz* was born in London in 1925 to American parents. She grew up in England and Europe and received her Master's degree in Political Economy from the University of Geneva. Her husband, Paul Booz, was a UN official and teacher, and their life together was spent largely in Asia. Elisabeth Booz's five children were each born in a different country.

She now divides her time between the United States and France, spending the winters in Washington DC, working for the National Geographic Book Division and the rest of the year as a freelance writer and illustrator on the shores of Lake Geneva. She still travels extensively. Her books for The Guidebook Company include *A Guide to Tibet* and *A Guide to New Zealand*.

# TIBET

Elisabeth B Booz

Copyright © 1997 Local Colour Ltd, Hong Kong
Maps copyright © 1997 Local Colour Ltd, Hong Kong

Distribution in the United Kingdom, Ireland and Europe by Hi Marketing Ltd, 38 Carver
Road, London SE24 9LT, U.K.
British Library Cataloguing-in-Publication Data
A catalogue record for this book is available from the British Library

Grateful acknowledgement is made to the authors and publishers for permissions granted:

B I Publications Ltd, Delhi for
*The Way of the White Clouds* by Lama Anagarika Govinda © 1960 Lama Anagarika Govinda

Peter Meixner for
*Seven Years in Tibet* by Heinrich Harrer, translation © 1953 Rupert Hart-Davis

HarperCollins Publishers for
*Danziger's Travels* by Nick Danziger © 1987 Nick Danziger

Cadogan Books for
*The Mystery Rivers of Tibet* by F Kingdon Ward © The Estate of F Kingdon Ward, first published in 1923

Lotsawa for
*Miraculous Journey—New Stories & Songs* by Milarepa © 1986 Lama Kunga and Brian Cutillo

Wisdom Publications for
*Warriors of Tibet* by Jamyang Norbu © 1986 Tibetan Information Office, Dharamsala

Wisdom Publications for
*Tibet is My Country* by Thubten Jigme Norbu & Heinrich Harrer © 1986 Thubten Jigme
Norbu & Heinrich Harrer

John Murray Publishers for
*Tibetan Venture* by André Guibaut © 1947

John Murray Publishers for
*India and Tibet* by Francis Younghusband © 1910

Revisers: Patrick Booz and Tom Le Bas
Design: De•Style Studio
Map Design: Tom Le Bas and Bai Yiliang

Photography Magnus Bartlett 8, 16, 31, 35, 42, 68–69, 72, 77, 83, 86–87, 91, 94–95, 104–105,
115, 118–119, 161, 168–169, 176–177, 180, 181, 192, 195, 199; Kate Kranzler 142; Herman
Wong 130–131, 172; Stone Routes 59, 146, 218; Jacky Yip 26–27, 46, 55, 123, 126, 158–159,
222–223; Charles Bell, by permission of the British Library 186–187; Charles Bell, Pitt Rivers
Museum, Oxford 23, 74, 150; Hugh Richardson, courtesy of the Trustees of the British Museum 18–19, 89, 108–109; Serindia Publications 5, 112; Altfield Gallery 59, 218; Patrick Booz
146; Front and back cover photographs by Tom Le Bas

Printed in Hong Kong

Front cover: Monks at Sera Monastery
Back Cover: (upper) Pilgrim, (lower) Tashilhunpo Monastery

*Medical thangka showing the Root of Physiology and Pathology and a presentation of*
*the lineage of medical teachings, from* Tibetan Medical Paintings, Serindia Publications, 1992

# Contents

·

*Monk outside Ngagpa chanting hall, Sera Monastery*

# Introduction

A first trip to Tibet is a marvellous experience. For many it comes after years of dreaming, reading and planning and the expectation is so high it can hardly be met, to the point where some people are unable to recognize real dangers, such as altitude sickness, in the midst of their rarefied hopes. Euphoria gives way grudgingly to the surrounding reality and the realization that the Tibetan Plateau is simply a place among others on this troubled planet, albeit one with special conditions, unique geography and a history and religion that often turned inward to the exclusion of the outside world. It is partly this feeling of penetrating a forbidden or hidden realm that elevates and excites the visitor.

Yet Tibet ultimately does not disappoint. It is certainly as exotic and unusual a destination as one might find, and a bit of effort can take a traveller to the threshold of a phantasmagoric world, where devotionalism and faith, knowledge of nature and mere physical survival exist at a level long forgotten in the West.

Just as it is necessary to acclimatize the body, it is as important to take the time to experience the beauty and mysticism of the country and the people. Every new sight and sound can surfeit the senses.

The famed friendliness of the Tibetans, their love of life, sociability and good humour are an added pleasure for the traveller. Tibetans respect nature and animals, and their lifestyle is dedicated to achieving a balance between the mundane chores of daily life and their spiritual aspirations.

The importance of religion frequently amazes those accustomed to faith being displayed in occasional rituals on high days and holy days. Observance is an integral part of daily existence—not for nothing have Tibetans been called the most religious people in the world. It is common to see women walk down the streets conscientiously twirling prayer wheels, gaining merit for a better reincarnation in their next life with every turn, while the market-places are decorated with hundreds of colourful cloth prayer flags. Wood from aromatic shrubs, particularly juniper, is burned in public places, as the smoke is believed to waft prayers up to the gods and ward off evil spirits. To fuel the thousands of butter lamps, people carry flasks of melted yak butter to the monasteries and everywhere there are shrines, stupas and chortens to inspire the faithful.

Tibetan Buddhism is a combination of Mahayana Buddhism, which came from India, and the ancient Tibetan spirit-worshipping religion called Bön. Although Buddhism from the start had the upper hand, in great part because it was introduced at the same time as the country's written script, many of Tibet's lamas have accepted Bön's superstitious animist beliefs with the result that its practices have been incorporated into everyday devotions. As every family was expected to send at least one son to the monastery, one fifth of the male population used to be monks. At their height, great monasteries, like Drepung and Sera, housed thousands of monks and wielded enormous power. Even today, many Tibetans dedicate years to pilgrimages to religious shrines, often prostrating themselves every inch of the way.

Life on the surface appears to be normal and indeed Lhasa is thriving economically as never before. But the outward calm should not lead one to believe that it has always been this way or will remain so. The recent past is instructive in helping to form a balanced view of the forces and aspirations that shape modern Tibet.

The lifting of martial law has allowed tourism to grow once again. Modernization is increasing apace and Tibetans are attempting to adjust to this and to the increasing population of Chinese whose residence is changing the face of Tibet. Foreigners are arriving in Central Tibet in large numbers, and nearly all enjoy themselves and have remarkable, unforgettable experiences that do not dissipate with time but rather become stories which are told over and again to friends and family. In the telling, also, should be Tibet's unique history, tradition and culture. In this way an awareness of that distant land, its people and trials becomes alive and palpable to all.

*- Amanda Reynolds*

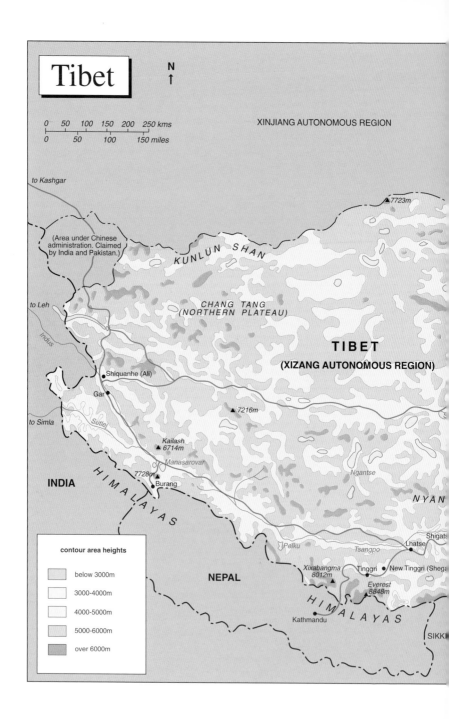

to Dunhuang,
Silk Road

to Xining

Beijing

TIBET

Shanghai

Chengdu

Golmud

to Xining

Hong Kong

QINGHAI PROVINCE

TANGGULA SHAN

Amdo

to Chengdu

Nagqu

Chamdo

SICHUAN
PROVINCE

to Chengdu

Namtso

Bamda

7088m

Mekong

Damxung

N TANGLHA

Nyingchi

Namche Barwa
▲7756m

Bomi

LHASA

Gonggar
✕ Airport

Tsangpo

Salween

Yangzi

Tsedang

Gyantse

Yamdrok

YUNNAN
PROVINCE

Phurma

Kulha Kangri
▲7538m

INDIA

dong

BHUTAN

Brahmaputra

MYANMAR
(BURMA)

borders shown on this map and all other maps
aring in this book are neither authentic nor correct

© Local Colour Ltd

# Geography and Natural History

In geological terms, the creation of the Himalayas and the rising of the Tibetan plateau are extremely recent events. The mountains originated less than four million years ago, making them among the youngest in the world.

About 80 million years ago India broke away from an early massive protocontinent. Slowly and steadily it moved across the ancient Sea of Tethys, collecting hard sheets of rock along the way. Eventually it rammed into the soft underside of Asia, which the rock easily penetrated and pushed up, creating the Himalayas. From sea level these mountains rose rapidly to a height of nearly 9,000 metres (30,000 feet). Today the succession of parallel ranges, running east to west for nearly 3,200 kilometres (2,000 miles), reveals this original plate boundary between India and Asia. In fact, the movement of sub-continental India is still forcing the Himalayas upwards at a rate of two centimetres (0.8 inches) per year in places.

The rivers of Tibet existed before the collision of India and Asia. As the soft sedimentary rocks that formed the bottom of the Sea of Tethys were folded up, the rivers were able to cut through them and maintain their original north-to-south course. (The Yarlong Tsangpo River is a major exception.) As a result there are many spectacular gorges and mountain ranges sliced up into individual massifs.

Much of Tibet, once well-forested, lush and fertile, is today one of the world's most terrifying, unforgiving places. As the Himalayas increased in height, less and less moisture reached the areas north of the range. The result has been a slow botanical death to the great northern plateau, the desertification of huge regions of Tibet and Xinjiang.

There are three distinct geographical regions in Greater Tibet. By far the largest natural region is the northern plateau, or Chang Tang, an enormous expanse of over a million square kilometres (386,000 square miles). It covers about half of Tibet's total surface area and is delineated in the west by the great Karakoram Range, in the north by the wall of the Astin Tagh, and in the northeast by the Nan Shan Range. The Chang Tang has one of the worst climates on earth, with strong winds every day and bitterly cold temperatures throughout the year. There is little rainfall and no outlet for the rivers. As a result, the region is characterized by myriad salty and brackish lakes.

These factors—constant wind, low rainfall and salt in the soil—severely limit the types of plant life that can survive, these being mostly grasses and herbs. There are fewer than 60 species of flowering plants, only three of which are woody.

One outstanding feature of the Chang Tang is the Zaidam or 'salt marsh' in the north. It used to be an enormous salt lake, which has now mostly dried up but retains some marshy areas. The Zaidam is distinguished by its large numbers of waterfowl and waders; more than 200 species of birds have been identified there. It should be noted that most of the Chang Tang is never visited by humans. The hunters and nomads who live permanently on the Northern Plateau generally confine their wanderings to the southern and eastern parts of that great wilderness.

The second main geographical region of Tibet, the outer plateau, extends in a great arc for nearly 3,500 kilometres (2,200 miles) from Baltistan in the west to beyond Xining, the capital of Qinghai, in the east. It is a relatively narrow strip, with the Himalayas forming the southern boundary. It is the most populous part of Tibet and contains almost all the major human settlements.

The outer plateau differs from the northern plateau in several important ways. First, the temperature and climate are milder, and consequently there is a richer distribution of flora and fauna. Secondly, agriculture exists in the outer plateau in many old and well-developed agricultural regions. The area around Shigatse and the Lhasa Valley are clear examples of this. Contrary to popular images of Tibet, Lhasa has a pleasant climate, with nearly all its rainfall occurring in the summer. For most of the year the weather is sunny and dry, mild during the day from April to October, and not unbearably cold in winter.

In the west, the outer plateau is an expanse of gravelly land, where vegetation is poor, but in the east it becomes a grassy steppe, running all the way to the Yellow River, where there is more rainfall, warmer weather and significantly more vegetation.

The other main geographical region is the southeastern plateau or 'river gorge country', comprising only one-tenth of the total area of Tibet. Plant and animal life here is vastly richer than in the other regions. Forests are very much a characteristic of the southeastern plateau; its western and northern boundaries follow the natural limits of trees.

The transition from the outer plateau to the southeastern plateau is gradual, though marked by a steady increase in trees and a decline in altitude. The lowest point in Tibet—1,615 metres (5,297 feet)—is near the great bend of the Yarlong Tsangpo River as it turns southward towards India. This region has an abundance of alpine and tropical plants such as laurel, rhododendron, azalea, bamboo, magnolia, oak, and even tea and banana, most of which appear in or near dense, moist evergreen forests.

The most dramatic geographical phenomena here are the deep river gorges formed by the upper reaches of the Salween, the Mekong and the Yangzi, three of Asia's mightiest rivers. These gorges erode and dissect the land, allowing moisture-bearing winds of the summer monsoon to reach the southeastern plateau.

*Ruins and desolate landscape between Nagarze and Gyantse*

Many animal groups are impoverished by the high altitude and severe climate of Tibet. There are very few amphibians or reptiles—or insects, limiting the number of insectivorous birds (fly-catchers, swallows, swifts), moles and shrews. Fish are generally members of the salmon and carp family. They abound in rivers and some large lakes, such as Namtso (see page 132), but many lakes have so much salt that no fish at all can survive.

Most of the animals of the northern and outer plateaux are desert and steppe species. These animals—particularly the hooved variety—are well adapted to the harsh conditions and wide open landscapes, which require them to migrate long distances in search of food.

The shaggy, powerful yak is a shining example of animal adaptation to the awful demands of Tibet. Another typical animal is the kiang, or wild ass. It often gathers in large herds, especially in western Tibet, and makes extremely long journeys in search of pasture. The kiang is the fastest runner on the plateau. Another remarkable and very beautiful beast is the Tibetan antelope, outstanding for its long, thin, almost vertical horns, which can attain 70 centimetres (28 inches) in length.

The most numerous mammals in Tibet are rodents, which are ubiquitous wherever there is sufficient plant material to support them. Predators such as wolves, foxes and bears rely to a large extent on these rodents. Another predator, and perhaps the most magnificent of all Tibet's creatures, is the extremely rare snow leopard.

More than 500 species of birds have been recorded in Tibet, and even the most casual observer can easily identify 20 or 30 separate varieties. This number can quickly be doubled with a bit of careful study or just a visit to one of Tibet's great lakes.

# Chronology of Tibetan History

500 BC     Birth of Buddha in India

AD 173     Birth of Tho-tho-ri-Nyantsen, 28th king of Tibet

233     Tho-tho-ri-Nyantsen receives a Buddhist scripture, marking the introduction of Buddhism into Tibet, an event of such importance that Tibetan currency notes were dated from this year

608–650     Reign of Songtsen Gampo, 32nd king. He sends scholars to India to study Sanskrit, and a Tibetan script is devised

634     Tibet sends envoys and tribute to China

640     Tibet occupies Nepal

641     Marriage of Songtsen Gampo to Chinese princess, Wen Cheng, daughter of Emperor Tai Zong. She and his Nepalese wife influence the spread of Buddhism in Tibet. Founding of the Jokhang

645     Songtsen Gampo sends a minister to the court of China requesting permission to build a temple on Mt Wu Tai in Shanxi Province. The request is granted

654–676     Tibetan conquest of state of Tuyulun and acquisition of Chinese territories in Central Asia

676–704     Tibetan expansion of Central Asian possessions and partial reconquest of these by the Chinese

704     Tride Tsugtsen (died 755) becomes king

707–710     Peace settlement with Chinese. Tride Tsugtsen marries Chinese princess, Jin Cheng

730     Another treaty negotiated with Chinese

755–797     Reign of Trisong Detsen, Tride Tsugtsen's son. Reconquest of Central Asian possessions

763     Tibetans invade Chinese capital, Changan, and withdraw 15 days later

*The great Kōku banner hangs from the Potala as onlookers gather under the Shö pillar*

| | |
|---|---|
| 779 | Foundation of monastery of Samye. Buddhism recognized as state religion |
| 783 | Peace treaty with China |
| 785–805 | Tibetan army advances westward to the Pamirs as far as the Oxus River |
| 797 | Muni Tsangpo, Trisong Detsen's son, becomes king |
| 799–815 | Reign of Sadneleg |
| 815–836 | Reign of Ralpachen, son of Sadneleg. Intense activity of translation of Buddhist texts |
| 821 | Peace treaty with China; the Tibetans retain most of their Central Asian possessions |
| 836–842 | Reign of Lang Darma, brother of Ralpachen. As a supporter of the Bön religion, he severely persecutes Buddhism |
| 842–1247 | Lang Darma murdered. Struggle for power ensues with small factions constantly warring or allying with each other |
| 978 | Rinchen Tsangpo, a famous translator, invites Indian teachers to western Tibet, marking the beginning of the renaissance of Buddhism. Monasteries are established in western Tibet. |
| 1040 | Birth of Milarepa (died 1123), great Tibetan poet and mystic |
| 1042 | Atisha (died 1054), a great Mahayana teacher from India, arrives in Tibet and carries out missionary activities in western and central Tibet |
| 1057 | Founding of Reting Monastery |
| 1071 | Founding of Sakya Monastery |
| 1182 | Birth of Sakya Pandit (died 1251), learned scholar of the Sakya Sect |
| 1189 | Genghis Khan (1167–1227) becomes leader of the Mongols |
| 1207 | Tibetans send delegation to Genghis Khan; friendly relations and tribute established |
| 1227 | Death of Genghis Khan. Tibetans cease paying tribute to Mongols |

1244    Sakya Pandit invited to meet Mongol Khan, and invested with temporal
        power over central Tibet

1252–53 Mongol invasion

1254    Kublai Khan grants Phagspa Lodro Gyaltsen (1235–80), Sakya Pandit's
        nephew, supreme authority over Tibet, thus forming a politico-religious
        relationship between the Mongols and the Tibetans (which later developed
        into the patron-lama link between the Manchu emperors and the dalai lama)

1354    Fighting breaks out between the Sakyapa Sect and the powerful Lang
        family. The might of the Sakyapa Sect declines and a reorganization of the
        state takes place

1357    Birth of Tsong Khapa (died 1419), founder of the Gelugpa or Yellow Hat
        Sect

1391    Birth of Gedun Truppa (died 1474), disciple of Tsong Khapa and head of
        the Gelugpa Sect. Posthumously named as the First Dalai Lama

1409    Founding of Ganden Monastery

1416    Founding of Drepung Monastery

1419    Founding of Sera Monastery

1434–   Constant power struggles, lasting more than 100 years, between the
1533    provinces of Ü and Tsang, whose leaders adhered to the Gelugpa and
        Karmapa sects respectively

1447    Founding of Tashilhunpo Monastery

1475    Birth of Second Dalai Lama, Gedun Gyatso (died 1542)

1543    Birth of Third Dalai Lama, Sonam Gyatso (died 1588). He visits Mongolia
        where Altan Khan confers the title 'dalai lama' on him

1582    Founding of Kumbum Monastery

1588    Birth of Fourth Dalai Lama, Yonten Gyatso (died 1616), conveniently the
        great-grandson of Altan Khan and the only non-Tibetan in the line of dalai
        lamas

1617 Birth of Fifth Dalai Lama, Ngawang Lozang Gyatso (died 1682), builder of the Potala. Collapse of the province of Ü and victory to the Tsang provincial forces resulting in a growth of power of the Karmapa Sect

1624–36 Jesuit missionaries arrive in western Tibet

1641–42 Gusri Khan of the Qosot Mongols overthrows king of Tsang and hands territory over to Fifth Dalai Lama

1642–59 Consolidation of the Tibetan theocracy. Many Karmapa Sect monasteries handed over to the Gelugpa Sect. Abbot of Tashilhunpo Monastery given title of 'panchen lama' by the Fifth Dalai Lama

1652 Fifth Dalai Lama visits China

1670–1750 Chinese conquest of Mongolia and Xinjiang and occupation of Lhasa

1682 Death of Fifth Dalai Lama; his death is kept secret by the regent

1683 Birth of Sixth Dalai Lama, Tsangyang Gyatso

1697 The Sixth Dalai Lama enthroned after death of Fifth Dalai Lama made public

1705 The Khan of Qosot, Lhanjang Khan, invades Tibet and conquers Lhasa

1706 The Khan of Qosot deposes Sixth Dalai Lama and sends him to China, but he dies en route. The khan declares Sixth Dalai Lama not to have been a true reincarnation and enthrones a monk of his own choice

1707 Italian Capuchin monks arrive in Tibet

1708 Another reincarnation of Sixth Dalai Lama discovered. For reasons of security he takes refuge in Kumbum Monastery

1716 Jesuit Father Ippolito Desideri arrives in Lhasa

1717–20 Junggar Mongols occupy and sack Lhasa, killing the Khan of Qosot. The Manchu emperor of China deposes the dalai lama appointed by the Khan of Qosot and recognizes claimant from Kumbum Monastery (Kelzang Gyatso), who is officially recognized as Seventh Dalai Lama in 1720

*A Gelugpa monk seated with religious objects: the yellow hat on his hand bell contains tea; skull drum; fruit. The staff is shaken to alert people to his presence that they might offer him food.*

1733–47   Pholhanas (died 1747) brings internal struggles to an end and, with the support of the Chinese, becomes effective ruler of Tibet

1751   After an attempted revolt against the Chinese garrison, dalai lama is recognized as ruler of Tibet but without effective political power

1757   Seventh Dalai Lama dies

1758   Birth of Eighth Dalai Lama, Jompal Gyatso (died 1804)

1774–45   First British mission to Tibet led by George Bogle

1783–84   British mission led by Samuel Turner. Chinese troops impose the Peace of Kathmandu following Gurkha incursions into Tibet

1806–15   The Ninth Dalai Lama, Lungtok Gyatso

1811–12   Thomas Manning, British explorer, reaches Lhasa

1816–37   The Tenth Dalai Lama, Tsultrim Gyatso

1838–56   The Eleventh Dalai Lama, Khedrup Gyatso

1846   Lazarist monks, Huc and Gabet, arrive in Lhasa

1854–56   Conflict with Nepal

1856–75   The Twelfth Dalai Lama, Trinley Gyatso

1876   Birth of Thirteenth Dalai Lama, Thupten Gyatso. Diplomatic conflict between Russia and Britain over contacts and privileges with Tibet

1890   British Protectorate over Sikkim

1904   British military expedition, under Col Younghusband, forces its way to Lhasa. Thirteenth Dalai Lama flees to Mongolia. Conclusion of agreement with abbot of Ganden Monastery

1909   Dalai Lama returns to Lhasa

1910   Restoration of Chinese control over eastern Tibet and dispatch of troops to Lhasa

| | |
|---|---|
| 1911 | Manchu Dynasty overthrown. Chinese Republic founded. Tibetan uprising against Chinese |
| 1912 | Dalai Lama resumes rule without Chinese influence |
| 1913–14 | Conference of Simla with British, Chinese and Tibetan plenipotentiaries: Chinese refuse to ratify agreement |
| 1920–21 | Mission of Sir Charles Bell to Tibet |
| 1923 | Ninth Panchen Lama flees to China |
| 1933 | Death of Thirteenth Dalai Lama |
| 1934 | Appointment of regent (abbot of Reting Monastery) |
| 1935 | Birth of Fourteenth Dalai Lama, Tenzin Gyatso enthroned in 1940 |
| 1947 | Indian independence and end of the British Tibet Policy |
| 1949 | Founding of the People's Republic of China |
| 1950 | Fourteenth Dalai Lama flees to border with Sikkim. Returns to Lhasa after receiving assurances from Chinese government |
| 1951 | Arrival of People's Liberation Army in Lhasa |
| 1954 | Dalai Lama visits Beijing |
| 1959 | Attempted uprising. Dalai Lama flees to India |
| 1964 | Tibet formally claimed to be an 'autonomous region' within the People's Republic of China |
| 1966–76 | Cultural Revolution |
| 1976 | Death of Chairman Mao Zedong |
| 1989 | Death of Tenth Panchen Lama in Shigatse |
| 1995 | Dispute over identity of Eleventh Panchen Lama |

(following pages) *Lamps, offerings and pilgrims at the Jokhang Temple, Lhasa*

# Facts for the Traveller

To visit Tibet, the legendary, forbidden land on the roof of the world, has been the dream of many Westerners. To be one of the first to travel here was once part of that dream, but today Tibet is no longer unspoiled. Nearly four decades as an occupied territory within the People's Republic of China have brought inevitable changes and the rapid development of tourism is tearing holes in its enticing aura of mystery.

Nevertheless, Tibet remains one of the most interesting, remote and undeveloped parts of the world. Its limited facilities for tourists are only now approaching a reasonable standard. Travel outside Lhasa can be difficult, expensive and dangerous.

This book does not attempt to cover all of Tibet. Bold individuals travelling by bicycle or hitch-hiking on trucks have penetrated nearly every corner, but this guide describes mainly those parts of southern and central Tibet that have been declared open to foreigners by the Chinese. Its aim is to help travellers who want to explore and to understand these areas.

Most visitors arrive by air in Lhasa, the capital. Not only is Lhasa the centre of administration and authority, the place to secure permission to visit other destinations, and to arrange transportation and buy supplies, but also many of Tibet's greatest cultural monuments are concentrated here. Its altitude—at 3,650 metres (12,000 feet)—makes it a good place to rest and sightsee while becoming acclimatized.

## Getting There

### By Air

Most visitors to Tibet fly from Chengdu, the capital of Sichuan Province. Flights are handled by China Southwest Airlines. Lhasa's airport is at Gonggar, in a broad stretch of the Yarlong Tsangpo Valley some 90 kilometres (56 miles) southwest of the capital.

**Chengdu–Gonggar** Two Boeing 757 flights operate daily in the early morning, taking two hours, and return to Chengdu mid-morning. Delays are caused frequently by adverse weather conditions. Cost is Rmb1,590 (one-way)

**Beijing–Gonggar** Boeing 757 flights operate on Sunday and Tuesday mornings, arriving four hours later after a stop in Chengdu. The return is in the middle of the afternoon, arriving four and a half hours later. Cost is Rmb2,690 (one-way)

In clear weather the flight from Chengdu offers a spectacular panorama of mountain ranges with peaks over 6,700 metres (22,000 feet). The best view is from the left-hand side of the plane. The many-crested Minya Konka massif, with its 7,556-metre (24,783-foot) peak, stands out dramatically after 20 minutes of flight. Half an hour later the southern horizon reveals 7,756-metre (25,447-foot) Namche Barwa, a magnificent pyramidal peak first climbed in 1992. The east-flowing Yarlong Tsangpo River hooks around north of the range before turning south, then southwest, to enter India as the Brahmaputra River. Between craggy ranges are glimpses of silver, pencil-line rivers at the bottom of precipitous gorges, including the upper reaches of some of the world's greatest rivers—the Yangzi, the Mekong and the Salween.

**Kathmandu–Gonggar** A twice-weekly Boeing 757 flight operates between Kathmandu and Lhasa from the beginning of April through October. The 55-minute flight goes on Tuesdays and Saturdays, with departure in both directions in the mid-morning, local time. The flight offers spectacular views of the Himalayas and the southern Tibetan plateau, but is often cancelled on short notice due to cloudy weather, especially during the monsoon season. As this coincides with the peak tourist season, outgoing travellers are advised to keep onward bookings from Kathmandu as flexible as possible. Tickets (around US$200 one-way) are available in Lhasa at the airline office on Niang Re Lu and in Kathmandu at China Southwest Airlines or any travel agent.

**Gonggar–Lhasa** International arrivals are met by airline buses at the landing strip at Gonggar and taken to the airport buildings a kilometre away for immigration and customs formalities and to meet their guides and vehicles. Domestic arrivals are met by guides and vehicles at the runway. Individual travellers can get from Gonggar to central Lhasa by airline bus (Rmb25) or taxi (about Rmb300). The trip takes one or one and a half hours.

If luggage is not available for collection at the airport, it should appear later at the airline office in Lhasa. Group guides arrange for luggage to be delivered directly to the group's hotel. It is prudent to carry overnight necessities in hand luggage, as delays in collecting luggage sometimes occur.

The paved road from Gonggar follows the south bank of the Yarlong Tsangpo River for 25 kilometres (15 miles), then skirts the foot of a granite outcrop (Chuwori, a sacred peak) and crosses the strategic Yarlong Tsangpo bridge. It then follows the Kyichu (Quxu) River north for 55 kilometres (34 miles). At Donkar Bridge and the confluence of the Kyichu and Tobing Chu, the valley divides, and the golden roofs of Lhasa's Potala Palace can be seen in the distance to the east. At this moment, Tibetan pilgrims on board call out prayers.

**Lhasa–Gonggar** With all flights leaving in the morning, most people find it necessary to spend the night before flying at Gonggar. CAAC buses depart every 30 minutes from 2pm until 4:30pm and cost Rmb25. Alternatively, taxis are available for around Rmb300. The Holiday Inn has its own car service to Gonggar for Rmb580. Those who opt to stay a night at Gonggar can choose between two hotels (see page 232).

## By Road

An approach that has great appeal for hardy and adventurous travellers is to enter or leave Tibet by road, following in the footsteps of explorers who for more than a century tried (and usually failed) to reach Lhasa overland (see page 197).

**Kathmandu–Lhasa** This trip takes at least three days, with overnight stops in Zhangmu or Nyalam and Shigatse. Organized tour groups from Kathmandu are met at the border (Zhangmu) by their guides and vehicles, but may still be delayed for a day or two around Nyalam if the weather is bad. Independent tourists can hire a jeep or landcruiser to Lhasa. The cost for such a hire ranges from Rmb1000–Rmb4000 depending on the quality of the vehicle and the itinerary to the capital. Typically, a landcruiser to Lhasa will include a guide and tours of Shigatse (Tashilhunpo Monastery) and Gyantse and will cost around Rmb3,500. Travellers should be prepared to spend some days in Zhangmu arranging transport. Tourists are not permitted to travel by truck.

The distance from Zhangmu to Lhasa is 830 kilometres (520 miles) via Gyantse (the route most tourists take), mostly on difficult gravel roads. It is a strenuous journey, especially for people who are not yet fully acclimatized to the high altitude. Within the first 90 kilometres (55 miles) from Zhangmu the road ascends almost 3,000 metres (10,000 feet) to the Lalung Leh Pass (5,050 metres or 16,570 feet). Less than 210 kilometres (130 miles) further on, it crosses the Jia Tsuo La, or Lhakpa La Pass at 5,220 metres (17,125 feet). It is a more pleasant and less exhausting trip when taken in the opposite direction after a period of travel and acclimitization in the region of Lhasa (3,650 metres or 11,975 feet).

**Golmud–Lhasa** Tibet's main northern road links Lhasa with Golmud, a bleak and dusty town in Qinghai Province that forms the nearest Chinese railhead. The entire length of the road (1,166 kilometres, 730 miles) is tarmacked. Individual travellers have found that Golmud is the open back door into Tibet; acquiring a bus ticket for the long trip is a straightforward affair. As of 1996, however, it is necessary to buy a ticket through CITS in Golmud (without one you will be turned back at the first checkpost) and these are not cheap—expect to pay around Rmb1,200. Prices from Lhasa are considerably cheaper at Rmb290 for the ordinary bus and Rmb550 for the "sleeper" bus (recommended). The 25- to 30-hour journey is spectacular and exhausting. Short stops are made at Amdo, Nagqu and Damxung, but passengers should bring their own food and some form of protection against the cold, as delays are common and snow-storms can occur on high passes at any time of year. Groups

*Entranceway to monastic chanting hall*

travelling between Tibet and Xinjiang do so via Golmud.

Foreigners are not permitted to travel by truck. Those who use fake student IDs to buy cheap tickets are increasingly at risk of discovery and a fine.

**Chengdu–Lhasa** Tibet's main eastern road crosses precipitous mountain ranges and river gorges from Chengdu by way of Kangding, Dege and Chamdo. (A more southerly route via Batang joins the main route at Bamda, between Baxoi and Rawu.) The road continues westwards through deep, forested river valleys past Bomi, Tangmai and Lunang to Nyingchi, thence through Kongpo to Maizhokunggar and Lhasa. The distance from Chengdu to Lhasa is approximately 2,400 kilometres (1,500 miles). Bridges frequently collapse during the summer rainy season, particularly between Bomi and Tangmai, and snow can block the passes in winter. There are few through buses, and in some places little local transport. A through bus ride with no delays takes ten days, but the journey usually takes much longer.

Travellers who have made this journey describe it as beautiful, dangerous and difficult. The route is closed to foreigners, and most who try it are turned back at the Sichuan-Tibet border. Routes up from Yunnan are also closed and closely watched.

**Kashgar–Lhasa** This fourth and longest road into Tibet crosses three spectacular ranges of the Kunlun Mountains, rising eventually to the Aksai Chin, a high, barren and uninhabited plateau. The road is high and difficult (sometimes fatal), with temperatures as low as -4.4°C (24°F) in July! 'Towns' marked on the map are usually single road maintenance huts. From Kashgar to Shiquanhe (Ngari or, in Chinese, Ali), the capital of Ali District on the upper Indus, is a seven-day drive, but delays usually add another week. Ali has a helpful Public Security Bureau and a keen local tourism company.

From Ali, a road leads south toward Burang (Taklakot), a trading town on the western border of Nepal, passing en route Mt Kailash and Lake Manasarovar. The road continues southeast across the northern plateau, the Chang Tang, to join the Nepal-Lhasa route near Lhatse. The journey from Ali to Lhasa usually takes at least five days. Buses run infrequently from Ali, but the police often prevent foreigners from boarding, even those with valid Aliens' Travel Permits for the route obtained in Kashgar.

# Visas

Chinese visas, available at most Chinese embassies abroad, and more easily through travel agents in Hong Kong, are generally valid for one month, although 60- and 90-day visas are issued (usually without difficulty) if requested. They commence from the date of entry into China or Tibet, though the entire life of the visa is usually three months from the date of issue, so it is advantageous to obtain a visa as close to the time of departure as possible. The Chinese embassy in Kathmandu will only issue visas to travellers on group tours. Visas can be extended within China for one-month periods at Public Security bureaux, usually for a total of three months of extensions, but sometimes longer. However, within Tibet extensions are normally sanctioned for four or five days so that transport arrangements can be made to *exit* Tibet, the exception being for those people who have an arranged tour itinerary. Extensions cannot be obtained more than two or three days before the expiration of the current visa or extension. In Lhasa extensions are granted by the Public Security Bureau on Linkuo Bei Lu (about half a mile north of the Banak Shöl Hotel), and cost Rmb25 (although some nationalities have to pay extra).

In addition to the visa, it is necessary to obtain an Aliens' Travel Permit (*luxingzheng*) for travel in Tibet. Costs vary widely—anywhere between US$20 and $100. This is included in the price of most tours, as well as the bus ticket from Golmud. Independent travellers arriving from Nepal must buy this permit at the border—this is usually arranged together with transport to Lhasa. To visit the closed areas of Tibet (check with the PSB which areas this applies to) tourists must obtain a further permit; this is only possible through a travel agent.

There is no system of trekking permits in Tibet. Exit visas are no longer required to travel overland to Nepal. Nepalese visas can be obtained at the Nepalese Consulate in Lhasa or at the border.

## Customs Regulations

Art objects and antiques in Tibet fall under special restrictions forbidding their export. Anything made before 1959 is considered an antique. Rugs may be bought and exported, so may the small religious objects that are sold in open markets, providing only one or two are taken as souvenirs. Customs officials have been known to confiscate jewellery or other objects if they consider that a tourist has purchased 'too much'.

## Climate, Clothing and Equipment

Tibet is cold in winter, cool in summer and generally dry, receiving only 450 millimetres (18 inches) of rain or snow. Sunlight is extremely intense. The thin air neither blocks nor holds heat, so sunshine feels warm, shadows are chilly, and

# Mystical Mountains

There are mountains which are just mountains and there are mountains with personality. The personality of a mountain is more than merely a strange shape that makes it different from all the others—just as a strangely shaped face or strange actions do not make an individual into a personality.

Personality consists in the the power to influence others, and this power is due to consistency, harmony, and one–pointedness of character. If these qualities are present in an individual, in their highest perfection, then this individual is a fit leader of humanity, either as a ruler, or a saint, and we recognise it as a vessel of cosmic power. If these qualities are present in a mountain we recognise it as a vessel of cosmic power, and we call it a sacred mountain.

The power of such a mountain is so great and yet so subtle that, without compulsion, people are drawn to it from near and far, as if by the force of some invisible magnet; and they will undergo untold hardships and privations in their inexplicable urge to approach and to worship the centre of this sacred power. Nobody has confered the title of sacredness on such a mountain, and yet everybody recognises it; nobody has to defend its claim, because nobody doubts it; nobody has to organise its worship, because people are overwhelmed by the mere presence of such a mountain and cannot express their feelings other than by worship.

The worshipful or religious attitude is not impressed by scientific facts, like figures of altitude, which are foremost in the mind of modern man. Nor is it motivated by the urge to 'conquer' the mountain. Instead of conquering it, the religious-minded man prefers to be conquered by the mountain. He opens his soul to its spirit and allows it to take possession of him, because only he who is inspired or 'possessed' by the divine spirit can partake in its nature. While the modern man is driven by ambition and the glorification of his own ego to climb an outstanding mountain and to be first on the top of it, the devotee is more interested in his spiritual uplift than in the physical

*Mountains of Eastern Tibet, seen on the flight from Chengdu to Lhasa*

*feat of climbing. To him the mountain is a divine symbol, and as little as he would put his foot upon a sacred image, so little would he dare to put his foot on the summit of a sacred mountain.*

*To see the greatness of a mountain, one must keep one's distance; to understand its form, one must move around it; to experience its moods, one must see it at sunrise and sunset, at noon and at midnight, in sun and in rain, in snow and in storm, in summer and in winter and in all the other seasons. He who can see the mountain like this comes near to the life of the mountain, a life that is as intense and varied as that of a human being. Mountains grow and decay, they breathe and pulsate with life. They attract and collect invisible energies from their surroundings: the forces of air of the water, of electricity and magnetism, they create winds, clouds, thunderstorms, rains, waterfalls, and rivers. They fill their surroundings with active life and give shelter and food to innumerable beings. Such is the greatness of mighty mountains.*

*But even among the mightiest there are some of such outstanding and position that they become symbols of the highest aspirations of humanity, as expresed in ancient civilisations and religions, milestones of the eternal quest for perfection and ultimate realisation, signposts that point beyond our earthly concerns towards the infinity of a universe from which we have originated and to which we belong.*

*In the dust-filled valleys and low plains of our daily existence we have forgotten our connections with stars and suns; and therefore we need the presence of these mighty signposts and milestones to shake up and arouse us from the slumber of self-complacency. Not many are there who hear the call or feel the urge to rise from under their thick blanket of petty self-interests, of money-making or pleasure-hinting, but the few whom the call has reached, and in whom the longing for greater things is still awake, form a steady stream of pilgrims who keep alive the tradition and knowledge of those sources of inspiration.*

*Thus it is above all the sacred mountains of the world the fame of Kailas has spread and inspired people since time immemorial. There is no other mountain comparable to Kailas, because it forms the hub of the two most important ancient civilisatons of the world, whose traditions remained intact for thousands of years; India and China.*

*. . . The mountain stands so completely alone in the centre of the Transhimalayan range that it is possible to circumambulate it within two or three days; and its shape is so regular as if it were the dome of a gigantic temple, rising above a number of equally architectural forms of bastions and temple-shaped mountains which form its base. And as every Indian temple has its sacred water-tank, so at the southern foot of Kailas there are two sacred lakes, Manasarovar and Rakastal, of which the former is shaped like the sun and represents the forces of light, while the other is curved like the crescent moon and represents the hidden forces of the night.*

*. . . Only he who has contemplated the divine in its most awe-inspiring form, who has dared to look into the unveiled face of truth without being overwhelmed or frightened—only such a person will be able to bear the powerful silence and solitude of Kailas and its sacred lakes, and endure the dangers and hardships which are the price one has to pay for being admitted to divine presence on the most sacred spot on earth. But those who have given up comfort and security and the care for their own lives are rewarded by an indescribable feeling of bliss, of supreme happiness. Their mental faculties seem to be heightened, their awareness and spiritual sensitivity infinitely increased, their conciousness reaching out to a new dimension, so that many of them see wonderful visions and hear strange voices and fall into trance-like states, in which all their former obstructions and difficulties disappear like in a flash of light that suddenly lights up what was hidden hitherto. It is as if their individual consciousness, which obscured or distorted their views or their conception of the world were receding and giving place to an all-embracing cosmic consciousness.*

Lama Anagarika Govinda, The Way of the White Clouds, 1960

*Lama Anagarika Govinda's personal account of a pilgrimage undertaken in the decades leading up to the Chinese invasion in 1950 illustrates how, unlike a simple journey, these travels are important as a spiritual awakening. 'The pilgrimage in the outer space is actually the mirrored reflection of an inner movement of development.' In Tibetan Buddhism clouds symbolise the creative power of the mind.*

## CLIMBERS OF MT EVEREST

Mt Everest reaches 8,848 metres (29,028 feet)—nearly nine kilometres (5.5 miles) high. English surveyors first measured the world's highest mountain in 1852 from the distant plains of India, as Tibet and Nepal were both closed. They named it after Sir George Everest, a great English surveyor, not knowing that it already had a name—Qomolangma.

For many years, John Noel, an English army officer, sought in vain for permission to visit the mountain. In 1913, he entered Tibet from Sikkim in disguise. He was discovered and turned back by armed Tibetans 64 kilometres (40 miles) from Everest, but by then he had seen a great deal. His lectures in England aroused passionate interest among mountaineers. In 1920, Sir Charles Bell, Britain's political officer for Tibet, persuaded the Thirteenth Dalai Lama to let English mountaineers climb Everest.

A reconnaissance group retraced Noel's route. The first expedition, in 1922, included John Noel and George Mallory, the best climber of that era. (It was he who, when asked why he had climbed Everest, gave the famous reply, 'Because it is there.') After a month-long trek from Sikkim, Noel and Mallory established a base camp at Rongbuk, where they first heard about the yeti—a mystery that intrigued the whole world. They used oxygen, but the climb was aborted by an avalanche that killed seven of their Sherpas.

Another expedition was mounted in 1924. Mallory and an able young companion, Andrew Irvine, were nearing the summit, when John Noel, watching from below, lost sight of them. They did not return, and their bodies have never been found. The possibility remains that they might have

temperatures can vary greatly within a day, exceeding 29°C (84°F) in desert areas in summer, and plunging below 4°C (40°F) the same night. Lhasa's night-time lows in winter are around -9°C (16°F). The higher you go the colder it gets, and the winds in winter are ferocious. Rainfall in southern Tibet occurs intermittently between May and September, bringing moisture to barley fields and greenery to the valleys. The most pleasant months for tourism are from April to October.

Clothing should be simple and consist of layers which can be added or removed as the temperature varies during the day. A warm windbreaker and stout comfortable shoes are especially recommended. Formal attire such as a necktie or dress is never needed—trousers and sweaters are the style.

reached the top and died on the return trip. There is no way of knowing.

Eight more expeditions attempted Everest from Tibet before World War II broke out. The greatest climbers in the world tried it, as well as amateurs. All were defeated by storms, snow and altitude.

When China closed Tibet in 1951, the British traced a new route up Everest through Nepal. In 1952, Swiss mountaineers very nearly succeeded but were halted by storms. A Russian team on the Tibetan side is believed to have lost six of its members on the mountain that same year.

On 29 May 1953, the peak was finally reached by New Zealander Edmund Hillary and Tenzing Norgay, a Sherpa who had climbed with the Swiss.

From that moment on, Everest became climbable. In 1956, four Swiss stood on top. In 1960, a Chinese team made it from Tibet. In 1963, six Americans took different routes to the peak. In 1965, nine Indians succeeded, followed in 1975 by one Chinese and eight Tibetans. There were failures, too, but by 1994, nearly 300 individuals had stood on the world's highest point. Nearly 20 of them made the ascent more than once, with the Sherpa Sungdare holding the record, having climbed to the top of Mt Everest four times.

In 1988, a huge combined Chinese/Nepali/Japanese expedition made a traverse of the summit, with parties crossing from one side to the other in both directions and even broadcasting live television transmissions worldwide by satellite from the summit. However, this technological feat pales next to Reinhold Messner's astonishing solo ascent from the Tibetan side—without porters, expedition backup or oxygen.

Lhasa now has many pharmacies (south of the Potala and in and near the Barkhor) selling Tibetan, Chinese and some Western medicines, including aspirin and antibiotics, which are available without prescription. It is simpler, however, to bring your own comprehensive first-aid kit. Soap, toothpaste, toilet paper, sanitary napkins (but not tampons), laundry soap, scissors, can-openers and other kitchen items are available in the half-dozen or so department stores in Lhasa. At a pinch, you can buy sunglasses here, but it is a good idea to bring sunglasses with good ultra-violet protection. Remember to bring sun block and lip cream, neither of which is available in Lhasa. A flashlight is important because many interesting sights are poorly lit. Do not bring small gifts as this has led many children to start begging.

# Transportation

In Tibet, distances are huge, many of the roads are bad, all gasoline must be trucked in, and long trips to remote areas can be expensive. Travellers can travel by bus on local or long-distance routes, hire vehicles for small or large groups, arrange landcruiser trips through travel agents in Lhasa, hire or buy bicycles, or bring their own bikes with them. There are no air routes within Tibet. Truck drivers are no longer permitted to offer rides; hitchhikers might succeed in getting a lift from a helpful but ignorant driver, only to land him in serious trouble at the next road checkpoint.

## By Bus

There are regular buses from Lhasa to Golmud, Tsedang and Shigatse, using fast, comfortable Japanese vehicles. The main bus station is on the corner of Minzu Lu, south of the Norbulinka. Tickets are put on sale two days before departure and usually sell quickly. Get seats in the front half of the bus for greater comfort on rough roads and better visibility through the dust. Buses go from these stations to a number of other destinations, but do not expect to be able to buy tickets for destinations not normally open to tourists. Watch out for thieves and pickpockets at both stations.

The local bus station is opposite Tibet University, at the southeast corner of town, near the bridge. Dilapidated buses run from here on routes to Maizhokunggar, Yangbajing, Damxung and other places in central Tibet. People planning to visit the Gonggar region can also use the bus service from the CAAC building to the airport and start walking from there. Take food and drink for the journey, as you cannot always count on the bus making stops en route.

## By Hired Vehicle

A wide range of vehicles suitable for long or short trips and large or small groups can now be hired. Toyota Landcruisers and Nissan Troopers are both comfortable and strong four-wheel-drive vehicles taking five passengers and heavy luggage. Modern Japanese buses and coaches seat between ten and 33 people. Beijing Jeeps, like those used by the army, are uncomfortable and slower (but cheaper), and there are also cheaper Chinese buses. A hired vehicle will normally come with an English-speaking guide.

Vehicles can be hired through any hotel or travel agency in Lhasa, who will make arrangements if they do not have suitable vehicles themselves.

Some trips, such as to Lake Namtso or Rongbuk, can be managed only by four-wheel drives. If the weather or road conditions look bad, operators may refuse to risk their vehicles being damaged or stranded.

Write out a detailed contract for the trip, including dates and an itinerary and covering every detail of the trip you plan. Specify all planned stops, otherwise the driver may insist on his own favourites. Do not expect a refund if you cut your trip short.

If all this sounds like a lot of trouble, check hotel noticeboards for other people who have already made all the arrangements and are looking for passengers to share the costs. You can also advertise that you are interested in a particular journey and want to meet others to share the organizing of the trip. The best noticeboards for ferreting out empty seats or filling them are at the Banak Shöl and Yak hotels. During the summer, a busload of tourists leaves for Nepal every day or two.

In addition to the agencies, the following places have their own fleets of vehicles:
**the Holiday Inn** has a fleet of Landcruisers, and buses seating from nine to 25.
**the Kirey Hotel** has its own fleet of Chinese-made jeeps, suitable only for short trips but cheaper.
**the Suns Hotel** is closely affiliated to Lhasa Travel Agency and shares management with them.

## BY BICYCLE

Touring Tibet by bicycle is becoming increasingly popular. Bicycles can be transported as baggage on CAAC flights or brought in from Nepal. Within Tibet, they can be carried on the luggage racks of local buses.

Mountain bikes are ideal for Tibet's rough, stony roads. Good pannier systems are essential for carrying camping and survival gear, food, fuel, spare parts (especially derailleurs, spokes and freewheels) and tools.

Chinese bicycles are mostly big, heavy models with thick 28-inch tyres and rod brakes. These can be hired in several places in Lhasa and Tsedang, including most hotels, for Rmb2 per hour. You must leave as security your passport or a deposit equal to the current cost of a new bike (about Rmb400). The Yak Hotel has some newer, lighter bicycles with 26-inch wheels, or even smaller, including some with ladies' frames, but these are not as strong as the bigger bikes.

An alternative to renting is to buy a bicycle. There are bicycle shops along Beijing Lu and bikes can also be bought in the second-hand bike market held every Sunday morning in the broad street outside the mosque. Ask for the little red registration book with the frame number; if this is not available the machine may have been stolen, and you will have difficulty selling it later. If you buy a new bike, get a shop receipt and retain it.

Shanghai-made Yongjiu-brand bikes are considered the most reliable, but careful maintenance is essential to keep even these from falling apart. Crank cotter pins, brake parts, bearings and spindles are the weakest parts. Everything becomes loose and falls off unless regularly checked and tightened.

*Return home by yak*

Bike thefts are common, especially around Lhasa. The little fitted frame locks can easily be broken off with a big Khampa knife, so buy extra cablelocks and lock the bike to something secure.

## By Horse

Though it sounds idyllic to roam the Tibetan highlands on the back of a horse gaily decorated with patterned carpets and saddles, there are some problems.

The first is that foreigners are not permitted to own and ride horses. Violators found on the main routes have been stopped by the police and forced to sell their animals on the spot.

Another problem is the limited supply of fodder. Grass grows only during the summer rainy season and, in upland areas, is so lacking in nutrition that it cannot sustain a horse over a long journey. Even in the valleys, many people have only enough fodder for their own animals and none to sell. During late summer, they may want to fatten their horses on the best grazing so that they will look good at the village horse races and archery festivals, and thus may not want to send them off on a gruelling journey. And, because Tibetan horses are quite small, you need two—one to ride, and the other for your luggage.

Thus, long journeys such as a Lhasa–Nepal trip are difficult, though determined individuals do succeed from time to time. Fewer problems are encountered when borrowing or hiring a horse to use within a remote valley and going to the uplands for only a day or two at a time. August and September are the best months.

# Altitude and Health

Because of Tibet's high altitude, travellers with a pre-existing problem of heart, lungs or anaemia should consult a doctor before considering a visit. Most other travellers, once they are acclimatized, rarely suffer more than mild discomfort from the altitude.

Acclimatization is the adjustment of the human body to the diminished supply of oxygen at high altitudes. Bone marrow produces quantities of extra red blood cells to take oxygen from the air in amounts needed for good health, a process that may take several days. Mountain sickness (also called altitude sickness) is caused by an insufficient flow of oxygen to the brain and other vital organs. It can affect anybody above 3,000 metres (10,000 feet).

Each person has a different tolerance for altitude that has nothing to do with age, sex or fitness. One person will get a headache at 3,400 metres (11,000 feet), another not until 5,500 metres (18,000 feet). The symptoms of mountain sickness include headache, nausea and shortness of breath, singly or together. About half the people arriving in Lhasa suffer at least one symptom in the first two days before recovering.

In nearly all cases, rest and two aspirins will relieve the discomfort. However, the serious—sometimes fatal—conditions of pulmonary and cerebral oedema also begin with these same symptoms. If a headache does not respond to aspirin or a good night's rest, if a dry cough with frothy sputum develops, or if there are any signs of severe lethargy or poor coordination, go to hospital at once. Better yet, take the next plane to Chengdu. A lower altitude is the surest cure.

Over-exertion contributes to mountain sickness, and dehydration may be a pre-disposing factor. Some precautions include:
–Stick to a schedule of very mild activity and rest for the first two days.
–Drink plenty of fluids. Four litres (seven pints) every day are recommended to maintain a clear, copious urine.
–Don't smoke, or at least keep it to a minimum.
–Avoid sedatives such as sleeping medicine or tranquillizers. They tend to depress respiration and limit oxygen intake.
–Diamox (acetazolamide), a mild prescription diuretic that stimulates oxygen intake, is used by doctors of the Himalayan Rescue Association in Kathmandu for climbers making sudden ascents. One 250 milligram tablet taken on the plane from Chengdu and another at bedtime the first night in Lhasa may help to forestall discomfort for

people known to be susceptible to mountain sickness. Consult a doctor. Diamox can cause unpleasant side-effects in some people.

It is not unusual to wake up at night at high altitudes gasping for breath. This complaint, known as 'periodic breathing' and caused by a change in the brain's control of breathing while you sleep, is normally quite harmless. Normal breathing can be quickly restored by relaxation, rhythmic deep breathing, and understanding that there is nothing to worry about.

# Other Health Concerns

Tibet has much less infectious disease than neighbouring countries because the spread of bacteria is limited by low temperatures, aridity and sparse population. However, a few visitors have contracted hepatitis in Tibet, and travellers arriving from hot, humid climates may already be carrying and incubating such illnesses as amoebic dysentery, giardiasis and hepatitis. These and normally less serious respiratory tract infections, such as colds, influenza, sinusitis and bronchitis, which reduce oxygen intake, can be devastating in Tibet, where your body's regenerative processes are occupied coping with climate and altitude. A standard traveller's first–aid kit should include a range of antibiotics and medicine for stomach troubles. Drugs such as Flagyl, Vermox and Tiniba for amoeba, worms and giardia should be used after consulting a doctor.

Drinking water should be boiled or treated with iodine tincture or compounds. Chlorine-based treatments do not kill amoebic cysts.

Dogs in Gyantse, Shigatse and small villages and encampments all over Tibet can be very aggressive. While the danger of dog bites is real enough, there is little danger of rabies. While the risk may be greater around Tangmai, Bomi, Yadong and the Chumbi Valley than in other places in Tibet, evacuation for a dog bite is generally considered unnecessary and is unlikely to be covered by your travel insurance policy. To prevent infection, bites should be washed at once with whatever clean fluid is available (even beer or soft drink, for lack of boiled or purified water), treated with an antiseptic, and bandaged. Then go to hospital. A clinic next to the Yak Hotel in Lhasa has information and treatment for rabies.

# Emergency Evacuation

Seriously ill travellers should not consider trying to leave Tibet by road, as the difficulties and uncertainties of such a journey pose unacceptable risks. Your only choice is to fly. You should have travel insurance to cover such contingencies. The hospital can give you a medical statement to use in claiming evacuation expenses.

A sick person, who can be accompanied by a relative or helper, can get on any CAAC flight without advance booking or notice. He should arrive at the airport at least an hour before boarding-time and should have letters in Chinese from a hospital or other competent authority stating the emergency and the need for evacuation. If the plane is full, other passengers will be taken off to make room. Emergency passengers can buy tickets on the spot at the airport, but must be carrying the exact fare in foreign exchange certificates. The pilot can radio ahead to Chengdu, giving details of the emergency and requesting preparations at the airport, so carry the medical statement (in Chinese) to show to the pilot and cabin staff.

Oxygen bags can be obtained from CITS at the Holiday Inn for the journey to the airport. As soon as the plane takes off, the cabin will be pressurized to sea-level pressure, bringing relief to patients with lung or breathing problems.

Travellers of any nationality can contact the US Consulate in Chengdu (the only foreign diplomatic presence in west China) for assistance. The staff is most helpful and can assist by arranging further hospitalization in Chengdu and contacting other embassies. You can telephone or telex them from Lhasa: at Room 135, West Wing, Jinjiang Hotel, Chengdu; tel Chengdu 51421; telex 60128.

You can go for check-ups or further treatment to the modern and excellent **West China Medical University Hospital** in Chengdu, which also has good dental care.

## Going to Hospital

If you are ill enough to need hospitalization, you should consider the following:
–Which first: hospitalization or evacuation? If altitude sickness is the problem, no medical treatment can do more than relieve some of the symptoms, and you will still need to evacuate to a low altitude. If you can safely be moved, it is best to do this by the next morning's flight. The later stages of oedema can make evacuation impossible.
–If you are travelling alone and staying at one of Lhasa's smaller hotels, you risk becoming very isolated if you have to stay in hospital for some time. Seriously ill patients are sometimes left unattended for long periods by the nursing staff. Before you go into hospital, tell as many friendly fellow travellers as possible and use hotel noticeboards to ask for help and visitors. You may need people to bring special foods, to take messages, to arrange your evacuation, and perhaps to lend foreign exchange certificates for an air ticket at short notice. Doctors, nurses and other health professionals can often be found amongst visitors at any of the hotels, and they may be willing to give you a diagnosis in Western terms and in your own language.

–Before going into hospital, consider checking into the Holiday Inn for access to their services, including taxis, international telephone and fax services, air-ticketing and—most valuable of all—help from the foreign management staff. When you are well enough to move, the hotel can make all the arrangements for your evacuation.

Ambulances are almost non-existent; taxis can be used during working hours but are difficult to find at night, except at the Holiday Inn. Mrs Tashi, the manager at the Yak Hotel, speaks good English and is very helpful toward sick people.

# Money

The cumbersome FEC (Foreign Exchange Certificate) system was scrapped in early 1994. Foreigners now use the same money as everyone else; *renminbi* (people's currency, abbreviated Rmb). *Renminbi* is divided into *yuan* (colloquially *kuai*), which equals ten *jiao* (colloquially *mao*) or 100 *fen*. In October 1996, US$1 equalled Rmb8.28. It is possible to buy and sell *renminbi* at the border, but not outside China.

In Tibet, only the Bank of China offers foreign exchange facilities. The bank's main office is in a white building near the Foreign Trade Centre west of the Potala Palace. There are several sub-branches in Lhasa. All can change travellers cheques (bring US$ denominations), and the main branch can give cash advances on major credit cards. Opening hours are 9 am–1 pm and 3.30–6 pm, Monday to Friday; the branch next to the Kirey Hotel is open from 9.30 am–5 pm Monday to Friday, and from 11.30 am–3 pm on Saturday and Sunday. Change all the money you think you will need before you leave Lhasa. A commission of 0.75 per cent is normal.

# Communications

International mail is reliable and quite fast if sent by airmail. In contrast, mail (especially parcel post) to or from other parts of China can be slow and unreliable. Telegrams are easily sent from any post office. This is the surest, most commonly used form of communication within Tibet. Fax services are available in the Holiday Inn for hotel guests and at the Telecommunications Centre, opposite the Ying Qiao Hotel.

Waiting time for an international call at the Telecommunications Centre can be anywhere from 30 minutes to three hours. Both incoming and outgoing calls can be routed through your hotel, but charges cannot be reversed. The sound quality is excellent.

Upmarket hotels in Lhasa have business centres with IDD phone and fax, as well

*Yak skin coracle on the Yarlong Tsangpo River near Tsedang*

as photocopying facilities. It is possible to make telephone calls within China from the numerous stores identified by a red telephone sign.

# Language

In Lhasa, some Nepalese traders and Chinese speak English, but few Tibetans do, as it was not taught in schools until recently. (Now, gifts of books and English-language cassettes are greatly appreciated.) Many Tibetans speak both Tibetan and Chinese, but few Chinese speak Tibetan. Most signs are written in Tibetan and Chinese. CITS and other travel agencies can provide interpreters if necessary, but most travellers manage without them. For a guide to basic Tibetan see page 238.

# Travel Agencies in Lhasa

China International Travel Service (CITS), also known as Liüxingshe, is the main organization responsible for looking after foreign tourists in China. CITS offers a comprehensive service covering visas, accommodation, food, sightseeing and transport. The Lhasa branch of CITS has guides/interpreters for English, French, German and Japanese, though the ability and experience of the guides varies considerably. Until recently, they were all young graduates from far away in China who knew less about Tibetan culture, religion and geography than many of their clients. Recently, however, CITS has taken on a number of young Tibetans, whose local knowledge is a great asset. The main CITS compound is opposite the Holiday Inn.

CITS normally operates with group tours and has less to offer to individual travellers, with their great diversity of needs. In addition, since the more profitable group tours must take precedence, individuals requesting transport, guides, or meeting/departure service during the peak tourism season between early summer and autumn may be disappointed.

Special-interest tours for groups such as botanists or art-historians can be arranged through CITS. CITS demands a large 'special licence fee' for unusual sporting activities, such as river-rafting, with the result that few people without commercial sponsorship can afford it.

A number of private trekking and guide companies have set up offices in Lhasa (see Travel Agencies, page 235) though they do not yet compare to services found in Nepal. Occasionally, Tibetans or Nepalese offer individual private arrangements. Prospective clients should check into the operator's reputation for reliability and honesty.

# Food and Drink

Traditional Tibetan fare consists of two basic items, salted tea mixed with yak butter, and *tsampa*, a coarse flour made from parched barley whose main virtues are that it is nourishing and (in a land where fuel is scarce) it does not need to be cooked. The tea, brewed in water, comes from bricks of tea that mostly originate from China's Yunnan and Sichuan provinces. This brick tea has been a major trade item for over 800 years. The brewed tea is poured into a long cylindrical churn made of wood banded with brass, along with salt and a small lump of butter. After vigorous churning, the opaque liquid is decanted into a teapot or a thermos, where it is kept for drinking throughout the day. (Sometimes a more concentrated brew is made with added wood-ash soda to bring out the colour, and later churned with added hot water, salt and butter.) The resulting drink is more like bouillon than tea as Westerners or Chinese know it. The body needs this extra fat intake to power its higher metabolic rate at high altitude, especially in cold weather. Tea provides a constant source of hydration and is everywhere socially important.

Mixed with *tsampa*, this tea makes an edible paste. Add some dried yak meat or *chiura* (dried cheese crumbs made from the residue of boiled buttermilk) and it becomes a meal. Tibetans have a deft technique for mixing the *tsampa*, kneading it with the fingers of the right hand while the left hand rotates the bowl; a visitor's first attempt at this invariably dumps half the contents on the floor, to gales of laughter from his Tibetan hosts. The best *tsampa*, like good coffee, is fresh-roasted and ground, enough for a week at a time, and has a nutty flavour.

*Drokpa* (nomad) yak-herders produce a wonderful yoghurt from the thick creamy milk produced by their *dris* (yak cows; a *yak* is actually a bull). Its strong flavour comes from the special process of manufacture. The milk from the evening milking is boiled, left in a pail overnight to turn into yoghurt, and mixed with boiled milk from the following morning's milking before being churned. It is this half-yoghurt mixture, not rancidity, that gives Tibetan butter its strong taste. In eastern Tibet, the evening and morning milk are churned separately to produce sweet butter, sometimes also found in the street market in Lhasa. In some low valleys around Lhasa, the milk comes from recently introduced cattle herds.

Nowadays the diet in the towns has greatly improved, due to the introduction of Chinese foods. Rice, fruit, soybean products and locally grown fresh vegetables are common. Fish, which was always abundant in Tibet's lakes and rivers but rarely eaten, is now a growing food item, though still rarely eaten by Tibetans. Restaurants have proliferated in Lhasa in recent years and all manner of food-stuffs are available from street shops. Moslem restaurants also sell steamed bread. One of the best dietary supplements is fresh yoghurt, peddled in glass jars along the Barkhor every morning.

Teashops in Old Lhasa serve sweet 'milk-tea'. The favourite local drink after tea, is *chang*, a greyish, flat, sour (though not unpleasant) barley beer. Beer and soft drinks are ubiquitous and a bit of searching will turn up useful foods for travelling and trekking. Chinese milk powder is available, but many brands have a great deal of sugar mixed in.

Restaurant menus are sometimes limited and the variety of vegetables is determined by Tibet's short grow-ing season and the produce that happens to be trucked in from neighbouring Sichuan and Gansu. Meat tends to be tough, chicken is scarce, but fish, if well cooked, can be a delicious source of protein. By most standards the restaurants lack hygiene, atmosphere and decor. If you do not speak Chinese or Tibetan, you can feel free to go into the kitchen, look over the food and point out what you want to have cooked for your meal. Be careful to ensure that each and every item you point at does not constitute one individual course, otherwise you will end up with a huge, expensive banquet.

Lhasa's Moslems, both indigenous Tibetans and recent arrivals from Qinghai, Gansu and Ningxia, have opened a number of **halal restaurants**. Blue and white banners written in Chinese (and sometimes Arabic) indicate their location. The fare is simple, predictable and reliable: noodles with beef

*Traditional Tibetan carpet from Nedong*

or beancurd in broth garnished with scallions, steamed bread and good aromatic tea. The tea—green, sweetened with rock sugar and flavoured with dried fruit—is worth a stop. The standard menu can be supplemented with seeds, peanuts or canned food usually available at the counter.

Tourist hotels in Lhasa offer yak burgers and other Western-style dishes.

# Shopping

In the midst of Tibet's fantastic sights it may sound mundane to talk about shopping. However, there are many odd, fascinating and beautiful things to buy. Tibet's culture continues to produce all sorts of objects for religious and other uses.

The best marketplace for curios is on and around the Barkhor, in the heart of Old Lhasa. Small shops carry colourful items like prayer flags, fur hats, horse bells and bridles, broad leather money-belts and copper teapots. The merchandise in small open street stalls changes from day to day. A curioseeker can find temple bells, conch-shell trumpets, rosaries, prayer wheels, amulets and a variety of jewellery made of turquoise (at least Rmb150 per string if old and genuine, cheaper if new and reconstituted paste), coral (also expensive, if old) and silver. Most of the prayer wheels, bracelets, necklaces and other small items are made by Tibetans in Nepal and India. A useful item is a wooden tea cup, with or without a lining of beaten silver.

Tibetan rugs can be found hanging on display along the Barkhor. Some of these have more individuality and appeal than the rugs produced for export in the Lhasa Carpet Factory (see page 113). Older house and horse rugs are of wool and usually have soft colours; newer rugs are usually of a wool mix and are brighter. As you amble clockwise around the Jokhang Temple you may be approached by Tibetan pilgrim-traders eager to sell you their own swords, inlaid knives, jewellery, Buddha figures and who knows what else. In the Barkhor's shops and stalls, and above all with individuals, you must bargain. As a loose guideline, you might get prices in shops down 20–25 per cent, but from stalls and individuals you should get nearer 50 per cent of the stated price. Haggling is a game that every Tibetan enjoys, and it should be played with perseverance, patience and good humour. The failure by tourists to haggle effectively has had a dramatic effect on prices. In addition, many popular items are becoming rare. Remember that too many souvenir 'cultural objects' may invite confiscation by customs officials when you leave the country.

For those who prefer fixed (if higher) prices, a fair variety of Tibetan handicrafts is on sale at the 'Selling Department for Tourist Products' on Beijing Dong Lu.

Any visitor to Lhasa notices the decorated tents, canopies and awnings that Tibetans use for numerous outdoor purposes. These are becoming a popular item for travellers to take home. At the Lhasa Tent and Banner Factory skilled artisans can copy and custom-make any design they are shown. They can make one-by-two-metre (three-by-six-foot) door curtains, awnings, canopies, small family tents for picnics or big ornate marquees for festivals or travelling lamas, with bestiary appliqué decorations in different colours. Prices vary greatly according to the complexity of the decorations.

For everyday practical items, there are four main department stores in New Lhasa. The General Department Store is a cavernous, L-shaped store at the west end of Yuthok Lu, and the Nong Ken Ting Department Store is a multi-storey building (with the Friendship Store on its top floor) halfway along the south side of the same street. The others are a large pale-green building in a fork in the road 300 metres (yards) east of the Holiday Inn, and a pale green building two-thirds of the way to Sera Monastery on the east side of Sera Lu. These stores and several other medium-sized shops stock comfortable cotton clothing, canteens, mugs, canned food, writing paper, envelopes, soap, towels and toothpaste. Toilet paper (*weisheng zhi*) can be found in most shops.

Lhasa's major bookshop, Xinhua, on Yuthok Lu, is not impressive but it does carry maps of Lhasa, posters, Tibetan primers, Tibetan-Chinese dictionaries, and Chinese and Tibetan paperback books. A bookshop with Tibetan literature is located just north of the Barkhor, west of the meat market.

# Photography

Visitors are generally allowed to take photos of buildings from the outside without charge. However, inside buildings (temples in particular) there may be a fee of about Rmb20 (up to Rmb100 in the Fifth Dalai Lama's Mausoleum), payable to the monks in charge. Avoid taking pictures of military personnel and police, bridges and communications installations.

# Trekking

Trekking is slowly developing as an important facet of the tourist industry in Tibet but still lags far behind Nepal. A few trekking companies do exist in Lhasa (see Practical Information, page 235), and they can organize some interesting trips such as a trek with pack-yaks to the Oracle Lake of Lhamo Lhatso. Some agencies in

Kathmandu, Europe and North America that specialize in mountain travel arrange group treks in Tibet.

As there are no equipment hire or sales outlets in Tibet, and renting gear from Kathmandu is expensive due to the inevitable delays in getting from Nepal to the Tibetan trekking areas, the best way to get equipped is to buy what you need at home, in Kathmandu or, if it is too late, to check noticeboards in hotels for used articles.

Tibet's unique environment—combining thin air and arctic conditions with sub-tropical sunshine—poses many problems, so even experienced trekkers should try a few short climbs and warm-up treks before setting out on anything ambitious. New arrivals and those suffering from a cold or flu should wait until they are better able to tolerate the altitude. All should plan their stages adhering to the dictim, 'climb high, sleep low', to minimize the effects of altitude and reduce the risk of waking up snow-bound—see page 43. (All precipitation above 4,500 metres (15,000 feet) is snow, regardless of the season.)

Protection from the sun requires good sunglasses and sunblock cream, a hat and perhaps even an umbrella. The desiccated air at most seasons parches the skin and lips and, coupled with dust, irritates the respiratory tract.

Surface water is hard to find, especially in high places. Snow tends to evaporate rather than melt, and even where there is sufficient snow or ice, melting it takes eight times more fuel than boiling the same amount of water. Dehydration (indicated by headache and a lack or darkening of the urine) is a serious risk, requiring a carrying capacity of at least two litres (3.5 pints).

Even those travellers who like butter tea, *tsampa*, noodles and dried yak meat cannot expect to live off the land while trekking, as the population is too sparse and impoverished to feed passing strangers, especially along the more popular routes. Trekkers should carry all the food they will need. That said, many Tibetans are delighted and honoured to offer hospitality to a foreign guest. They will refuse all payment, but are happy to receive such gifts as photos of the Dalai Lama, cords blessed by lamas, scissors, cloth gloves, hairpins and sewing needles.

Unlike Nepalese and Indians, Tibetans have no tradition of hiring out as porters or guides. Yaks, *dzos* (yak-cattle hybrids), donkeys and horses can sometimes be hired as pack animals or for riding. Additional expenses are a day rate for the handler (who brings his own food and bedding) and, for one-way trips, payment for the return journey (at about half the loaded rate). Prices are highest in the west and lowest in central Tibet; prices for animal hire vary by the season and the beast, but are generally Rmb25–40 per animal per day.

Examine the animals carefully; if they look too weak, they probably are. Pay only part of the money up front.

Nomad camps and herders' villages are usually guarded by very aggressive dogs, including huge Tibetan mastiffs. Extra care should be taken after dark, as the dogs are often left loose to keep away wolves and foxes. It is best to stop about 200 metres (yards) away and shout to the inhabitants, who will leash their dogs before inviting you in. Stones and a walking stick can offer some protection.

Tibet may be an unfenced wilderness, but there are still places you cannot go. The ongoing border dispute with India has made several beautiful and interesting areas in the Himalayas, around Sikkim and Bhutan and east to Burma, too sensitive for tourism. The considerable military presence has led to the closing of other areas, but trekkers are unlikely to stumble into trouble unless they deliberately choose sensitive areas.

The most popular treks are to Everest Base Camp (see page 209), from Dagze (Dechen) Dzong to Samye Monastery (see page 160), from Ganden Monastery to Samye (see page 162), and to Lake Namtso. Oracle Lake (Lhamo Lhatso) and the Kailash *kora* are for the hardy, experienced few.

Various side valleys to the north and south of Lhasa offer opportunities for easy warm-up treks with lots of contact with village people. You can stay in villages or camp out, making side trips into the mountains and returning at night to sleep low. This approach is good for people without experience or equipment. Some suitable areas are the long valley north of Samye Monastery, up to and around Yamalung, Tsürphu Monastery and its beautiful valley, Pembo and Reting (north of Lhasa), Drigung (further to the northeast), Mindroling, and the Yarlong and Chonggye valleys, near Tsedang. Victor Chan's *Tibet Handbook—a pilgrimage guide* covers all trekking destinations in detail.

*A monk with newly printed scriptures, Derge Monastery*

## How Buddhism Emerged in Tibet

Buddha means 'the enlightened one'. Sakyamuni (Saviour of the Sakya Clan) is a title of respect for the man named Siddharta Gautama, who was born a prince in north India around 500 BC. He grew up in luxury, shielded from contact with human misery, and married young. One night curiosity led him outside, where he saw shocking examples of disease, old age and death. Determined to find a way to save mankind from suffering, Sakyamuni left his wife and child, renounced his princehood, and spent long years wandering as an ascetic. At last, fasting and meditating under a tree, he received enlightenment.

Buddha's insight into ultimate reality was embodied in the Four Noble Truths and the Eightfold Path. He wished to be a guide, not an authority, and early Buddhism was a way of life rather than a religion. Its teaching encouraged people to take full responsibility for their thoughts and actions and to progress along a path to spiritual growth.

Buddha's followers formed open communities of monks and nuns, who lived disciplined lives and sought wisdom, their prime virtue. For 500 years, while Buddhism spread throughout India, all teaching was oral. In the third century BC this early form of Buddhism in India, called Theravada, took root in Ceylon and spread into other parts of South and Southeast Asia.

In the north, a new form of Buddhism appeared, called Mahayana or the Greater Vehicle, which appealed to many more people. Though sharing basic doctrines with Hinayana (Theravada), its emphasis changed. Compassion was its chief virtue, and its ideal was the bodhisattva, a perfected individual who gave up release from the cycle of rebirth in order to return to earth and help all sentient beings.

Buddha was now treated like a god. Countless mythical Buddhas were invented to embody all of his aspects, and their images were worshipped in temples. By the first century AD, scriptures, called sutras, laid down doctrines and monastic rules and recorded Buddha's sermons as they were remembered. Mahayana Buddhism spread to Central Asia, China, Korea and Japan.

A third type of Buddhism saw man's harmony with the universe as the key to salvation. Adepts of Tantrism in India tried to manipulate external forces by magic, while followers of Chan in China induced inner harmony through meditation.

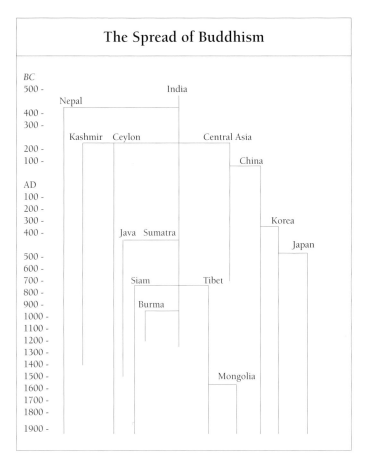

# The Spread of Buddhism

Buddhism died out in India around 1200, as Hinduism revived and harsh Moslem invasions destroyed Buddhist centres. But Buddhist doctrines and scriptures lived on in Tibet, where Buddhism was promoted by the kings. The faith almost vanished with the end of the monarchy in the ninth century. When it arose again, Tibet's decentralized conditions allowed Buddhism to split into some 20 sects. The following five became the most important:

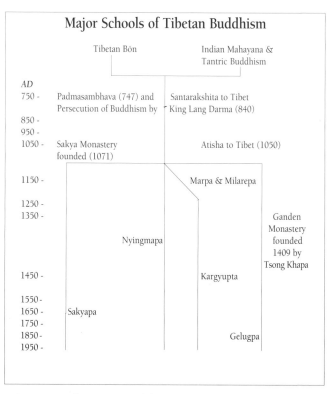

## Major Schools of Tibetan Buddhism

Tibetan Bön

Indian Mahayana & Tantric Buddhism

AD
750 - Padmasambhava (747) and Persecution of Buddhism by

Santarakshita to Tibet
King Lang Darma (840)

850 -
950 -
1050 - Sakya Monastery founded (1071)

Atisha to Tibet (1050)

1150 -

Marpa & Milarepa

1250 -
1350 -

Ganden Monastery founded 1409 by Tsong Khapa

Nyingmapa

1450 -

Kargyupta

1550-
1650 - Sakyapa
1750 -
1850-
1950 -

Gelugpa

**Nyingmapa**, the Ancient Ones, began around 750 with Padmasambhava. It absorbed the Bön faith and produced *The Tibetan Book of the Dead*.

**Kahdampa** began with Atisha after 1050. Its tradition laid stress on the scriptures and discipline, and it formed a link with India's sages.

**Kagyupa** began around 1060 with the teachers of Marpa and Milarepa. Most typically Tibetan, it stressed yoga as the way to seek enlightenment.

**Sakyapa** arose in 1073 at Sakya Monastery, which later governed Tibet. It was worldly and practical in outlook, less concerned with metaphysics.

**Gelugpa**, the Virtuous Ones or Yellow Hats, began with Tsong Khapa in 1407. It absorbed Kahdampa and carried on Atisha's tradition. It dominated Tibet after the 17th century, leaving other sects to play a minor role.

*Tibetan Khaden, or sleeping carpet, c. 1900–1920, courtesy of Altfield Gallery. The traditional arrangement of dragons and phoenix symbolize a happy home or marriage.*

# Lhasa

The city of Lhasa, population over 300,000, lies in the valley of the Lhasa (Kyi Chu or Quxu) River. Its altitude is 3,650 metres (11,975 feet). Its barren surrounding mountains average over 4,800 metres (16,000 feet), high enough that a night of summer rain in Lhasa can mean a ring of snowy peaks the next morning.

Two high, craggy hills stand up in isolation from the valley floor. One, Red Hill, is topped by the Potala Palace, a spectacular edifice whose golden roofs soar high above the town. The other, Chakpori or Iron Hill, is crowned by a tall antenna. Chakpori, one of the four holy mountains of Central Tibet, used to be the site of a famous 17th-century monastic medical school until it was demolished by the Chinese in 1959.

Lhasa consists of two distinct parts with different architecture, population and lifestyle. Old Lhasa, the Tibetan section, centres around the Jokhang Temple, the holiest site in Tibet. Its streets are narrow, between whitewashed stone houses whose walls slope inward as they rise. Windows are framed in black trapezoids, with protruding, fan-shaped eaves above. Many houses have brightly painted woodwork. The heart of Old Lhasa is the Barkhor, a street encircling the Jokhang. It is a sacred pilgrim path, a lively marketplace and a social centre that attracts a cross-section of Tibetans: traders from Kham (east Tibet) with high boots and daggers, their long hair wound in cockscombs of red yarn; shaggy nomads in sheepskins; maroon robed monks; women twirling hand-held prayer wheels, adorned in turquoise jewellery and wearing their long hair in 108 braids, a sacred and lucky number in Tibet. Pilgrims chant earnestly at the curbside, while others, covered in dust, progress by body-lengths around the Jokhang in devotional prostrations. All move in a clockwise direction as decreed by Buddhist custom. Long after the colourful shops and street stalls have closed for the night, crowds of Tibetans continue their circular walk by the light of sacred juniper fires in an atmosphere of sociability and good humour. Before 1985 the Jokhang and the Barkhor were totally hidden inside the old city. Now several blocks have been torn down to front the temple with a landscaped plaza and an avenue leading into New Lhasa.

New Lhasa, the Chinese section, was built in the last 40 years around the base of the Potala. It is characterized by straight, broad streets and utilitarian buildings that house Chinese-style department stores and all kinds of government offices. Most Chinese and some Tibetans live in 'work units'—barracklike buildings inside walled compounds with impressive gateways. These 'units' extend throughout the suburbs of New Lhasa and carry out functions ranging from foreign affairs to truck repair.

Lhasa's unprecedented building boom has changed forever the face of the city, and what was once a beguiling, mysterious and peaceful town is now on the surface a loud, crowded metropolis. Many people are appalled at the change, of which the influx of Chinese migrants is the most obvious manifestation.

Nevertheless, the place still has a soul, and walking the circuit of the Barkhor at any time of day or night is one of the strangest, most wonderful experiences in life. Wandering the alleys of Old Lhasa and befriending a Tibetan family is also deeply rewarding.

## Getting Around

One of the most pleasant ways to get around Lhasa is by bicycle (see page 41). Tricycle rickshaws are found in Barkhor Square, bus stations and outside the Holiday Inn. Negotiate the fare in advance. These are not recommended for long distances, such as to Sera or Drepung monasteries; buses make the trip every morning. The Holiday Inn runs buses to important sites around Lhasa and sometimes further afield. Vehicles can be rented by the day or half-day. Taxis are fairly plentiful; expect to pay Rmb15 or 20 from the Holiday Inn to the Jokhang. Minibuses charge a flat fee of Rmb2.

## Historical Background

The greatest sights around Lhasa proclaim Tibet's unique past, which is the story of a religion rather than of a nation. The Tibetan people and their religion are inseparable.

Their origins are lost in myth. Long ago, they believe, the bodhisattva of compassion, Chenrezi, sent his disciple, a holy monkey, to be a hermit in the mountains. While meditating in his cave, the monkey heard an ogress crying among the crags and took pity upon her loneliness. (Some say she threatened to marry a demon and to people the world with their offspring.) The monkey obtained Chenrezi's permission to marry the ogress. In due time they had six children, who grew up to be human beings with noble traits from their father, such as generosity, bravery and piety, and base ones from their mother, such as greed, envy and lust. They multiplied and became the Tibetan people, whose first kings descended from the sky. The Tibetans practised Bön, a faith filled with demons and magic.

Recorded history began with the reign of King Songtsen Gampo (AD 608–50), a young warrior king who unified all Tibet and made Lhasa his capital. He posed a sufficient threat to China to be able to demand a Chinese princess as his bride. Emperor Tai Zong, the first of the Tang Dynasty, sent his adopted daughter, Wen

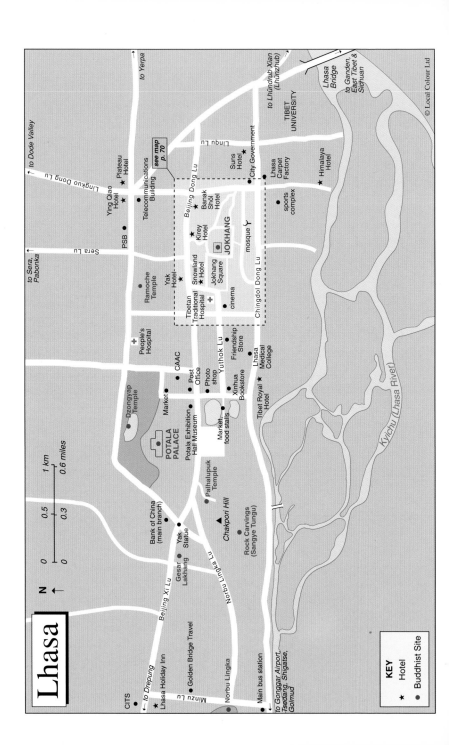

Cheng, to Tibet with pomp and ceremony, along with a gold Buddha statue as her dowry. Songtsen Gampo made another alliance by marrying Princess Tritsun of Nepal. His three Tibetan wives gave birth to the children who founded Tibet's Tubo Dynasty.

The two foreign princesses, both Buddhists, converted the king from the Bön faith to Buddhism and persuaded him to wear silk instead of sheepskins. Songtsen Gampo built a fortress on Red Hill (the first Potala) for them to live in, and he built the Jokhang and Ramoche temples in Lhasa to house their sacred Buddha statues.

The king then sent a bright young man, Tönmi Sambhota, to India to learn a system of writing. Sambhota invented a Tibetan orthography based on that of Kashmir and adapted its script to his complicated language—a brilliant feat. Ancient annals show that within 20 years it had come into wide use in Tibet for documents and laws, as well as for writing translations of Buddhist texts. Much later, when lamas ruled Tibet, Songtsen Gampo, the first 'religious king', was declared an incarnation of Chenrezi, the bodhisattva of compassion, and the patron saint of Tibet. His image is frequently seen in temples (see page 64).

After Songtsen Gampo, four generations of kings devoted themselves to wars of conquest. Buddhism made headway by absorbing many features of the old Bön faith and also of Indian tantrism—a branch of Buddhism that included esoteric and sexual elements and paranormal powers. This threefold mixture is sometimes called Lamaism. A lama was a highly learned monk. Although a lama must be a monk, relatively few monks became lamas.

The second great king of the Tubo Dynasty was Trisong Detsen (755–97). Like his ancestor, Songtsen Gampo, he was a notable military commander. His armies campaigned from Samarkand to Chang'an, the capital of China. But he is best remembered for his role as Tibet's second 'religious king', who definitively rooted Buddhism in Tibet. Trisong Detsen called in famous Buddhist teachers from India and China, among them a great Indian tantric mystic named Padmasambhava (or Guru Rinpoche), who so terrified the Bön priests that they eventually forced him to leave. Padmasambhava had a far-reaching influence and became the patron saint of early Tibetan Buddhism. His image can be seen in many temples (see page 64).

Trisong Detsen founded Samye, Tibet's first monastery, in 779 (see page 151) where Tibetans could be trained as monks. When fundamental conflicts appeared between the doctrines of India and China, the king staged public debates at Samye between masters of contending schools of thought. The Indians won hands down. Thereafter, Indian philosophy held sway in Tibet, although some elements of Chinese Chan (Zen) Buddhism did enter Tibetan Buddhism.

During Trisong Detsen's reign, the influence of monks on Tibetan life began to grow. It reached its climax 50 years later when his grandson turned over his whole administration to a monk. That blindly pious king was assassinated, and his brother,

# EASILY RECOGNIZED FIGURES

In the phantasmagoria of figures that populate Tibetan art in sculpture, mural paintings and *thangkas*, some important historical people and religious beings can be recognized by their iconographic conventions.

**King Songtsen Gampo** (AD 608–50). Introduced Buddhism to Tibet. Founded Tubo line of kings. Always wears high orange or gold turban with small Amitabha Buddha head peeping out of the top. Chinese wife, Wen Cheng, always on viewer's right. Nepalese wife, Tritsun, on viewer's left.

**Padmasambhava** (or Guru Rinpoche, eighth century). Invited from India to Tibet in 747. Exorcized demons by supernatural powers. Founded earliest Tibetan Buddhist sect. Wears magical, crown-like, red hat. Severe expression, curled moustache. Carries *dorje* (see page 96) and magic sceptre with skull-heads.

**Tsong Khapa** (1357–1419). Great reformer of Tibetan Buddhism. Founder of the Yellow Hat Sect. Always seated. Wears pointed yellow cap with long ear flaps. Usually smiling, with a bulbous nose. His image is often repeated with large and small versions of himself sitting side by side.

**Fifth Dalai Lama** (1617–82). Greatest of all the dalai lamas. Unified Tibet and made Yellow Hat Sect the state religion. Built the Potala. Wears pointed yellow cap with ear flaps. Portly, with double chins and popping eyes. Often has small moustache.

**Sakyamuni** (fifth century BC). The historical Buddha (see page 56). His enlightenment and teachings set in motion the Buddhist faith, which today claims 300 million followers. Often has blue hair with a cranial bump on top, but sometimes crowned. Usually sits cross-legged on a lotus-flower throne.

**Chenrezi**, the bodhisattva of compassion. (Tibetan manifestation of India's Avalokitesvara, or China's Guan Yin.) In full splendour he displays 11 heads (of which one is wrathful) and multiple pairs of arms. Sometimes encircled by 1,000 hands. In simpler forms he is hard to distinguish from other crowned Buddhas.

**Tara**, the most beloved of female deities. Special protectress and saviour of the Tibetan people. Symbolizes fertility. Believed to fulfil wishes. Green Tara associated with night and Tritsun; White Tara with day and Wen Cheng. Usually seated. Wears pagoda-shaped crown. Delicate features. Has seven eyes on face, hands and feet.

**Yamantaka** the Terrible. Favourite of the eight guardians of the faith, popularized by Tsong Khapa. A wrathful form of the bodhisattva of wisdom. Coloured blue with horned bull's head. Many arms. Body draped with skulls. Tramples on human forms representing stupidity, sloth and nihilism. Often shown in sexual embrace (*yab-yum*) with his female partner, Prajna (Wisdom), symbolizing the union of compassion and insight.

**Four Heavenly Kings**, guardians of the four directions. Usually found as large statues or murals in temple porches and entrances. East is white, carries a musical instrument. South is blue, carries a sword. West is red, usually carries a stupa or *dorje*. North is orange and carries an umbrella. The chief of the four kings is East.

Lang Darma, seized the throne. Lang Darma (reigned 836–42) then set out to extinguish Buddhism. Monasteries were systematically disbanded, monks were persecuted, and religion in Tibet went into eclipse for more than 100 years. Lang Darma himself was murdered by an avenging monk, and with that the monarchy came to an end. Tibet collapsed into enclaves ruled by rival clans.

Gradually, peace returned and Buddhism trickled back. In 1042, a famous tantric master from India named Atisha journeyed northward just when Tibet was ready for a religious revival. Under his influence, a number of Tibetans formed communities to study aspects of Buddhist doctrine. Thus arose the sects, known by the colour of their hats, who fought for control of Tibet during the next 500 years. The Red Hats and Black Hats were the strongest of these sects.

New monasteries were founded at this time, the greatest of which was Sakya (see page 205). When Genghis Khan, the Mongol tyrant, forced Tibet into submission, Sakya's abbot converted the Mongols to Buddhism. The next abbot, Phakpa, went to Peking as mentor to Kublai Khan, the emperor. (Phakpa's diary mentions meeting Marco Polo there.) As a favour, the emperor granted Sakya Monastery the right to rule Tibet in 1254. Rival sects resented this privilege, and 90 years later other monasteries, with princely Tibetan patrons, seized control.

During this period of struggle for power, a saintly scholar named Tsong Khapa (1357–1419) founded Ganden Monastery near Lhasa and began a new sect, the Gelugpa (Virtuous Ones), also known as the Yellow Hats. Strict morality, celibacy and a purified doctrine that followed Atisha's teachings marked the Yellow Hat monks. Tsong Khapa's disciples founded Lhasa's huge monasteries of Sera and Drepung and popularized their master's theological writings. The Yellow Hat Sect eventually became Tibet's state religion. The image of Tsong Khapa, its founder and Tibet's great reformer, appears in temples and monasteries almost as frequently as that of the Buddha (see page 64).

One line of Yellow Hat abbots were known as *dalai lamas* (see page 76). They had equal status with high lamas of other sects until the Fifth Dalai Lama (1617–82) ensured their permanent supremacy. With the help of an army supplied by a Yellow Hat Mongolian prince, the Great Fifth unified Tibet under his own leadership, subdued the nobility and ended any secular role for the Red or Black Hat sects. To solidify Yellow Hat control, he gave his own revered teacher the title of *panchen lama* (see page 173), with spiritual powers equal to his own, and placed him in Shigatse.

The Fifth Dalai Lama built the vast Potala Palace as his centre of government. He declared all dalai lamas (as well as King Songtsen Gampo) to be reincarnations of Chenrezi, thus making them god-kings. High lamas wielded great power throughout Tibet as regents or members of ruling councils. The tax-exempt land-owning monasteries accumulated huge wealth.

An unchangeable theocracy prevailed in Tibet until 1951. The outside world was feared and shut out. No subsequent ruler approached the stature of the Great Fifth until the Thirteenth Dalai Lama (1876–1933). This able man made concerted efforts to bring Tibet into the 20th century, but with scant success. When China entered Tibet in 1951, there were no public schools and no roads outside Lhasa.

The Tibetan uprising of 1959 brought fierce reprisals from the Chinese. The Dalai Lama and 80,000 followers fled. All the old institutions vanished, monasteries were dismantled, and Tibet was forced into a modern socialist world. Wanton destruction during the Cultural Revolution (1966-76) wiped out much of the physical evidence of Tibetan culture. Only a tiny number of many thousands of monasteries remained standing, and many magnificent landmarks were gone forever.

Tibet started to stir again in 1980, when new policies in Beijing allowed the people more religious and economic freedom. Worshippers and traders resumed their pilgrimages to Lhasa, and money was provided for the repair of famous historic buildings by Tibetan artisans under Tibetan foremen, many of whom were former monks. Visitors to Lhasa can now detect echoes of Tibet's amazing cultural past. If they keep their eyes open and are not afraid to explore, they may discover surprising corners that are not on any tourist itinerary—a hidden nunnery, a sculptor at work in a tiny unmarked temple where the religious culture of Tibet is now recreating itself. Please remember, however, that repression still lurks in Tibet; be careful of your activities because they might inadvertently get Tibetans into trouble.

# Sights Around Lhasa

## JOKHANG TEMPLE

The Jokhang is the spiritual centre of Tibet, its most holy place, the destination, over time, of millions of Tibetan pilgrims.

The oldest part of the Jokhang dates from the seventh century AD. It was one of two temples built by King Songtsen Gampo to house the statues of Buddha that his two foreign wives brought to Tibet from China and Nepal. Legend says that Songtsen Gampo threw his ring into the air, promising to build a temple wherever it landed. The ring fell into a lake and struck a rock where a white stupa miraculously appeared—an auspicious sign. Workmen filled in the lake with stones, and the Jokhang was built over it by craftsmen from Tibet, China, Nepal and Kashmir. Even today, a pool exists under the Jokhang's main courtyard.

Following removal of part of the Barkhor in 1985 to make way for a plaza, three monuments that stand in front of the Jokhang were enclosed in walls. The pillar on

*(following pages) The roof of the Jokhang looking east*

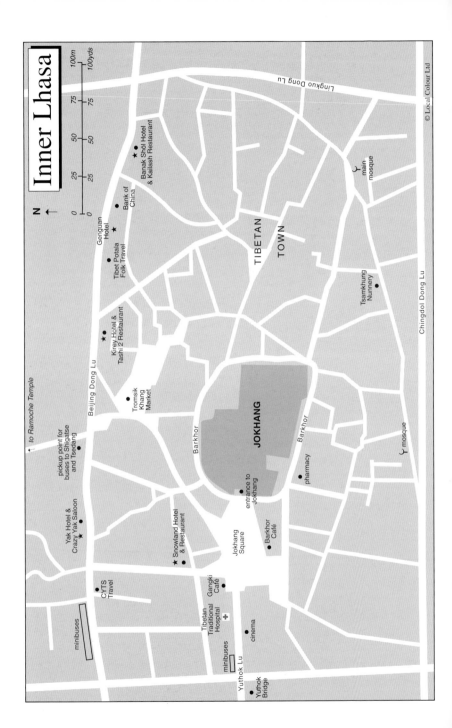

# Inner Lhasa

N

0   25   50   75   100m
0   25   50   75   100yds

© Local Colour Ltd

to Ramoche Temple

Beijing Dong Lu

Genguan Hotel

Tibet Potala Folk Travel

Bank of China

Banak Shöl Hotel & Kailash Restaurant

Kirey Hotel & Tashi 2 Restaurant

Tromsik Khang Market

pickup point for buses to Shigatse and Tsedang

Yak Hotel & Crazy Yak Saloon

minibuses

CYTS Travel

Snowland Hotel & Restaurant

Barkhor

JOKHANG

Barkhor

entrance to Jokhang

Jokhang Square

Barkhor Café

Jokhang Square

Gangki Café

Tibetan Traditional Hospital

cinema

minibuses

Yuthok Lu

Yuthok Bridge

TIBETAN TOWN

Tsamkhung Nunnery

pharmacy

main mosque

mosque

Lingkuo Dong Lu

Chingdol Dong Lu

the left is a treaty stone recording an alliance between the king of Tibet and the emperor of China in AD 823. On the right, the more visible of the two tablets was erected by the Chinese in 1794 to announce procedures in case of a smallpox epidemic. The tablet was partly eaten away by people who thought the stone itself had curative powers.

The outer courtyard and porch of the temple are usually filled with pilgrims making full-length prostrations towards the holy sanctum. Its innermost shrine contains the oldest, most precious object in Tibet—the original statue of Sakyamuni (the historical Buddha), which Princess Wen Cheng brought from Chang'an 1,300 years ago.

### ■ LAYOUT

The Jokhang was enlarged eight times between the seventh century and 1660, when the Fifth Dalai Lama added its last embellishments. It consists of an elaborate porch leading to a frescoed cloister around an open courtyard. Outside runs a long gallery of prayer wheels. A passage leads into a main hall with numerous small chapels around it. The sacred shrine holding the ancient Buddha statue is centred at the rear of this main hall. Above, another floor has historically valuable murals. At the top, a three-level roof is a world unto itself. Although monks have been attached to the Jokhang for centuries, its eminence rests on the sacred statuary and shrines of the temple, not on the fame of the monastery.

Unlike the lofty Potala, the Jokhang has intimate, human proportions. Pilgrims inch their way clockwise towards the Holy of Holies, crowding through low chapel doorways in semi-darkness with gifts of yak butter to fuel the myriad flickering votive lamps, or with white scarves to honour the deities. The murmuring of mantras sounds like a distant swarm of bees.

In recent years sad events have taken place in the Jokhang. Many early wall paintings, some over a thousand years old, have been removed for the sake of 'restoration'. With the exception of one 11th-century mural in the Sheray Lhakhang and some much later mandalas in the Songtsen Gampo Chapel on the west side, all of the wall paintings of the Jokhang's first floor have been removed and replaced with modern murals. The loss of so many world-class works of religious art is a great cultural disaster.

The **Main Hall** is entered through a corridor graced by guardian statues—fierce on the left, benign on the right. Here a delightful set of murals, thankfully still intact, depicts Wen Cheng's procession arriving in Tibet with the statue enthroned in a horse-drawn carriage, and then the building of the Jokhang. In the middle of the hall sit huge images of Padmasambhava (left) and Sakyamuni (right). Between them, a delicate, 11-headed Chenrezi expresses infinite compassion. Above, beams carved

with human-faced lions show influence from Persia via Kashmir. Numerous small chapels enshrining a variety of Tibetan deities progress to the back wall.

The **Holy of Holies** During mornings, late afternoons and holy days pilgrims can circumambulate the shrine. The statue, gilded many times, crowned, encrusted with jewels and placed in an elaborate setting, originally represented Sakyamuni aged 12. On both sides of the shrine are altars with images of Songtsen Gampo and his two wives (see page 64).

The **roof** is a conglomerate of pavilions, craftsmen's workshops, monks' living rooms and gold roofs adorned with bells, figures, birds, beasts and dragons. At the front, two golden deer holding the Buddhist 'Wheel of Dharma' recall the Buddha's first sermon in a deer park. There is a splendid view over the Barkhor to the Potala. Photography is permitted. Open mid-morning to 5 pm.

## POTALA

This world-famous architectural wonder is built on the escarpments of Red Hill and rises high above the valley floor. The awesome Potala can be seen from all directions for miles around.

A stronghold probably existed on Red Hill as early as the seventh century AD, when King Songtsen Gampo built a fortress on it for his two foreign wives. He is reputed to have studied the Buddhist scriptures there after his conversion from the Bön faith. Fires, lightning and wars took their toll, yet 1,000 years later two of the original rooms still remained.

The present Potala was built mainly in the Fifth Dalai Lama's reign, between 1645 and 1693. It became the winter palace in 1755, when the Seventh Dalai Lama made the Norbulingka into a summer residence. The Potala remained the centre of political and religious power for the dalai lamas.

With over 1,000 rooms, it contained the living quarters of the dalai lamas while they lived, and their sumptuous golden tombs when they died. Regents, tutors and other high lamas also had apartments in the palace. The Potala held the offices of government, a huge printing house at its base where Buddhist scriptures were hand-printed from woodblocks, and a seminary to train government officials, run by the élite order of monks of Namgyal Monastery who surrounded the god-king. Hundreds of elaborately decorated chapels and shrines, halls and corridors contained thousands of gilded statues—Tibet's pantheon of Buddhas, bodhisattvas, saints and demons. The round, outside towers were fortifications, but legend says they are wings to fly the Potala to safety from a future devastating flood.

Beneath the splendid ceremonial areas of the palace lay a warren of soot-blackened cells for monks and servants, and two great treasuries—one for the dalai

*Tibet's holiest statue, the Jowo Sakyamuni, housed in the Jokhang Temple*

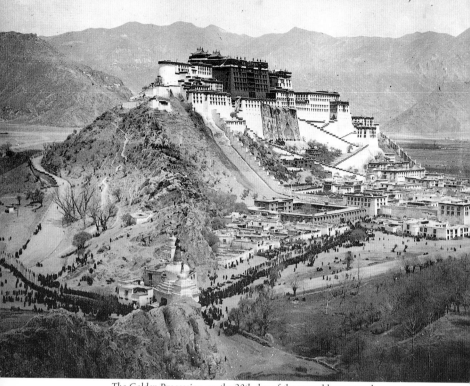

*The Golden Procession, on the 30th day of the second lunar month,
makes its way around the Potala*

lamas and regents, and the other for the state. Still lower lay granaries and store-rooms filled with pilgrims' gifts and enough yak butter to fuel the Potala's countless votive lamps for years. At the base, carved from living rock, were the dungeons, the dreaded Cave of Scorpions, from which enemies of the rulers rarely emerged.

Today the Potala is a state museum with a group of caretaker monks, but to many thousands of Tibetan pilgrims it remains a beloved shrine. Visitors should respect Buddhist custom by moving clockwise around the rooms when possible.

### ■ LAYOUT

The Potala consists of a White Palace and a Red Palace, with one small yellow portion between them. The first White Palace was built in the lifetime of the Fifth Dalai Lama, then extended to its present size by the Thirteenth Dalai Lama in the early 20th century. The Great Fifth moved to the Potala from Drepung Monastery in about 1650. His death in 1682 was concealed for ten years by the regent, who explained his absence as a series of religious retreats. During those years the Red Palace was built.

The White Palace was for secular use. It contained living quarters, offices, the

seminary and the printing house. The Red Palace's function was religious. It contained gold stupas (see page 153), which were the tombs of eight dalai lamas, the monks'
assembly hall, numerous chapels and shrines, and libraries for Buddhist scriptures:
the *Kanjur* with 108 volumes, and the *Tenjur* with 227. The yellow building between
the main palaces housed giant banners (*thangkas*) embroidered with the Buddha and
holy symbols that hung across the Potala's south face during the last day of the
second lunar month.

Construction of the Potala was a huge undertaking. It is 13 storeys (100 metres
or 330 feet) high, 400 metres (1,310 feet) east to west, and 350 metres ( 1,150 feet)
north to south. Its inward-sloping stone walls are, on average, three metres (ten feet)
thick, fully five metres (over 16 feet) thick at the base. Copper was poured into the
foundations to help them withstand earthquakes. So much earth was dug up for
mortar behind Red Hill that the pit was turned into a lake. (The flighty Sixth Dalai
Lama later added a pavilion in the middle of it for his dalliances).

The upper parts of the Potala have such finely joined wooden brackets, beams
and eaves that no nails were needed. The upper exterior walls are made from twigs
rammed end-in and painted brownish-red—a uniquely Tibetan style reserved for
sacred buildings and houses of nobles in high authority. The roofs are made of gilded
copper. Murals in the Red Palace's lower gallery show the building of the Potala in
splendid detail.

Tour groups are brought by bus up Red Hill to enter the Red Palace at the
western end. Individuals and pilgrims approach through Shö, a village at the base of
Red Hill formerly enclosed within the Potala's compound wall. A steep climb up the
main east-central flight of steps leads to the eastern portal of the White Palace. The
approaches to both entrances are decorated with *mani* stones (see page 97), small
cairns, prayer flags and knotted garlands of yak hair left by pilgrims as devotional
offerings.

Only a relatively small part of the Potala is open to the public, but it is still easy to
get lost. Bring a flashlight.

The central yellow-painted courtyard, or Deyangshar, of the **White Palace** is
reached from the East Portal by a broad corridor that climbs upward between thick
walls to an entrance with hanging drums. The large, open court is surrounded by a
two-storey gallery of rooms (former offices) embellished with sacred emblems (see
page 136). On the west side is the exterior of the dalai lama's living quarters, from
whose upper windows the god-king watched religious ceremonies and performances
below. On the east is Tsedrung Seminary (left) and its dormitory (right). A souvenir
shop and tour guide office are located on the north side.

The **roof** is reached by a series of ladder-stairs from the west side of the court

# THE DALAI LAMAS

'Dalai lama' was the title of Tibet's rulers for over 500 years. Fourteen dalai lamas ruled in succession, each one a reincarnation of his predecessor, according to Tibetan belief. The title dalai, or 'ocean' (presumably ocean of wisdom), was given to the Third in 1578 by a Mongol king, and applied posthumously to the first two. The Fifth named himself, his four predecessors and all future dalai lamas as incarnations of the bodhisattva of compassion, Chenrezi, thus adopting divine status.

When a dalai lama died, a search for his reincarnation began at once. Helped by the state oracle, portents and dreams, high lamas scoured Tibet for a boy with special physical traits, such as big ears and long eyes, who, in addition to other tests, could identify the late dalai lama's possessions among a pile of similar objects. In case of rival candidates, they drew lots. Until the new dalai lama was 18, a regent wielded unlimited power. The Fifth and Thirteenth were the greatest dalai lamas.

The First Dalai Lama (1391–1474) was a disciple of Tsong Khapa. He founded Tashilhunpo Monastery, at Shigatse, and was its first abbot.

The Second (1475–1542) served as the abbot of three great Yellow Hat monasteries while disputes raged between rival Tibetan sects.

The Third (1543–88), an abbot of Drepung Monastery, succeeded in reviving Buddhism in Mongolia. Altan Khan, the king, became his patron.

The Fourth (1588–1616) was conveniently discovered to be the great-grandson of Altan Khan—the only non-Tibetan in the line of dalai lamas.

The Great Fifth (1617–82) was a mighty scholar, politician and architect. Aided by a Mongol prince, he unified Tibet under his rule and suppressed all rivals of the Yellow Hat Sect. The Potala is his monument.

The Sixth (1683–1706) preferred women, wine and poetry. Angry Mongolians killed the regent and kidnapped the Dalai Lama. He was never seen again.

The Seventh (1708–57) was installed with Chinese help after Mongols imposed a false dalai lama.

The Eighth to the Twelfth (1758–1875) are of minor importance. Most died young (probably poisoned), while their regents held on to power.

The Great Thirteenth (1876–1933) withstood a British invasion in 1904 and made Tibet independent in 1912 after China became a republic. An able, intelligent ruler, he tried in vain to modernize Tibet's institutions.

The Fourteenth (b 1935) was only 16 when Mao Zedong's China took over Tibet. He ruled in partial capacity under the Chinese for ten years but fled in 1959 with 80,000 followers to India, where he keeps an active headquarters. He is still held in great esteem in Tibet.

The First Dalai Lama is entombed at Tashilhunpo Monastery; the Second, Third and Fourth at Drepung Monastery; and all the others (except the Sixth, who has no tomb) inside the Potala.

*Statue of Tsong Khapa and Yellow Hat disciples, Potala*

# A Sacred Quest

Naturally the fascinating question of who was to be the Fourteenth Dalai Lama occupied our monastic community more and more the longer the Delegation maintained its headquarters in Kumbum—and, as I have already said, they stayed there for no less than two years. It was only much later that I heard the details of the visits paid by the ambassadors of the Government to my old home, visits which finally led to the declaration of my younger brother Lhamo Döndrub as the incarnation of Chenrezig; and then it was in Lhasa from a monk named Kesang of the Sera Monastery who was a member of the Government Commission which carried out the search. Kesang was in the retinue of Kyetsang Rinpoche when the Rinpoche subjected my brother to a searching interrogation and examination in our family home.

Kyetsang Rinpoche had gone to Tengtser with Kesang and one or two others. They were travelling as merchants on their way to Chakhyung, and they asked my mother for permission to make themselves tea in her kitchen. In order to obtain the best possible insight into any circumstances he met with Kyetsang Rinpoche had chosen the role of servant to the rest, who were outwardly Bönpos, and thus his masters and superiors. On going into our courtyard for the first time he had been struck by the bizarre shapes of our wooden gutter pipes; the same that had so often stimulated the imagination of my playmates and me years before. It appeared that the Regent in Lhasa had had a dream in which he had seen the as-yet-unknown Fourteenth Dalai Lama standing under just such extraordinary roof gutters. In consequence Kyetsang Rinpoche now decided to subject the background, and in particular the little Lhamo Döndrub, to a much closer investigation. He therefore told the others to ask for lodgings for the night, and this was willingly granted to them by my parents. That evening he and his companions played for a long time with Lhamo Döndrub and were greatly impressed by him.

Now Kyetsang Rinpoche had a number of things with him which had belonged to the Thirteenth Dalai Lama, and the normal procedure was to bring them quite casually to the notice of such children of whom it was thought that they might conceivably be the long-sought-for incarnation. Now no sooner did Lhamo Döndrub catch sight of the rosary of the dead Thirteenth Dalai Lama in the possession of Kyetsang Rinpoche than he addressed him indignantly, declaring that the rosary was his; and he refused to let himself be persuaded, and continued to insist that the rosary was, in fact, his. Lhamo Döndrub was an unusually lively and high-spirited child, and he insisted that Kyetsang Rinpoche should hand over 'his' rosary. But not only that, the child told the disguised Kyetsang Rinpoche to his face that he was a lama from Lhasa. And the visitors could hardly believe their ears when the child addressed them in Lhasa dialect. Then the same thing happened with a walking-stick and a damaru, or small double drum, both of which had previously belonged to the Thirteenth Dalai Lama. Lhamo Döndrub seized them, declared them to be his own, and refused to be parted from them any more. In fact he was so excited about the whole affair, and so indignant at what he regarded as the attempt to deprive him of his possessions, that he was near to tears.

> Thubten Jigme Norbu and Heinrich Harrer, Tibet is my Country:
> Autobiography of Thubten Jigme Norbu,
> Brother of the Dalai Lama
> translated by Edward Fitzgerald, 1960

In his autobiography, Thubten Jigme Norbu recounts a countryside childhood, his recognition an a reincarnated lama, his training in the monastery of his previous life from the age of eight and many details of his later life including exile in the United States.

# Arrival

Within seconds of our arrival Tibetans had surrounded us, pressing up against the van's windows, hands and faces flattened there by the weight of others behind them trying to get a look.

Their piercing eyes were both soft and threatening.

Their clothes, hats and shoes were made from animal skins, furs and wool. A bulky, knee-length sheepkin coat was the main article of apparel, worn off the shoulder with the loose arm wrapped around the waist, forming a pouch-like overhang which seemed to be concealing a beerpot. The coat was knotted around the waist, and a knife was stuck in the waistband. The hats were of fox fur, and the colourful boots made of wool with a leather sole. The mens' hair was quite often worn uncut—a mane wrapped round the head and decorated with ribbons, bones and jewellery. The women's coats were longer, reaching right down to the ground and decorated on the lower half with bands of red and green material. Their hair was worn in pony-tails plaited with brightly coloured threads—red, pink, blue, purple, green and orange. Babies slept wrapped in blankets on their backs. Sometimes the babies were carried by sisters not much bigger than themselves, staggering under their weight. The air was crisp and the sky was bright.

Nachu's architecture was unlike anything I had seen. The typically Tibetan edifices were made of stone and rose at an inwardly-sloping angle. Their solidity reminded me of the buildings of the Incas. The windows also sloped, but they were protected from above by a jutting wooden ledge which was decorated with painted crenellations. The temple was concealed from view by the buildings that surrounded it. The streets were so narrow that our vehicles only just managed to squeeze along them, but we reached the little temple square at last, where worshippers prostrated themselves in the dust and dirt in front of the building. I wondered if I should go in or not, *but Wangchuk led the way forward. As my eyes adjusted to the candlelit dimness of the interior I was filled with awe—I was on the edge of discovering a new world once more. And this magnificent, alien treasure house meant even more to me that the Caves had done, for it was alive, now! I smelt the burning rancid butter; I heard the muttered incantations of the lamas and the heart-stopping sound of the temple drum, which stilled the soul, just as the clash of the cymbals freed the spirit. We passed by empty rows of cushions which would normally be occupied by lamas, and I saw that in the empty places their habits lay—just as if their owners had been magically lifted from this world. Uninitiated in their mysteries, I trod carefully in Wangchuk's footsteps, admiring the temple's magnificent murals and its rich thankas—free-hanging paintings or emroideries on silk—and bowing my head as I passed its golden Gods. They were unforgiving, their expressions variously sinsiter, sarcastic, mocking, serene or wise. Offerings of yak butter were poured from thermos flasks. Bowls of money. The spinning of a hand-held prayer wheel. A photograph of the Dalai Lama on the altar in front of his Gods.*

*The scenery beyond Nachu became even grander, and was never without its sprinkling of yaks. Approaching Lhasa I had a hint of what was to come: the Roof of the World—bleak, barren and yet majestic. A land at one with its religion. We passed pilgrims making their way to the holy city on foot. Alone or in pairs they took three steps forward and then prostrated themselves, before retracing their steps to fetch their cart of belongings and tow it after them. Never have I seen such laborious progress so patiently made. It was an almost inhuman patience. They would take 90 days to reach the city, starting from Golmud—a journey we would make in our vans in about 36 hours.*

*At last there were only twelve kilometres between us and Lhasa. I had tried to keep my excitement in check, telling myself that the Potala was bound to be a disappointment, but then we rounded a bend and there in the distance it stood astride a hill against the mountains.*

*I was almost choking with excitement as we passed beneath it on our way to the guesthouse.*

*Nick Danziger,* Danziger's Travels, *1993*

*In 1982, Nick Danziger was awarded the Winston Churchill Memorial Trust Fellowship to follow ancient trade-routes. He set off in 1984 and* Danziger's Travels *was the result. Danziger is an artist and photographer by training and his photographs have appeared in many newspapers and magazines worldwide.*

(above) *Tsong Khapa statue detail;*
(below) *Exterior view of the Potala's southern face*

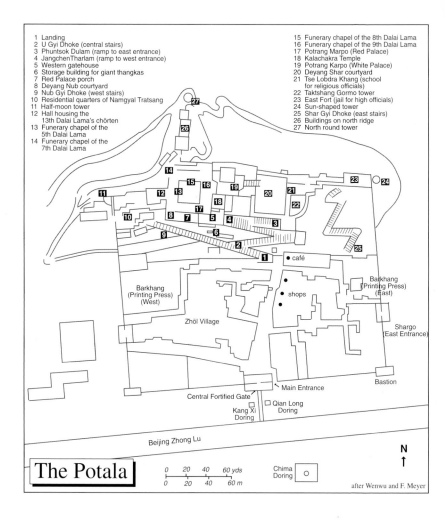

| | |
|---|---|
| 1 Landing | 15 Funerary chapel of the 8th Dalai Lama |
| 2 U Gyi Dhoke (central stairs) | 16 Funerary chapel of the 9th Dalai Lama |
| 3 Phuntsok Dulam (ramp to east entrance) | 17 Potrang Marpo (Red Palace) |
| 4 JangchenTharlam (ramp to west entrance) | 18 Kalachakra Temple |
| 5 Western gatehouse | 19 Potrang Karpo (White Palace) |
| 6 Storage building for giant thangkas | 20 Deyang Shar courtyard |
| 7 Red Palace porch | 21 Tse Lobdra Khang (school |
| 8 Deyang Nub courtyard | for religious officials) |
| 9 Nub Gyi Dhoke (west stairs) | 22 Taktshang Gormo tower |
| 10 Residential quarters of Namgyal Tratsang | 23 East Fort (jail for high officials) |
| 11 Half-moon tower | 24 Sun-shaped tower |
| 12 Hall housing the | 25 Shar Gyi Dhoke (east stairs) |
| 13th Dalai Lama's chörten | 26 Buildings on north ridge |
| 13 Funerary chapel of the | 27 North round tower |
| 5th Dalai Lama | |
| 14 Funerary chapel of the | |
| 7th Dalai Lama | |

• café

Barkhang
(Printing Press)
(East)

Barkhang
(Printing Press)
(West)

• shops

Zhöl Village

Shargo
(East Entrance)

Bastion

← Main Entrance

Central Fortified Gate

Kang Xi
Doring

Qian Long
Doring

Beijing Zhong Lu

**The Potala**

| 0 | 20 | 40 | 60 yds |
|---|---|---|---|
| 0 | 20 | 40 | 60 m |

Chima
Doring

N
↑

after Wenwu and F. Meyer

yard. The first hallway contains an edict of the Fifth Dalai Lama, copied from the original and signed with the Thirteenth Dalai Lama's handprint. Opposite, murals depict construction in the seventh century AD. The flat roof has some fine examples of the golden roof ornaments and finials that are typical of Tibetan religious architecture. There is also an unsurpassed view of the Lhasa Valley.

The **apartments** on the east side of the roof belonged to the Thirteenth and Fourteenth dalai lamas. The Chamber of Eastern Light, with a throne and library, overlooks the main courtyard. Proceeding clockwise through formal living rooms, one reaches the suite of the present Dalai Lama, who is now in India. The innermost room contains his yellow iron bed and personal belongings, such as a clock and calendar, left almost exactly as they were on the day of his departure.

From the west side of the roof, a chapel with a giant Maitreya statue gives entry to the Sixth Dalai Lama's chanting hall and formal rooms. A corridor beyond leads to the Red Palace through a hall that houses the tombs of the Seventh, Eighth and Ninth dalai lamas behind red doors with gold grills. Here, too, sits a statue of the Sixth. He has no tomb because he disappeared, aged 23, after being kidnapped (see page 76).

The **Saint's Chapel**, on the north side of this hall, is the Potala's holiest shrine. A big gold and blue inscription over the door was written by the 19th century Chinese emperor Tong Zhi, proclaiming Buddhism a 'blessed field of wonderful fruit'. This chapel, like the Dharma Cave below it, dates from the seventh century. It contains a small, ancient, jewel-encrusted statue of Chenrezi with two attendants. On the floor below, a low, dark passage leads into the Dharma Cave, where Songtsen Gampo is believed to have studied Buddhism. Here in the company of many divinities are images of Songtsen Gampo, his wives, his chief minister and Tönmi Sambhota, the scholar who developed Tibetan writing.

The layout of the **Red Palace** is complicated. Its centre is the Great West Hall with four large chapels. Light comes in from a free-standing pavilion built directly overhead, around which are three levels of open galleries like a hollow square. Chapels open off these galleries.

The **Great West Hall** and its chapels proclaim the glory and power of the Fifth Dalai Lama. The hall is noted for its fine murals, reminiscent of Persian miniatures, depicting events in the Fifth Dalai Lama's life. The famous scene of his visit to Emperor Shun Zhi in Beijing is located on the east wall just outside the entrance. Special cloth from Bhutan wraps the hall's numerous columns. Four important chapels open off the Great West Hall, which should be visited in a clockwise sequence.

The **North Chapel** (where tour groups enter) centres on a crowned Sakyamuni Buddha (left) and the Fifth Dalai Lama (right), seated on magnificent gold thrones. Their equal height and shared aura imply equal status. Far left is the gold stupa tomb of the Eleventh Dalai Lama, who died as a child, with two rows of benign Medicine Buddhas, the heavenly healers. On the right are Chenrezi and his historical incarnations, including Songtsen Gampo and the first four dalai lamas. Scriptures (loose leaves wrapped in silk between wooden covers) form a pigeonhole library.

The **East Chapel** is dedicated to Tsong Khapa, founder of the Yellow Hat Sect. His central figure is surrounded by lamas from Sakya Monastery, who briefly ruled Tibet from the mid-14th century to the mid-15th century and formed their own sect until many were converted by Tsong Khapa. Other statues include the alert-looking dalai lamas.

(following pages) *Resplendent doorway at the Potala*

The **South Chapel** centres on Padmasambhava, the eighth-century Indian magician-saint (see page 64). His Tibetan wife, a gift from the king, is by his right knee. Left, eight of his holy manifestations meditate with inturned gaze. Right, eight wrathful manifestations wield instruments of magic power to subdue demons of the Bön faith. Beautiful thangkas hang above.

The **West Chapel** contains five golden stupas. The gigantic central one contains the mummified body of the Fifth Dalai Lama. This stupa, built of sandalwood, is coated with 3,720 kilograms (8,200 pounds) of gold 'as thick as a cow's hide' and studded with semi-precious jewels. It rises for more than three storeys, 14.8 metres (48.5 feet) high. On the left is the funeral stupa of the Twelfth Dalai Lama, and on the right that of the Tenth. The stupas at both ends contain scriptures.

On the floor above, the **First Gallery** has windows that give light and ventilation to the Great West Hall and chapels below. Between the windows, superb murals show the Potala's construction in fine detail.

The **Second Gallery** gives access to the central pavilion, where visitors can rest, have a cup of tea, and buy souvenirs. This gallery also has excellent murals with scenes from Tibetan history.

The **Third Gallery** has, besides fine murals, a superb three-dimensional Kalachakra mandala in gold and copper, about four metres (13 feet) in diameter

and 2.5 metres (eight feet) high, in its own special chapel. Take your flashlight! The Seventh Dalai Lama's chanting hall and apartment are on the south side. On the east, an entrance connects with the Saint's Chapel, and on to the White Palace.

A trip to the **Thirteenth Dalai Lama's Tomb** must be in company with a monk and a Potala guide (none of whom speak foreign languages) or a CITS guide. Located west of the Great West Hall, it can be reached only from an upper floor. Built in 1933, the giant stupa contains priceless jewels and a ton of gold. It is 14 metres (46 feet) high. Devotional offerings include elephant tusks from India, porcelain lions and vases, and a pagoda made of 200,000 pearls. Elaborate murals in traditional style show many events from the Thirteenth Dalai Lama's life in the 20th century. Open 9 am–noon; closed Sundays.

## NORBULINGKA; THE SUMMER PALACE

The Norbulingka, meaning Jewel Park, lies three kilometres (two miles) west of the Potala, near the Holiday Inn. Palaces, pavilions, a zoo, gardens and woods cover 40 hectares (100 acres). It has the finest trees in Lhasa and its light-hearted air makes it less demanding than most sights in the city. The Seventh Dalai Lama put up his first summer palace in 1755, and each successive ruler added his own buildings. The current Dalai Lama built a new palace in the 1950s shortly before he left Tibet. Although considerably damaged, the Norbulingka has been restored.

One of Lhasa's greatest annual pageants used to be the Dalai Lama's springtime move from his winter to his summer palace. In a magnificent procession of lamas,

*Wild Yak Dancers at the Curd Festival*

90

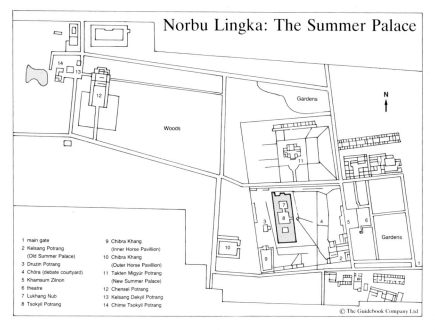

**Norbu Lingka: The Summer Palace**

Gardens

N

Woods

Gardens

1 main gate
2 Kelsang Potrang
  (Old Summer Palace)
3 Druzin Potrang
4 Chöra (debate courtyard)
5 Khamsum Zilnon
6 theatre
7 Lukhang Nub
8 Tsokyil Potrang

9 Chibra Khang
  (Inner Horse Pavillion)
10 Chibra Khang
  (Outer Horse Pavillion)
11 Takten Migyür Potrang
  (New Summer Palace)
12 Chensel Potrang
13 Kelsang Dekyil Potrang
14 Chime Tsokyil Potrang

© The Guidebook Company Ltd

nobles in the costumes of their rank, soldiers, musicians on horseback, and banners, the god-king was borne along in a gilded, curtained palanquin while monks carried his belongings wrapped up in yellow silk. The dalai lama, his family and high dignitaries entered the inner walled gardens containing the palaces, while teachers, servants and bodyguards occupied the surrounding buildings. During the summer, nobles were invited to watch operas and other open-air performances.

The elaborate gate of entry, guarded by comical white lions and huge red doors, was built by the Thirteenth Dalai Lama in this century. A road to the right leads past ragged lawns to the **New Summer Palace**, which stands inside a spacious walled garden. Its traditional Tibetan architecture is modified by large windows and a double-storey entrance with painted eaves in Ming-Dynasty style. Visitors can enter, after removing their shoes, and are conducted in groups by a palace guide. The rooms on view upstairs include a main throne hall above the entrance, the Dalai Lama's private apartment, an audience hall and his mother's apartment.

The style throughout is a bizarre mixture of religious-traditional and modern. The main throne hall is bright and airy with a statue of young Sakyamuni occupying the higher of the two thrones. Opposite, a superb mural tells Tibet's mythical early history from its founding by the holy monkey through to Songtsen Gampo's building of the Jokhang. The adjacent wall recounts the founding of Samye Monastery.

The palace remains exactly as the Dalai Lama left it in 1959. His own apartment juxtaposes carved Tibetan cabinets with heavy, Art-Nouveau armchairs hauled over the Himalayas. Sacred images look down on an antique Russian radio and a Philips console still containing his old 78 rpm records. One amusing detail in the Audience Hall is often overlooked: on the left-hand wall when facing the throne, near the back corner, is a mural like a photo-montage showing the Dalai Lama's family and an international delegation of diplomats mingled among gods and demons.

The artificial lake, usually dry, and the Thirteenth Dalai Lama's little temple are in a walled compound adjoining the garden of the New Summer Palace. Two pavilions with charming, carefree murals stand on a small island. On the east side, through another wall, an inner, unkempt garden backs up to the Old Summer Palace;

*Pavilions inside the Norbulingka*

it contains small buildings formerly used for studying, meeting and living, still un-repaired. The 18th-century **Old Summer Palace** is reached from the road outside. Its dark, low-ceilinged, elaborate rooms have been restored.

To the west is a small, fairly well-kept **zoo** with a collection of Tibetan animals such as snow lynx, white-bibbed Himalayan bears, fanged deer (*lageh*) and red, ring-tailed lesser pandas.

Not to be missed is the furthest temple group, called the **Kasang.** The main tem-ple contains one of the finest collections of thangkas anywhere. Bring a flashlight. Some 70 hanging thangkas depict mandalas, scenes from Buddha's life, a herbal phar-macopoeia, a bestiary, and more—a magnificent array. One wall displays the dalai lama's throne and 48 jewelled, brocaded bodhisattvas and Taras in glass cases. Just west of the main temple, the small Deki Hall with steep steps has delightful murals. Open 9 am–5pm.

## DREPUNG MONASTERY

Drepung lies eight kilometres (five miles) west of Lhasa on a main road, then three kilometres (two miles) north on a steep, unpaved road. Its name means Rice Heap, after its jumble of white buildings piled up against Mt Gambo Ūtse. This was the biggest and richest monastery in Tibet. Its lamas, who helped to train each young dalai lama, could guess how a new god-king would rule—as a leader or as a tool of the regent.

Drepung was founded in 1416 by a disciple of Tsong Khapa, with a noble family as patron. The Fifth Dalai Lama enlarged it and ruled there while the Potala was be-ing built. At its height, Drepung had over 10,000 monks. It governed 700 sub-sidiary monasteries and owned vast estates.

Of the 6,000 monks who lived here in 1959, half, including all the high lamas, fled with the Dalai Lama. The rest went home, took up trades, and married. A hand-ful of elderly monks stayed on at the monastery, labouring on a 20-hectare (50-acre) farm that the Chinese let them keep. Today, about 400 monks and novices live there, turning a profit from their orchards, which produce the best apples in Lhasa.

The monastery was divided into four tantric colleges which, at the highest level, specialized in different branches of knowledge. Each had its own chanting hall, dor-mitories, kitchens and offices. The entire monastic community assembled only for special ceremonies and festivals.

The chanting halls are all built on a similar plan, facing south with a courtyard in front. A big vestibule, with stairs to the roof at its east end, has large murals that typically include the Four Heavenly Kings (see page 65) and the Wheel of Life (see page 137). These are worth careful study. The chanting hall, hung with thangkas and 'victory banners' (see page 137), has closely spaced pillars with rows of cushions between, each holding a monk's robe and cap. Murals decorate the walls. Stairs on the left lead to the roof. Walk along the north wall in a clockwise direction. It is often dark, so bring a flashlight. The roof contains a hollow pavilion whose windows illuminate the chanting hall beneath. It is surrounded by a painted gallery. The higher roof levels hold chapels. The top level, supporting the golden finials, has a splendid view.

The gravel road approaching Drepung winds up through orchards and groves (full of hoopoes in spring and summer) before arriving at a car park; at the back is a small shop, and to the right are food stalls, a garage that functions as the monastery's apple shop in the autumn, and a restaurant serving simple Tibetan fare—*thukpa* (noodles), *momo*s (dumplings) and sweet tea.

Stone steps lead up to the monastery city, arriving first at the chanting hall of **Loseling College**. Splendid murals on the south wall show a finely detailed Chenrezi in a circle of hands and eyes (left) and Yamantaka (see page 65) with the Eight Guardians (right). Gold stupas on the altar and in the chapel are tombs of the Second, Third and Fourth dalai lamas. Butter and *tsampa* sculptures (see page 97) fill a glass case on the altar. The chapel behind has fine drawings on its plain red walls, and in a glass case is a doll-size oracle in full regalia, with crown and armour, prophesying with open mouth. The oracle appears in various forms all through the monastery, recognizable by the circular mirror on his chest.

The monks do not mind visitors going clockwise around the edge, if chanting is going on, but discretion should be used in taking photographs. Drums and cymbals sometimes accompany the chanting. Periodically, a bell sends teenage novices dashing out for jugs of butter tea to fill the wooden bowls of older monks. A kitchen just east of the chanting hall uses medieval stoves and gigantic churns, urns, cauldrons and utensils.

Uphill to the west is the **Main Assembly Hall** (Tshomchen). East of the entrance, there is a small porch, instead of a vestibule, with a dais overlooking the courtyard. The dilapidated, half-empty interior is redeemed by a huge thangka, the old weapons tied on to pillars on the west side, and eight fine bodhisattvas in the westernmost chapel. The roof, housing Drepung's treasures, has on its west side a chapel fronted by a covered porch. This contains the Holy of Holies, a giant gilded Buddha, whose head and chest alone are visible. The cluttered chapel also holds, nearly hidden under white scarves, a sacred conch shell with counter-clockwise whorls. Pilgrims come here to prostrate themselves. To the east is a chapel containing oracle dolls said to have spoken to special lamas in olden times and Tsong Khapa's tooth in a gold reliquary.

(following pages) *The Tshomchen, Main Hall at Drepung Monastery*

## MONASTERIES AND MONKS

For 1,000 years Tibet was run by its monasteries or *gonpas,* which overlooked every town and settlement. A handful were great monastic cities, such as Drepung and Sera, with thousands of monks. Several score, like Samye, housed about 500. Most were small, without land holdings, supported by the monks' relatives. Monasteries were the pillars of Tibet.

Under the rule of the dalai lamas, monasteries were free from taxation and they formed independent economic units. If they owned land, they held the local people as serfs. Trade and commerce were an integral part of their existence. The bigger ones accumulated vast wealth.

Every family in Tibet was expected to give at least one son to the monkhood. It is estimated that about one-fifth of Tibet's male population was celibate monks. The religious life, open to all, was the only avenue to education, improved social status or power. A monk brought honour and merit to his family and might, after long study, become a lama. The monasteries were the only centres of learning, art, literature and medicine in Tibet. They embodied every formal aspect of the culture.

The structure of authority throughout Tibet depended on 'incarnate lamas'—monks, discovered as small children, who were thought to be the reincarnations of previous abbots or lamas and were not infrequently found in the families of powerful nobles. About 2,000 of these *tulkus* existed at

any one time. At the pinnacle stood the dalai and panchen lamas, who were acclaimed as incarnations of a bodhisattva and a Buddha. Tibet was governed by the dalai lama, along with his regent, cabinet and a council made up of the abbots of principal monasteries and lay noblemen, who owned much of Tibet's land and were rich and influential in their own right.

Boys generally became monks at the age of seven; girls—far fewer in number—became nuns at ten. Only the brightest entered a scholarly life within the monastery schools. Many more became clerks, craftsmen, builders, artists, cooks, housekeepers or monk-soldiers feared for their ferocity.

Those who became educated followed a long course of study, examinations and initiations that lasted for 20 to 25 years. Examinations took the form of debates between the student monk and more-learned lamas. Only after mastering logic, rhetoric, theology and close analysis of the Buddhist sutras could he become a lama himself. When he reached an advanced state of learning, he was considered eligible to follow the path of esoteric or occult doctrines and could develop paranormal powers.

Life for a monk, regardless of his status in the monastery, was rigorous. He rose before dawn and was occupied all day with religious services, administrative tasks, study, vigils, sutra-chanting, recitation, memory work, and the never-ending chores of communal life.

## Common Religious Objects

Throughout Tibet, monks and laymen have always used religious articles as part of their daily lives. Some of those most commonly encountered are listed below:

**Prayer Flag** Found in clusters fluttering on roofs, at mountain passes, strung across rivers, above paths, etc. Prayers and mantras printed by woodblock on five colours of cotton cloth are thought to be carried heavenward by the wind.

**Prayer Wheel** A hollow cylinder containing printed prayers or mantras. Every rotation equals a recitation of the contents. All sizes. Most are hand-held or hand-turned in fixed rows around temples; some are turned by water or heat.

**Dorje and Bell** *The dorje* represents a thunderbolt. Fundamental symbol of tantric faith. It is used with the bell in all rituals. The note of the bell, or *trilpu*, is said to drive away evil by its magic music.

**Mani Stone**  A smooth stone inscribed with the universal mantra *Om Mani Padme Hum*. Found in piles near temples and beside pilgrim paths.

**Juniper Hearth**  Large stupa-shaped fireplace found near temples and holy spots, fuelled with juniper wood, whose sacred, fragrant smoke constitutes an offering and bestows blessing.

**Butter and *Tsampa* Sculpture** *Torma* or 'holy food', ritually presented to the gods, is usually a cone of coloured *tsampa* (barley meal) supporting decorated medallions of butter. Elaborate, gilded versions made at New Year remain on altars in glass cases throughout the year.

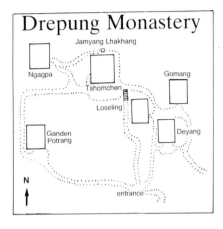

# Drepung Monastery

Jamyang Lhakhang

Ngagpa

Tshomchen

Gomang

Loseling

Deyang

Ganden
Potrang

N

entrance

Behind this building is the carved rock face on which Drepung was founded. It now forms the wall of a little temple with white stupas on either side. The stick with which the founder beat his disciples is kept here in a silver scabbard by a lama who uses it to bless pilgrims, tapping them on their backs and shoulders with mock ferocity.

The small chanting hall of **Ngagpa College** nearby deserves a visit for the exquisite gold drawings on its red doors, portraying the history of the dalai and panchen lamas. Straight down the hill from there is the **Ganden Podrang**, a three-tiered building from which the Fifth Dalai Lama reigned while the Potala was under construction. It should be entered from below to get its full effect. Steep steps lead up from its unimpressive front yard to an inner courtyard and a sudden, stunning view of its majestic façade.

## TREK TO MT GAMBO ÜTSE

This ridge, rising to 5,200 metres (17,000 feet) above Drepung, is one of Lhasa's four sacred mounts. On the night of the full moon of the fifth lunar month (usually in June) there is a great pilgrimage to the summit, traditionally led by the Dalai Lama riding a white yak. At least 1,500 people make the climb, holding a huge party at Ritü Hermitage on the way up and burning juniper incense and hanging prayer flags on the summit as the moonlit night gives way to dawn.

There is a difficult and little-used track up the rocky east ridge, but the main trail starts behind Drepung Monastery, passing some trees by the northwest corner of the *kora* (circumambulatory) path. Four hours' climb on rocky paths brings you to Ritü Hermitage, high on the side of the mountain. Fill your waterbottles at the springs here, as the mountain above is completely dry. Flowering plants such as wild briar roses and blue poppies make this a pleasant place, and you can stay overnight at or beside the little ruined hermitage *gompa*, which is populated by young Drepung monks tending the monastery herds.

Another hard three hours' climb brings you to the summit, a rounded dome strewn with thousands of prayer flags covering the ruins of a little palace and stones stacked into two-metre-high (six-foot) columns all around. The views are immense:

on a clear day you can see over 200 kilometres (125 miles) to snow peaks in Bhutan in the south-southwest, to the peaks beyond Lake Yamdrok Yamtso in the southwest, and to Nyenchen Thangla in the north-northwest. Lhasa lies a mile below, and the Potala looks minute. The descent takes about five hours, for an 11- or 12-hour round trip.

## NECHUNG TEMPLE

Nechung Temple, visible on the right as you approach Drepung, was the home of the state oracle of Tibet until he went into exile in 1959. At a bizarre ceremony, the special protector of the Tibetan government, Dorje Drakden, who was consulted before any major decision was taken, would speak through the oracle in a trance. The monastery was severely damaged during the Cultural Revolution and has only recently been restored.

You enter the monastery through the main doors, with their startling paintings of flayed human skins, and come to a hall. The chapel of Dorje Drakden is on the left. It contains the remains of a tree-trunk where the deity is believed to have taken residence, two thangkas depicting him in peaceful and wrathful aspects, and a statue of Padmasambhava. The other groundfloor chapel contains a statue of Sakyamuni and some fine thangkas. A side door to the right of the main entrance leads up to the first floor, with the dalai lama's audience room on the left and a room dedicated to Tsong Khapa on the right, and then up to a chapel at the top of the building containing a fine new statue of Padmasambhava.

The group of buildings to the east is a monastic school of Buddhist logic attended by more than 130 young monks of many sects from all over Tibet.

Nechung is well worth a visit on the way down from Drepung. Soft drinks and jars of yoghurt can be bought from a stall by the entrance.

## SERA MONASTERY

Sera lies on the northern edge of Lhasa at the base of Tatipu Hill. Sera means Merciful Hail, denoting its rivalry with the Rice Heap (Drepung), since hail destroys rice. Sera was smaller than Drepung, with 7,000 monks, but very rich and comparable in power. Today it has about 300 monks, and some of its buildings house a farm.

Sera was founded in 1419 by one of Tsong Khapa's eight disciples. It became famous for its tantric teachings, while Drepung drew fame from its governing role. The monks of Sera were considered clever and dangerous. Its small army of warrior-monks, the *dob-dobs*, were admired as athletes but also feared. Sera's rebelliousness sometimes posed a threat to the state. In 1947, its leaders planned to kill the regent and install a rival. The plot failed, but witnesses recount that shops in Lhasa were

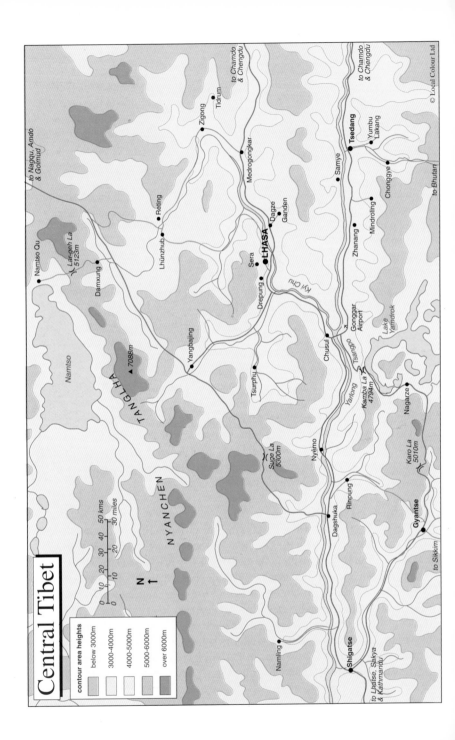

# Central Tibet

**contour area heights**

- below 3000m
- 3000-4000m
- 4000-5000m
- 5000-6000m
- over 6000m

N

0  10  20  30  40  50 kms
0    10    20    30 miles

to Nagqu, Amdo & Golmud

Namtso Qu

Largeh La 5123m

Reting

Tidrum

Zigong

to Chamdo & Chengdu

Lhünzhub

Damxung

Medrogongkar

Dagze
Ganden

Sera
**LHASA**

Drepung

Kyi Chu

Yangbajing

NYANCHEN

TANGLHA

▲7088m

Tsurphu

Suge La 5300m

Namtso

Chusul

Gonggar Airport

Tsangpo

Yarlong

Kamba La 4794m

Lake Yamdrok

Nagarze

Samye

Zhanang

Mindroling

**Tsedang**

Yumbu Lakang

Chongye

to Chamdo & Chengdu

to Bhutan

Nyêmo

Dagshuka

Rinpung

Karo La 5010m

**Gyantse**

to Sikkim

Namling

**Shigatse**

to Lhatse, Sakya & Kathmandu

© Local Colour Ltd

barricaded and the nobles armed their servants for fear of rampaging monks.

A central lane and fairly simple layout make Sera easy to visit. Stalls by the main gateway sell soft drinks and snacks. A long driveway leads up to the monastery. Sera had three colleges similar to those at Drepung, but the chanting halls and chapels seem dark, heavy and more awe-inspiring.

Near the west side of the lane is the chanting hall of **Sera Je College**. Its holy west chapel contains an awesome, horse-headed demon-god, Hayagriva, whose origins go back to the pre-Buddhist Bön religion.

Next to this building is the **Debating Garden**. Monks can be seen preparing for monastic examinations by staging mock debates in the ritual way. Some sit cross-legged under the trees, while others run from group to group giving vigorous hand-claps to end a statement or make a point. Master and dignitaries sit on the raised tiers when a real examination takes place. In Tibetan Buddhism, the debating garden is the whetstone on which the mind is sharpened, and the importance of the institution cannot be stressed too strongly. Years of study, memorization, meditation and intellectual struggle produce monks with outstanding abilities who keep alive a profound religious tradition.

Sera's rock paintings are on the east mountainside. Notable are a blue Yamantaka with Prajna (see page 65), Tsong Khapa above and Sera's first abbot, Sakya Yeshe, at the top. From here you can enter the **Assembly Hall** (Tsokchen) at roof level and, in an east chapel, find the greatest treasure of Sera—a gilded Chenrezi with hundreds of hands and eyes. A colossal Maitreya can be seen from both the roof and the chanting hall.

Across the lane, **Ngagpa College** has many interesting objects, but the chanting hall of **Sera Me College** down the hill is truly remarkable. It has the best vestibule murals anywhere, its Wheel of Life being particularly noteworthy.

One kilometre east of Sera is an isolated rock where 'sky burials' take place at dawn—Tibetans learned to break the bodies of their dead into small pieces and feed them to the birds. Thus, their last earthly act is to make a compassion-ate gift of their body to feed other creatures. Vultures, ravens and kites swoop down when

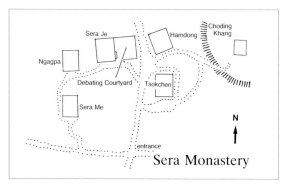

the body-breakers, called *domdens,* have done their work. The whole gruesome process takes about two hours, the dead Tibetans literally vanishing into thin air. In the past, thrill-seeking tourists have outraged local feeling by arriving in car- or bus-loads and demanding to take photos and videos, and so tourists are now banned by law from intruding. Notices to this effect are posted in hotels. Take heed.

## CHAKPORI HILL

Chakpori Hill is one of central Tibet's holy mountains; because of their sacred nature such mountains were considered to be the soul of the country. They preserved and protected the pilgrims who visited them. Chakpori has since caught up with modern times and is now topped by a tall, steel antenna.

Legend tells that the first doctor and founder of Tibetan medicine, Yutok Gampo, made his home on Chakpori during the reign of King Songtsen Gampo. At the same time, one of the king's Tibetan wives made a temple in a cave on the east side of the hill. Much later, in the 17th century, the Fifth Dalai Lama established a monastic medical college on its summit, which remained the chief one in Tibet for 300 years. It was shelled during the uprising of 1959, and the ruins were removed in 1983 to make way for the antenna.

The middle slopes are encircled by a pilgrim footpath. Prayer flags, rock paintings, small shrines, piles of *mani* stones and juniper fires punctuate the route. A small crater is worn into the limestone cliff where devotees have scratched away powder to place on their tongues, believing in the medicinal properties of the mountain itself. At the southwest end of the hill is Sangye Tungu, a spectacular collection of rock paintings.

## PALHALUPUK TEMPLE

This small, ancient cave-temple just off the main road in front of the Potala should not be missed. A lane, festooned with prayer flags, turns south at the foot of Chakpori Hill, opposite the spot where the rocky outcropping at the west end of the Potala meets the road. This used to be the site of Lhasa's massive West Gate. The little temple, recently extended and gaily painted in red and yellow, is built into the hillside above the lane, 100 metres (yards) along it.

Palhalupuk was one of five temples built by King Songsten Gampo's wives. The Jokhang, popularly attributed to Wen Cheng, the Chinese princess, was more probably founded by his Nepalese wife, Princess Tritsun. Ramoche was Wen Cheng's temple. His first Tibetan wife chose the caves on Medicine King Hill as the site for hers. The other two Tibetan wives founded a shrine named Pabongka above the present site of Sera Monastery and a temple 20 kilometres (12 miles) south of Lhasa.

Palhalupuk Temple, ascending the face of a cliff, is hardly more than a façade enclosing the cave within. Other buildings cluster in steps around it, housing a little community of monks. The gateway, at street level, leads into a courtyard where a deep cave has recently been refurbished to include numerous images set in glassed niches. Steep steps lead up to a hospitable antechamber a few steps below the original cave. This room serves as the monks' all-purpose room for chanting, doing household tasks and making large *tsampa* and butter sculptures (see page 97). The cave itself is hollowed out around a central rock column with stone Buddha statues carved into its four sides. The walls display a frieze of relief sculptures, including one contemporary figure of Songtsen Gampo. Small and friendly, ancient Palhalupuk Temple has more charm than many of Lhasa's grand sites.

## Lingkhor

The Lingkhor was Lhasa's circular, outer pilgrim road, matching its inner twin, the Barkhor (see page 60). The Lingkhor was eight kilometres (five miles) long, encompassing Old Lhasa, the Potala and Chakpori. In former times it was crowded with men and women covering its length in prostrations, beggars, and pilgrims approaching the holy city for the first time. The road passed through willow-shaded parks where Tibetans loved to picnic in summer and watch open-air operas on festival days. New Lhasa obliterated most of the Lingkhor, but two sections remain, one running along the west end of Chakpori to a great vertical rock wall, known as Sanjia Gudong. This wall of beautifully carved and painted bas-relief images dates from the eighth and ninth centuries and is thus among the oldest extant cultural sites in Tibet. 'The finest wall I've ever seen' is a comment of visitors who make the effort to find Sanjia Gudong, a kind of holy holdout in the midst of military compounds and general squalor. The central figure, painted blue, is Dorje Sampa, surrounded by hundreds of bright, lively, archaic images. In the late afternoon sunshine the wall glows and shimmers and is an altogether beatific sight.

The other stretch is also west of Chakpori but further south. A bridge about a kilometre (half a mile) west of the Potala on the main road, with green buildings beyond it on the right, is the landmark. The Lingkhor goes left before the bridge between walls and willow trees. After making a turn to the right at a small stream, it peters out at a duck pond. Open-air Tibetan operas are still performed within earshot of this pond on high festival days, one of which often falls in June (see page 224).

As the old Lingkhor was simply a great circular path around the holy city, Tibetans have adapted to the new city plan, and the Lingkhor now follows new roads and pathways. It runs past the People's Hospital and north of Ramoche Temple, then

*(following pages) Alleyway and silhouette of monks, Sera Monastery*

# King Gesar of Ling

England has King Arthur and the Knights of the Round Table. India has Rama, in the tales of the Ramayana. Tibet has a beloved epic hero named King Gesar of Ling, who lives on in a host of songs and stories. Tibet's popular literature has been overshadowed by a wealth of philosophical and religious writings. Yet a lively oral tradition existed among common folk outside of the monkhood, a tradition of songs, jokes, poems, proverbs, lampoons and—above all—the stories of Gesar.

There are many versions, but all agree that Gesar came to establish order on the earth and bring an end to injustice and violence. The tales were chanted by wandering bards of nomadic origin, who spread them throughout Tibet. No bard knew them all but each had his own repertory, which he chanted at gatherings or festivals. Most would deny that they had learned the poem by heart, insisting that they were inspired by Gesar himself, or some other divinity, who put the words into their mouths.

There may have been a historical king named Gesar. The songs place his country of Ling in the north, although the customs described are those of eastern Tibet. Some episodes originate in the old, magical Bön faith; others are borrowed from Chinese or Indian folk tales. But as Buddhist thought permeated Tibet, Gesar became the incarnation of a bodhisattva, sent to earth by Padmasambhava to fight the demons that gripped mankind. Gesar was born miraculously to a beautiful Naga water sprite who worked in the

turns south past the Telecommunications Centre and west past the mosque. It follows the main road to the new river embankment before taking an alley marked by a huge cairn up to the south foot of Chakpori. From there, it follows small paths and alleys northwards to circle the Potala. Each year, there is a great pilgrimage around the Lingkhor, and thousands of Lhasa people walk the circuit, making offerings of juniper incense, *tsampa*, and *changon* fires all the way round. A happy, leisurely walk ends up with a huge picnic near Lukhang Temple, in the lake of Ching Dröl Chi Ling Park, north of the Potala. The Lukhang is also known as the Naga Chapel, a small square building erected by the Sixth Dalai Lama on an island in the lake. The chapel's central image is the King of the Nagas, lord of the waters and the snake-like creatures that have the capacity to both help and harm humans. The Lukhang murals are

service of a king. People believed, therefore, that the boy was a prince.
Gesar made a bargain with Padmasambhava before accepting his mission
on earth. One condition was that he should have a brave uncle who was a
good strategist. Something went wrong, and Gesar was saddled with a
cowardly, miserly, greedy, treacherous step-uncle named Todong, who is a
stock character in all the stories, offering comic relief and a raw, human
touch. Todong and the jealous queen tried every means to kill Gesar, but
the boy always escaped. They finally banished him to Tibet's high
wilderness, where he learned the skills of the nomads. When the old king
died, Gesar returned and won a horse race, in which he outwitted Todong
and won not only the crown but also a beautiful, loyal wife as well.

Gesar and his army undertook many campaigns against demons, giants
and evil kings. His bold adventures were touched with high drama and
romance. In the end he established order and justice on earth, and even
made peace with Todong, who had become a buffoon in his old age.

His work done, Gesar retired to a mountain cave to meditate, and from
there passed on to the mythical land of Shambala. Many Tibetans believe
that he will come again. They say he will return with his army, when Tibet
is in great trouble and Buddhism is dying, to take vengeance on its enemies
and once more usher in an era of peace and justice.

exceptionally fine in their depictions of meditation scenes, yoga and yogins, anatomy
and the weird visions that await us in the after-death state.

## RAMOCHE TEMPLE

Often erroneously referred to as 'Little Jokhang', Ramoche stands among small lanes
in the north part of Old Lhasa. It originally housed Wen Cheng's statue of Sakyamuni, now the Holy of Holies of the Jokhang. In the eighth or ninth century, an exchange was made (nobody knows why), and the Nepalese princess's small bronze
statue of an eight-year-old Sakyamuni was enshrined at Ramoche instead.

The temple was gutted and partly destroyed in the 1960s, and the bronze statue
disappeared. Many years later, half of it was found in a rubbish pit in Lhasa, and the
other half was found marked as scrap-metal in Beijing. Now repaired and temporarily

(following pages) *Monks with banners prepare for a procession around the Potala*

housed in the Jokhang, it will be returned to Ramoche and to the care of its 30 monks when restoration of the building is completed. The roof of the temple gives a fine view over Old Lhasa and down into the courtyards where Tibetans live.

## MOSQUE AND MOSLEM QUARTER
Many people are surprised to learn of Lhasa's substantial Moslem community. Moslems from Ladakh were known in Tibet from early times as traders. When the Fifth Dalai Lama took Ladakh into his religious sphere of influence in the 17th century, a small community of Moslems established itself in Lhasa, many of them working as butchers. Later, they were eclipsed by immigrants from Moslem areas north of Tibet. Today, Lhasa's Moslem quarter, lying southeast of the Barkhor in Old Lhasa, comprises about 1,000 families. The mosque of mixed Tibetan and Islamic architecture is its focal point for Friday prayers and Moslem holidays. A curious feature is that it contains numerous clocks—hung on every pillar! Another small mosque has recently been built, further west past Ani Sangkhung Nunnery. Several nearby restaurants serve *halal* food (see page 237).

## TIBETAN TRADITIONAL HOSPITAL
The hospital, which includes Mendzekhang Medical College, is on the north side of Yuthok Lu (Mimang Lam), one block west of the Jokhang Temple. It gives some interesting insights into the ancient tradition of Tibetan medicine.

Throughout history, few Tibetans have benefited from medical care, relying instead on charms, amulets and common sense. Their lack of hygiene, still all too evident, belies the existence of a profound and complicated medical tradition.

Tibetan medical theory evolved from various sources. King Songtsen Gampo was treated by the famous Galen of Persia, who was invited to Tibet by his wife, Queen Wen Cheng. Chinese and Indian physicians were also present at his court, and the Tibetan Medicine King, Yutok Gampo, exerted his influence from Chakpori Hill. The appearance of numerous Medicine Buddha images in the tenth century points to a close connection with Indian medical theory and practice.

Knowledge of anatomy came from Chinese texts and diagrams and from Tibetan *domdens,* the body-breakers who dismembered corpses for 'sky burial' (see page 101). Complex surgery, including probes into the heart and brain, is known to have been carried out up to the ninth century, when the king permanently banned surgery after his mother died during an operation.

Tibet's first medical school was set up by King Trisong Detsen (see page 63) in the eighth century. The second was the renowned Chakpori school established by the Fifth Dalai Lama in the 17th century. Even with several smaller monastic schools in operation, a need for more doctors prompted the modern-minded Thirteenth Dalai Lama to found a third major school, Mendzekhang Medical College, in 1916.

Future doctors spent at least 11 years studying Tibetan medical theory, which was based on eighth-century tantric texts. By committing thousands of pages to memory, a student became familiar with a fundamental theory of 'humours', not unlike those known to medieval Europeans: 'wind' moving within the skeleton, 'bile' in the blood, and 'phlegm' in the flesh, fat and fluids. Good health resulted from a stable balance among all three—which could not have been easy to achieve considering that the *tantras* enumerated 84,000 different illnesses.

After grasping the theory, a student visualized a huge, schematic Tree of Medicine, whose roots, trunks, twigs and leaves represented all branches of medicine from embryology to pharmacology. Months were spent in wild areas collecting and identifying the herbs that went into the making of some 2,000 drug preparations. Minerals and animal products, such as ground tiger's tooth and pearls, also went into medicines.

Finally, the student doctor encountered patients and learned the vital tool of Tibetan medicine, pulse diagnosis. A doctor had to develop his sensitivity until six of his fingers each had two distinct points for monitoring his patient's pulse and gathering information about all the internal organs. Certain pulses were described by weird comparisons: a vulture attacking a bird, who stops, plunges, beats his wings quickly, stops again and resumes flight; of a moribund patient, the saliva of a drool-ing cow, moving in the wind. Acupuncture, moxibustion and blood-letting were traditional areas of study.

Today, the students at Mendzekhang Medical College, half of whom are women, complete their core studies in four years, but many aspects of their training remain unchanged. Surgery is still eschewed. (This is handled in Lhasa by the four top Chinese hospitals.) The hospital expanded into its present building in 1978. It has only 25 beds, which are used for emergencies, but it routinely handles 600–700 outpatients a day. The top floor houses a library containing the medical tantras wrapped in silk, and magnificent teaching thangkas (see page 114). Anatomical charts mounted on brocade are over 300 years old. Finely detailed drawings in colour depict medicinal plants, minerals and animal parts. An ancient view of embryology is remarkably accurate by modern standards. A senior physician may be observed taking a patient's pulse with deep concentration. Across the hall is the arcane Astrological-Astronomical Institute, where research goes on into astrological diagnosis. Star maps, charts and compilations of symbols fill the walls. Doctors pore over religious texts and diagrams of the heavens, making calculations on trays of sand. They not only work out astrological signs for years ahead, but also predict the weather.

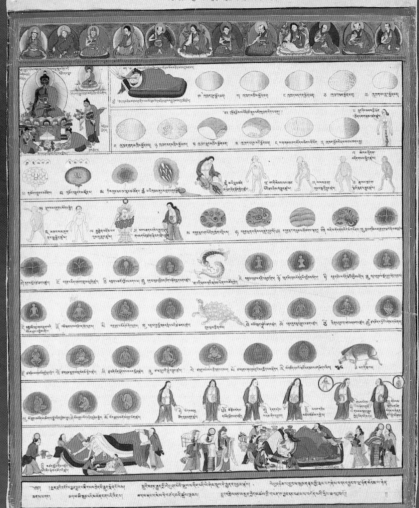

The two lower floors are given over to small clinics. Some of them administer purely traditional medicine, including herbal treatment, acupuncture and moxibustion. Others have relatively modern equipment like electrocardiographs and X-ray machines. Patients can choose the type of clinic they prefer.

The central lobby of the hospital is filled with Tibetans waiting with fistfuls of prescriptions outside a vast pharmacy-cum-dispensary. Be sure to arrange a visit inside, where there are hundreds of orderly drawers, hand-decorated cabinets, vats and tubs, and mountains of herbs, seeds, roots, pills, tablets and elixirs. Twenty-two pharmacists, grinders and mixers make up the medicines, which are dispensed through small windows to the lines of patients waiting outside in the lobby.

## LHASA CARPET FACTORY

The factory is just south of Jinzhu Dong Lu (Tsang Gyu Shar Lam), near Tibet University. It produces traditional Tibetan rugs for export worldwide through Guangzhou. Although the actual weaving and finishing are done by hand, using old-style vertical looms, some stages of the process, such as spinning, are now mechanized, and the dyeing is not done here. This factory is more modern than either the one in Gyantse (see page 196) or in Nedong (see page 149). Traditionally, Tibetan women are the weavers and men the spinners, but today both work on rugs.

The rugs are typically quite small, with bold designs, bright colours and a deep, even pile–about 60 knots per square inch. Rug weaving is an ancient craft in Tibet, but because it was not for sacred use it was never considered an art. As a result, there are no rugs veritably earlier than the 19th century. Chemical dyes first appeared in Central Asia around 1870 and are now very widely used. Durable cotton warps and wefts were introduced into Tibet in the early 20th century. A one-by-two metre (three-by-six foot) rug costs about Rmb400.

## TIBETAN PERFORMING ARTS SCHOOL

This school, also known as the Tibet Song and Dance Group, has a compound south of the main road, facing the Potala Palace. It was founded in 1980 and has over 100 students aged 12 to 20. The director, Mr A Ke, is a well-known Tibetan dancer and choreographer. By arrangement, visitors can watch the students practise Tibetan dances in the studio. Some will become members of cultural groups or the Tibetan Opera, which performs throughout Tibet and China and occasionally abroad. Others will remain in the school as teachers. Although the operas are no longer restricted to revolutionary themes, some still have obvious influences from Beijing opera, with women singers using a shrill sing-song style. Other operas are now performed entirely in the traditional manner, with religious and mythical themes.

*Medical thangka, presenting the Tibetan understanding of conception and human embryology, from* Tibetan Medical Paintings, *Serindia Publications, 1992*

## THANGKAS

Thangka is the name for the scroll-banners seen hanging in every temple, monastery and family shrine in Tibet. They carry painted or embroidered pictures inside a broad, coloured border and can range in size from the page of a book to the façade of an entire building. The picture is usually made on paper or cotton canvas protected by a thin dust-cover; the mounting is of colourful silk. A heavy wooden stick at the base allows a thangka to be rolled up like a scroll for storage or transportation, or to hang securely without flapping.

Thangkas first appeared in Tibet around the tenth century AD. The scroll form seems to have been borrowed from China; the style of painting probably came from Nepal and Kashmir. Apprentice thangka painters studied under experienced lamas, and their works were consecrated before they could be hung.

Thangkas were widely used in monastery schools as teaching tools because of their convenient movability. Common folk hung them in homes as protection against evil spirits. At the highest level of religious practice, mystics in a state of meditation would become one with the deity portrayed.

Thangkas can be simple in design or very complicated. They can deal with a great number of subjects, of which a few are Tibetan theology, astrology, pharmacology, the lives of Buddhas, saints and deities, and mandalas.

## MANDALAS

Mandalas are graphic, geometric representations of the cosmos—psycho-cosmograms' symbolizing the order and harmony achieved by a truly enlightened mind. They have great power, being seen as concentrated areas where the forces of the universe are gathered. (*Manda* means essence, while *la* means container.)

The design is symmetrical, based on circles and squares, with a central focal point. In tantric Buddhism, where the mandala is used to support meditation, adepts seek to absorb its power. Sometimes a mandala takes the form of an elaborate, four-gated city—a palace of knowledge—which the practitioner mentally enters, approaching the centre, in order to achieve a state of mystical unity with the Buddha.

Although not created primarily to please the eye, mandalas are often works of art with great stylistic elegance and beauty. They are most frequently displayed on thangkas but are also seen on the walls of temples and monasteries. A few monasteries, such as Sakya and Tashilhunpo, still create magnificent mandalas of coloured sand.

*Fresco of Sakyamuni Buddha on a lotus throne,*
*flanked by disciples*

The music studios, where various instruments and singing are taught, can also be visited. One group of graduates performs with one of Lhasa's opera companies. A costume rehearsal provides a chance to get some colourful and exotic photographs.

The unit also has a modern dance band, with bass and electric guitar, two keyboards, flute, drums and two vocalists. Most of the players are young Tibetans; all studied music in Shanghai or Beijing. Their repertoire includes disco music via India, quicksteps, foxtrots and American 60s pop.

There are regular **disco dances** on Saturdays at the school and at a cultural hall one block south of the main cinema. Occasional discos are also held at the Potala Exhibition Hall Museum and at the Holiday Inn. The music is a mixture of Chinese, Indian, and western-style dance music, both recorded and live.

## GRAPHIC ARTS

Lhasa's first **art gallery** was set up in 1987 west of the main post office, on the right side of the yard leading to the Potala entrance. Tibetan and Chinese artists display paintings and drawings, ranging from traditional Chinese watercolour to modern styles, from thangkas and rubbings of old stone carvings to Tibetan modern art. There is also a display of prints by local photographers. The work on display is for sale.

The **Teahouse School**, opposite the main Public Security Bureau compound, occasionally hosts painting exhibitions by younger artists in a rough tea-and-*thukpa* ambience.

The **Traditional Arts and Crafts Centre**, known commonly as Guo Jian Du, is a large cooperative for art restoration. Thangka painters, sculptors, woodworkers and makers of Tibetan handicrafts work at many sites around Lhasa and elsewhere in central Tibet. Tourists with specific ideas for a painting or other work of art can commission artists directly. The headquarters are east of the Jokhang, just north of the mosque.

A score of art galleries and painting shops stand in clusters near the south base of the Potala.

## POTALA EXHIBITION HALL MUSEUM

This small museum is on the corner opposite the main post office, south of the Potala. It has sections on recent modernizations and improvements in Tibet and on traditional Tibetan life, including the interior of a nomad tent. The room containing exhibits showing the alleged horrors of Tibetan feudal society has not been open recently

# Sights Outside Lhasa

## BUMPORI HILL

This small, rocky peak south of the Lhasa River, near the bridge, is often called Little Everest by trekkers. It is a good first warm-up climb of about 600 metres (less than 2,000 feet), taking only three hours up. The path on ledges through vertiginous crags is approached from the northwest but hard to find. There is also a steep, slippery path up the west side. The top is strewn with colourful ropes of prayer flags and affords a wonderful view across Lhasa. In summer, tasty wild rhubarb grows in the rock crevices, but there is almost no water on the mountain, so take plenty with you.

## DROMA LAKHANG TEMPLE

This small temple, 27 kilometres (17 miles) south of Lhasa on the main road to Gonggar, has a community of monk caretakers and is dedicated to the memory of Atisha, who stayed here during his history-shaping visit to Tibet in the 11th century (see page 66), and to his special deity, Tara. It consists of a vestibule with restored murals and a white stupa, a prayer wheel gallery around the main hall, and the hall itself, which is divided into three chapels. The first two have richly adorned figures of goddesses and several copper stupas (see page 153); Atisha himself is believed to have introduced these ubiquitous domed towers to Tibet from India. The third chapel, dominated by giant statues, contains the stone throne from which Atisha preached to the people. A small statue of Atisha in a glass case now sits on the throne. Myth has it that after Atisha taught the Tibetans, he crumbled a piece of stone in his hand and blew on the dust, causing the giant figures to take form. The three biggest are male Buddhas—Amitayus at the back, Kashyapa to the right and Dipankara to the left. The eight grand, elegant, standing bodhisattvas, often presented as an iconographic unit, complete the excellent sculpture in this chapel.

The two white stupas outside are particularly venerated; the one on the left is said to contain Atisha's robes.

## RATÖ MONASTERY

This historically important monastery, founded in the 11th century, lies hidden in a side valley to the west of the Kyichu River Valley. Six kilometres (four miles) south of the large, painted rock Buddha by the main road, turn right at a pipeline and follow the dirt road for three kilometres (two miles) to Ratö.

The monastery originally belonged to the Sakyapa sect but was converted to the Yellow Hat Gelugpa school by one of Tsong Khapa's disciples in the 15th century. It

(above) *Entranceway at Sera Monastery, with mural of the Guardian Kings;*
(below and opposite) *Close-up images of the Yellow and White Guardian Kings*

# Marriage Rites

When I was twenty, my parents wanted me to marry. They had already selected a girl, the daughter of the Chieftain Chigo Tsang, the clan leader of Khongshe. Although my family was a modest one and my father only the Arrow Chief of a sub-tribe, he had a great reputation as a scholar and a man of integrity. Thus the marriage was arranged and in the course of time, I was informed. I made a few protests just to show my parents that it was my marriage, and after an initial show of reluctance I finally gave my consent. The girl, Nyima Tso, was nineteen and very beautiful. At dances and festivals I had always tried to look my very best in her eyes. I think my parents must have known that. In a small community like ours, nothing could really be kept a secret for long.

The first thing that happens at this sort of wedding is the formal preliminary conference at which the two families meet and make the rather unromantic but necessary deals. This is accomplished in a traditional manner during a modest but formal banquet. Some years earlier both parties would have observed the custom of singing boasting songs. But because of the drinking common on such occasions, quarrels, fights and other inauspicious incidents used to occur and so this custom had been wisely discontinued.

My father had to pay the rather stiff price of thirty dotses, three thousand silver dollars for the girl. Since she was from a very prosperous family, her share of her family's wealth would be considerable, and so in the long run it would be no loss to us. In fact she brought in much more than we had ever expected. On a later occasion when my fortunes fell drastically, she generously gave up all her jewellery and ornaments to get me out of my predicament. But that is another story.

Fresh chang had been brewed, arak distilled and all other preparations made. Astrologer monks had been consulted, and since all the omens were favourable my wedding-day was finally arranged. The night before, Nyima and three other close friends had ridden to the girl's home to deliver a fine female yak, as a present for the girl's mother. This is known as the 'milk price' and is supposed to compensate the mother for the loss of her daughter. They had also delivered the other required gifts of silk scarves, religious books and a brand new wooden basin for the girl to wash her hair in. A feast was then held, with much singing and dancing. When it ended they presented ceremonial scarves and packets of currency to all the young people present, as was the custom.

It was a fine morning, and I was waiting, dressed in a new outfit. Everybody in the house was rushing around putting final touches to the preparations, and the kitchen was a pandemonium of cooks, helpers and relatives. Everyone seemed to have something to do and no-one paid me any attention as I strolled around feeling somewhat nervous. Outside, lined up on either side of the pathway, were the old people of the village with casks of fresh water before them. This was considered auspicious, and they were to receive gifts from the bridal party. Most of the young people from the village had departed earlier to welcome the bride.

The bridal party appeared in the distance and my family and I went to receive them. The party halted at the boundary of our land, and one of my friends went over to lead the bride's horse over to our side and up to our house. She looked very beautiful in her silk robe and rich jewellery. Her dark shining hair was arranged in long plaits and decorated with coral ornaments. She wore a jewel-encrusted charm box around her neck.

She looked at me with her dark sloe eyes and smiled shyly. I smiled back and felt a great happiness in my heart. She dismounted onto a tea-chest covered with silk, and my mother led her into the courtyard, where both of them thrice circled a large barrel full of fresh water. Then we all sat down on mats and performed a short ritual prayer, conducted by the monks, to bring luck to the family. After this, the bride was taken to the kitchen where she was given a bowl of milk. She dipped the tip of her third finger into it, and flicked a few drops into the air as an offering to the gods. We were then both led to the family chapel where the monks and the lama, Chandi Rinpoche (my brother), gave us their blessing. Then we proceeded to the family Treasure House where the luck of my family was kept in the shape of a mystic arrow.

After all that, there was endless feasting for three hectic days. My friends and relatives came to offer me and my bride their congratulations, ceremonial scarves and presents. Everyone, including my father, got truly and magnificently drunk and there was much singing and dancing. We have songs to suit every occasion, and marriages are no exception.

> The good steed is like a swift bird,
> The golden saddle is like its feathers,
> When the bird and its feathers are together
> Then the great Highlands are easily crossed.
>
> The ornamental musket is like thunder in the sky,
> The black powder is like lightning in the sky,
> When both lightning and thunder meet
> Then the hills are illuminated.
>
> The young tiger man is like the sun,
> The young girl is like the full moon,
> When the sun and the moon meet
> There is happiness in the village.

After three days, we rode over to my wife's home where a similar ceremony took place. For three days they also held a great feast after which my wife and I returned home to begin our new lives together.

I have never found any occasion to doubt the wisdom of my parents' choice of a wife for me. Although happy marriages are more the exception than the rule, I guess I inherited my father's luck in this matter. Nyima Tso was a wonderful woman, more than I ever deserved. Sha was everything a man could ask for—beautiful, gentle, hard-working and religious like my mother. Though she had a streak of toughness in her, and did not readily agree with all my decisions, she was immensely loyal and stood by me till the last of her days.

Jamyang Norbu, Warriors of Tibet, 1979

This lyrical account of the history and pre-invasion life style of the Khampas is the true life story of Aten, a Khampa from Eastern Tibet. Aten escaped to India in 1960 after his family was murdered.

*Gold stamp with multiple Buddha images*

was designated as a centre of logic training and debate; its reputation was built on this rigorous philosophical foundation. Today 60 monks are here from a former community of 400.

One can see how the entire village of Ratö was once part of the monastery. Four religious structures remain and many others are used by farmers.

The central building and main hall is Ratö Tratsang. Its most important image is a small Tara statue, said to have come from India in the 11th century. The murals at Ratö are outstanding for their brightness, quality of preservation and age, many dating back 600 years.

GANDEN MONASTERY

The ruins of this great monastery lie about 45 kilometres (28 miles) east of Lhasa. The main road east is good tarmac to beyond Dagze Dzong and then rough gravel for the last few kilometres. A track turns south past two villages then zig-zags for nearly 600 metres (2,000 feet) up the mountainside to the monastery. A pilgrim bus leaves every morning from the north side of the Barkhor, by the juniper hearth behind the Jokhang, sometime after 6 am, when full.

Situated at 4,300 metres (14,100 feet) in a bowl like an amphitheatre, Ganden was Lhasa's second biggest monastery and at times the strongest of the three that dominated the government. Tsong Khapa established it in 1409, earlier than either Drepung or Sera, as a place to train moral, disciplined monks and to work out the reformed version of Tibetan Buddhism that soon evolved into the Yellow Hat Sect (see page 56). Today, Ganden's massive effort to rebuild after the disaster of the Chinese invasion goes on, largely with the help of local volunteer effort; about 200 monks have returned.

Amongst the great expanse of ruins a number of buildings have been reconstructed. There is a guest room with dormitory beds in the first building on the right for those who want to absorb monastery life for a day or two. Few facilities for guests exist so take provisions. The courtyard of a teahouse is used as a workshop by craftsmen repairing statuary rescued from the rubble.

The second building on the right is **Ngam Chö Khang**, a small temple containing statues of Tsong Khapa and his two chief disciples,

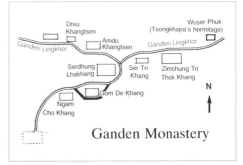

Ganden Monastery

and a protectors' chapel (closed to women) with images of Pelden Lhamo, Mahakala, Dharmaraja and Yamantaka.

Below the next building (monks' quarters) is the **Debating Courtyard**, where this essential training method is practised most mornings.

The path continues uphill, past a large *chorten* (stupa), to a large building with red-painted walls. This is **Serdhung**, or **Tsong Khapa's Golden Tomb.** You enter an open inner courtyard, and opposite is a protectors' chapel containing a large image of Dharnaraja (also closed to women). Stairs lead up to a chamber called the Yangchen Khang, containing the great silver and gold chorten, which holds the few fragments of Tsong Khapa's remains left after the original chorten and building were destroyed by Red Guards. In a corner at the top of the building, an old monk makes impressions in small tablets of *tsampa* from one of Tsong Khapa's teeth set on top of a small silver stupa; these are eagerly accepted by pilgrims.

Higher up to the left among the buildings is the **Amdo Khangtsen**, containing chapels and accommodation for monks. This building was traditionally used by visiting monks from Amdo (now Qinghai) who came here for training. In the same area is **Dreu Khangtsen**, another residence. The kora circuit starts just beyond this building and crosses the ridge to the west side.

To the right of Ser Dung is a tall, narrow building with red-painted walls called **Ser Tri Khang**, or the **Golden Throne Room.** A steep climb up some steps leads to the chapel, which holds a throne reserved only for the dalai lama and the head of the Gelugpa Sect, the Ganden tripa. Ganden Tri Rinpoche lives in exile in India.

The next building, **Tri Thok Khang**, is the residence of the Ganden tripa. It has a number of interesting rooms and chapels. The basement contains four shrine rooms, including the room where Tsong Khapa died and the room where the dalai lama stayed during visits. Upstairs is a chapel which holds a complete set of the *Kanjur*, books containing teachings attributed to the Buddha.

Two more residential buildings, **Nyare Khangtsen** and **Ngari Khangtsen**, complete the list of major buildings. These are downhill from Tri Dok Khang.

Pilgrims proceed directly to the kora path, which offers spectacular views. . The small building set in the east side of the hill above the path is Tsong Khapa's hermitage, where he stayed in retreat. Pilgrims also climb a hundred metres (yards) or so to the hilltop above to burn incense. The popular four- or five-day trek on the pilgrims' path to Samye starts from this hill (see page 162).

## TIDRUM HOT SPRINGS

An adventurous and rewarding trip far beyond the normal tourist routes involves a journey of at least three days (round trip) to the mountain hot springs of Tidrum.

The site is approximately 120 kilometres (75 miles) east-north-east of Lhasa. Travel first to Medrogongkar, then turn north to Zigong (Zhigong) and follow a road to the right (east) along the river's south bank, soon after Zigong. After one hour reach the village of Menpa and soon turn northwards to Tidrum. If you go straight the road leads to Drigung Til Monastery.

At Tidrum expect to walk the last few kilometres down to the village and hot springs. Beyond and above is a nunnery with friendly, welcoming people. Enquire here about lodging but plan to bring your own food for the entire trip. The nunnery

*Ruins and reconstruction at Ganden Monastery*

is religiously important for being the meditation retreat of the great eighth-century adept Yeshe Tsogyel, consort of Padmasambhava. It stands on the site of her cave.

Beautiful villages, breathtaking scenery and the exhiliration of being in a wild, unspoiled place are the reasons for coming here. An arduous, day-long circuit (*lingkor*) of the hot springs region is highly recommended in order to complete the experience.

Every 12 years, in the Year of the Monkey, a festival occurs to honour 'women, children and the richness of fertility'; it is called Drigung Powa Chenmo and will next take place in 2004.

The excursion to Tidrum can be combined with an entire circuit of special sites northeast of Lhasa, including Drigung and Reting.

**Drigung Til Monastery**, farther to the east, is a Kagyu centre that was established in the 12th century. It has always had a strong tradition of meditation training.

**Reting Monastery** lies to the northwest of Tidrum and can be reached by returning to the main road, continuing northwest to the town of Lhünzhub, then following the Kyichu River northeast for an hour.

Reting was founded by a disciple of Atisha in the mid-11th century. Tsong Khapa trained here as a monk and developed his ideas and writings that eventually led to the creation of the Gelugpa school of Tibetan Buddhism.

The site of Reting is beautiful, in a valley with juniper trees, though the monastery was largely destroyed by the Chinese after 1959. Slowly, in stages, the buildings are being revived.

## TSÜRPHU MONASTERY

Tsürphu Monastery is the principal shrine of the Karmapa branch of the Kagyupa sect of Tibetan Buddhism, and is the seat of the Karmapa Lama. The Kagyupa was once one of the most powerful religious orders in Tibet until it was suppressed by the Fifth Dalai Lama. The first Karmapa, Dusumkhyenpa (who founded the monastery in 1187), instigated the establishment of *tulkus*, whereby an existing lama could predict and provide clues regarding his next incarnation. This system was later adopted by the Gelugpa for the succession of dalai lamas and panchen lamas. The Seventeenth Karmapa Lama (born in 1984) was installed in 1992. Many pilgrims travel to Tsürphu to receive his blessing. The monastery was badly damaged in the Cultural Revolution, but today there is extensive rebuilding and renovation in progress.

It is possible to reach Tsürphu from Lhasa by pilgrim bus; these depart from the western end of the Jokhang square in the early morning, returning in the afternoon and cost Rmb15. Most tourists opt for a guided tour day trip, travelling by landcruiser. Costs are typically around Rmb500 including a guide (Rmb125 per person for a group of four). The 70-kilometre (45-mile) journey takes two hours; from Lhasa the route follows the Golmud road until, 40 kilometres (25 miles) from Lhasa, it turns off onto a dirt track (four-wheel-drives only) heading west up the picturesque Drowolung Valley. Tsürphu is 30 kilometres (20 miles) from the turnoff at an altitude of 4,300 metres (14,100 feet).

## DAMXUNG AND LAKE NAMTSO

A visit to Namtso, Tibet's largest salt lake, involves a two-day round trip from Lhasa of 420 kilometres (260 miles) and an overnight stay in Damxung or at Tashi Dorje Monastery, right on the lake shore. This is becoming an increasingly popular organised trip from Lhasa. It is a fairly rugged trip off the beaten track, but the rewards are considerable. At present this is the best opportunity open to travellers to see nomads on the move with their yak herds and to get the flavour of Tibet's high grazing lands. The lake itself is spectacular and still totally wild.

The altitude exceeds 4,300 metres (14,100 feet) for most of the journey, and one mountain pass is around 5,200 metres (over 17,000 feet), so warm clothes are essential. A windproof and waterproof outer garment and gloves are advisable. The weather is subject to abrupt, unpredictable changes, and it is not uncommon to encounter a snowstorm on the pass between Damxung and Lake Namtso even in midsummer. Bring food and soft drinks from Lhasa. Beer is available in Damxung.

The road from **Lhasa to Damxung** follows Tibet's main route to Golmud and Qinghai for 167 kilometres (104 miles). Lake Namtso lies about 40 kilometres (25 miles) further, on the far side of the Nyanchen Tanglha Mountains. A rocky mountain track, requiring a four-wheel drive vehicle, leads over a high pass and crosses the flat grassland near the lake.

After leaving the road junction 11 kilometres (seven miles) west of Lhasa, the route follows the Tölung River valley north through fields of rape and barley, passing small villages. Greenery and dwellings become sparser as the valley narrows. The road enters a steep, rocky gorge 80 kilometres (50 miles) from Lhasa and climbs beside the tumbling river for several kilometres. When it emerges on Tibet's northern plateau, a totally new landscape greets the traveller. Windswept grasslands alternating with gravel desert stretch between snowcapped mountains and a chain of steep, bare hills. This is the land of nomads, too high for farms and villages. Settlements are few, but the first town is reached almost immediately.

**Yangbajing** is an 'electricity town' built around a thermal power plant 87 kilometres (54 miles) north of Lhasa, halfway to Damxung. The altitude is 4,300 metres (14,100 feet). Yangbajing borders on a flat area of hot springs covering 16 square kilometres (six square miles). Steam and geysers can be seen rising from the plain. These feed two new geothermal electricity generating stations and a huge geodesic greenhouse that uses warmth and humidity from the steam to produce unseasonal vegetables. If nomads are in the vicinity, yaks graze right up to the wire fence, apparently unperturbed by the racket of gushing steam and modern technology on the other side. The sprawling town on the left of the road consists of houses and private facilities for workers at the power plant. A roadside village next to it provides services for truck drivers who stop at this junction on the northern route to Shigatse, now rarely used.

The power plant, which supplies a large part of Lhasa's electricity, is the first and biggest thermal development in China, established in 1976. The electricity produced is vital to Tibet's economic development, as all other kinds of fuel, except yak dung and wood, have to be trucked in. The plant can be visited by arrangement with CITS. A technician answers questions and conducts a guided tour of the steam-powered generators, cooling towers and steam-heated greenhouses where vegetables grow throughout the year.

The road runs northeast from Yangbajing through a long, straight, upland valley usually dotted with nomad encampments and herds of yaks. The nomads who roam over vast areas of northern Tibet make up about a quarter of the population of central and western Tibet. They produce the wool that has been Tibet's chief export for centuries and contribute an essential part of the country's diet in meat and dairy products. It is hard to be precise about their numbers, as nomads sometimes live a half-settled life, especially in eastern Tibet. One tribe with the same name and same chief may be engaged in two entirely different occupations, sharing and exchanging roles as farmers and shepherds. Some nomads have fixed winter homes where they return for a few months a year. Others scarcely see four walls during their whole lives.

Nomads are big, handsome people—tough, cheerful and independent. At sacred places throughout Tibet they stand out in their sheepskin *chubas* (long coats) as the most ardent and joyous of pilgrims. They put high value on honesty and can dispense rough justice. It is said that nomads always return a kindness twofold—and repay a bad turn twofold.

Nomads live with family or relatives in easily movable black tents made of yak-hair felt or woven wool. Tents invariably contain a fire-pit for cooking and an altar. Women and children usually work close to camp, but men cover long distances alone on horseback. A typical family commands an impressive array of skills and can live for long periods without touching settled areas, their only outside essentials being tea and *tsampa*.

The animals—yaks, sheep and goats, often numbering in the hundreds, are the

(following pages) *Tents on the grasslands, northeast Tibet*

family's private property. Men, women and children all use a sling and pebble with incredible accuracy to control the herd's movements, and dogs give some assistance, too. The woollen sling cracks like a whip as a pebble flies from its leather pouch, and a moment later a straying yak can be seen galloping at full speed back to its herd.

**Damxung** is a bleak little settlement of low, barrack-like buildings. It is also the administrative centre of Damxung County, founded in the 1960s. Its altitude is 4,400 metres (14,430 feet). Unlike towns in the southern farming areas, Damxung has no old Tibetan village at its heart. Its main street has the raw look of an American Wild West frontier town, with stocky nomads' horses hitched to the posts of open-front stores. A small ghost-town stands near an abandoned airstrip. The wind never ceases and the treeless plain stretches unbroken to the distant mountains. The nearest towns are Yangbajing, 85 kilometres (53 miles) to the south, and Nagqu, 160 kilometres (100 miles) north.

Damxung is an important spot in this region for government functions and general supplies. It has a barn-like department store where basic necessities and sturdy clothes can be bought. Open-front stores by the road sell items nomads like to buy—such as plastic flowers and plaster Buddha statues! Truckers stop here for gasoline and food. A major festival called Dajyur draws nomads to Damxung from all directions at the beginning of the lunar calendar's eighth month (solar September) for ten days of festivity: horseracing, bicycle-riding contests, rock-carrying competitions and other forms of merriment.

A track from Damxung crosses the plain and follows a stream up a steep, rocky valley into the mountains. Local Tibetans say that wolves, bears and leopards still live in the **Nyanchen Tanglha Range**. A stark crag and a stone pile mark the top of the **Lar-geh La Pass**, 5,132 metres (16,833 feet) high. This route leads to the tiny settlement of Namtso Qu. The route to Tashi Dorje Monastery traverses the 5,150-metre (16,900-foot) **Kong La** pass, a short distance to the west of the Lar-geh La.

Occasionally, cars meet a caravan of several hundred yaks heading through the pass laden with hand-woven bags of sheep's wool. This is a wonderful sight. Steered by mounted, sling-wielding outriders and circling dogs, they fill the narrow passage. Although yaks look large and clumsy at first sight, they are surprisingly graceful on the move.

Yaks rank with camels as the most efficient, all-purpose animals in the world, supplying almost everything a nomad needs. They give butter, milk and meat for food, and wool for clothing and tents. Their dung, sun-dried into hard bricks, can be used as fuel or building material for wind-shelters. They provide transportation, as saddle or pack animals. Unfortunately, they are also extremely ill-natured and stubborn, but when bred with domestic cattle, they produce the versatile *dzo*, which is frequently seen in Tibet's valleys.

Just beyond the pass, a dramatic view opens over the boundless expanse. Bright sapphire-blue **Lake Namtso** stretches away to the southwest, 4,591 metres (15,060 feet) above sea level. This is the second biggest salt lake in China (after Koko Nor, or Qinghai Hu), with a surface area of 1,940 square kilometres (750 square miles). A nomad, moving steadily, needs 18 days to circle it. This part is its narrow eastern tip. The road descends rapidly to the plain where it continues over the grassland, fording shallow streams. Mt Nyanchen Tanglha's white head soars 7,088 metres (23,249 feet) in the west, and the tin roofs of Namtso Qu, a tiny county station, can be seen near the foothills far off to the east.

To reach the lake's edge, a four-wheel-drive vehicle must leave the track and make its own way. Several kilometres west, a group of isolated hills extends into the lake.

Water birds skim the water and, in June, hundreds of wild geese nest close off shore on banks of reeds. Colour abounds everywhere, in tiny, jewel-like flowers underfoot and in distant mountain rocks. To take a short walk and experience the immense distances, the timelessness and the total silence of the plateau is perhaps to understand the nomads' deep love for this land.

# On the Trail of the Blue Poppy

*Great rolling masses of cloud, which rubbed against each other and continuously altered their form, hung over this magnificent rampart throughout its length, or rested lightly as thistledown on the tips of the mountains. A breeze fluttered the pages of my notebook and carried one loose one eddying into space. Reluctantly I turned my back on the threshold of a land flowing with milk and honey, and descended through the fir forests to the village.*

*. . . Next day we ascended the valley which is dominated by the highest peak on this part of the range, a ponderous blunt-headed buttress of dark rock, where snow lies in the gullies all the year round, though the glaciers have long since disappeared.*

*At first we followed the flower-girt stream which now wandered with divided waters over a flat sandy channel, starred with red and white saxifrage, and anon rushed noisily between bush-clad gravel banks where tall yellow poppies nodded to us as we passed. Presently, leaving the stream and ploughing knee-deep through Rhododendron we began to climb more steeply over very uneven hummocky country, interrupted here and there by grassy alps, where numbers of yaks were browsing. The black tents of the herdsmen were visible at the foot of the slope just across the stream.*

*It was rather dangerous work climbing over the enormous piles of lichen-fretted boulders which here encumber the valley, for they were partly covered by a loose growth of small shrubs concealing holes and crannies in which one was liable to trip. Amongst these boulders grew tall hollow-stemmed herbs, such as Meconopsis Prattii, the yellow gentian with its hanging bells, and a stately Umbellifer, bearing aloft plate-shaped inflorenscences arranged in meticulous order. On our left bare screes stretched up to the the splintered cliffs of the ridge, a thousand feet over our heads.*

*Presently shrubs grew more scattered and finally died out. Masses of pale-grey rock lay in disordered heaps. Small level pockets of sand occurred here and there along the stream, and before us the stony ground rose steeply in every direction, barren and forbidding. We were again in the land of the blue poppy.*

*Of this magnificent plant (Meconopsis speciosa) I will give some details. One specimen I noted was 20 inches high, crowned with 29 flowers and 14 ripening capsules above, with 5 buds below—48 flowers in all. Indeed the plant seemed to go on throughout the summer unfurling flower after flower out of nowhere—like a Japanese pith blossom thrown into water—for the stem is hollow and the root shallow. Another 8 bore fruits, 15 flowers and 5 buds, and a third, only 15 inches high, had 6 flowers, each 3.5 inches across, besides 14 buds. But for a certain perkiness of the stiff prickly stem, which refuses any gracefulness of arrangement to the crowded raceme, and the abscence of foliage amongst the the blooms, these great azure-blue flowers, massed with gold in the centre, would be the most beautiful I have seen. The Cambridge blue poppy is, moreover, unique amongst the dozen species of poppy-wort known to me from this region, in being sweetly scented. On one scree I counted no less than forty of these magnificent plants within a space of a few square yards.*

F Kingdon Ward, The Mystery Rivers of Tibet, 1923

## Common Tibetan Symbols

Some symbols recur on the walls of almost every temple, shrine and monastery, or on the walls of private houses. The most common decorative motifs of all are the Eight Sacred Emblems of Buddhism, as follows:

**Dharma Wheel** (*chakra*) represents the unity of all things and symbolizes Sakyamuni himself.

**Umbrella** (*gdugs*) is a token of loyalty and symbolizes the protection of the Dharma (faith).

**Conch Shell** (*dun*) used in Buddhist worship as a trumpet or offertory vessel and symbolizes the '.spoken word'.

**Golden Fish** (*gser-na*) as water allows fish to swim freely, so Buddhist belief emancipates the soul. They symbolize spiritual liberation.

**Lotus flower** (*padma*) as the flower rises from muddy roots, so Nirvana arises from this shabby world and thus it symbolizes purity.

**Vase** (*bum-pa*) is used as a strorage urn or a sacred receptacle and thus symbolizes hidden treasures.

**Banner of Victory** (*dpal-be*)
a unique Buddhist object, the cylindrical layered banner symbolizes victory over ignorance and death.

**Endless Knot** (*apal-be*) an auspicious geometric diagram, it symbolizes the unity of all things and the illusory character of time.

Some other common symbols are as follows:

**Wheel of Life** Found in vestibule murals. The hub shows the three poisons: ignorance, hatred and greed (pig, snake, cock). The six main sections show all realms of existence Heaven (top); demi-gods (top left); humankind (top right); Hell in awful detail (bottom); hungry ghosts with big bellies but tiny necks (low right); animals (low left). The demon of impermanence holds the whole wheel.

**Mystical Seal of the Kalacakra** Usually among vestibule murals. It symbolizes the highest of all initiations into occult knowledge, which can be performed only by a dalai lama or about a dozen other high lamas.

**Swastika** Found in mosaic floors or painted on homes. Ancient symbol. In Tibet it means good fortune. Strict followers of Buddhism draw it clockwise, followers of Bön anti-clockwise.

**Wind Horse** *(lung-ta)* Printed on prayer flags. Symbol of good luck with Three Jewels of Buddhism on his back. He takes prayers to Heaven by wind.

**Allegory of Co-operation** Found among murals. Bird brings a seed from afar and plants it. Rabbit manures the tree while eating grass under it. Monkey waters it while eating sweet fruit. Elephant comes to enjoy its shade and protect it. Thus was the Earth prepared for mankind.

**Sun and Moon** Painted on village houses. Ancient archetypal symbol for the source of light, union of opposites. In Tibet it is a folk sign for good luck and protection against evil spirits.

# Tsedang and the Yarlong Area

Southeast of Lhasa is a large administrative region known in modern times as Shannan (South of the Mountains). At its heart lies the ancient Kingdom of Yarlong, the cradle of Tibetan civilization. Tsedang, its capital, is at the foot of Mt Gongbori, one of central Tibet's holy mountains. Tibet's creation myth tells how, in a cave at the back of this small mountain, a saintly monkey and an ogress gave birth to the Tibetan people (see page 61). Their early history, including the reigns of some 30 semi-mythical kings, unfolded in this section of the Yarlong Tsangpo Valley. Tsedang means 'Playground', where the monkey came to frolic.

Tsedang (altitude 3,400 metres or 11,150 feet) and the adjacent town of Nedong follow the familiar pattern: both are cosy, old Tibetan towns surrounded by the modern, utilitarian buildings of new, larger Chinese sections which, in this case, run together as though they were one city, with a combined population of 25,000. Nedong, the smaller part, is the administrative capital of the Shannan area. Tsedang, which is socially and economically more important and growing fast, is a municipality. Both towns are small enough for a visitor to get around to most places on foot. The ruins of several monasteries can be seen in the old sections and the surrounding hills.

The outstanding physical features of Tsedang are the wide Yarlong Tsangpo River flowing just to the north of the city, Mt Gongbori overshadowing it to the east, and the profusion of trees all around that make the town an oasis in a strange, high-altitude desert.

## Getting There

Tsedang and the nearby areas of Yarlong and Chonggye (Qonggyai) are open to all travellers, but note that if you are including a side trip to Samye Monastery, you need a travel permit (see page 33).

Fast, luxurious Japanese buses leave Lhasa for Tsedang at 8.30 each morning, with tickets on sale two days before. You can break your journey at the Samye ferry point, near kilometre stone 155. The road is tarmacked the whole way to Tsedang. The journey of 190 kilometres (118 miles) takes about three hours. Buses returning from Tsedang leave at 9 am from near the central roundabout. Other (older) local buses leave earlier and go as far as Gonggar. These are good for getting to the Samye Ferry, as bus companies often refuse to sell short-haul tickets on long-distance buses.

# Along the Yarlong Tsangpo

After crossing the bridge over the Yarlong Tsangpo, the road rounds **Chuwori**, one of the sacred mountains of Tibet, and passes the ruins of **Gonggar Dzong**. Easily visited from the main road is the large, yellow-painted **Gonggar Chöde Monastery**. This monastery, following the Sakya tradition, has some fine murals. Coats of whitewash had to be scraped off many of these during the slow work of restoration. Sixteen kilometres (ten miles) further on, having passed the airport, the road passes another Sakyapa monastery, **Rawame**, which has over 30 monks. However, all its murals were defaced during the Cultural Revolution.

Beyond, in the village of Chitishö, is **Dunbu Chökor Monastery**, also Sakyapa, and founded in the 11th century. It is 300 metres (yards) away through the village on the right. From Chitishö, it is possible to cross the Yarlong Tsangpo by coracle or motor boat to visit the famous Nyingma monastery of **Dorje Drak**, beautifully sited at the foot of a high mountain spur next to the river. This is slowly being restored, and a few monks have returned.

The road continues east along the south bank of the Yarlong Tsangpo. Though close to the river, there is little agriculture. In places the stony mountains and sand dunes resemble a moonscape. Trees and irrigated fields of wheat and barley surround the occasional villages, but the greenery soon peters out into faded plots, and the desert takes over once again. Near Tsedang, planted forest belts of willow and poplar radiate from the river and agriculture intensifies. This region is famous for its apple and pear orchards.

# Historical Background

Archaeologists agree that agriculture appeared first in Tibet in the Yarlong region, confirming the Tibetans' own belief that they originated here as a people and a civilization. The earliest building still extant in Tibet lies just south of Tsedang. Tibet's first monastery was founded across the river nearby.

Mythology places the first Tibetan king's arrival from the sky near Tsedang. The Kingdom of Yarlong was the heart of Tibet until the seventh century AD, when King Songtsen Gampo moved the capital to Lhasa (see page 61). Even thereafter, the kings' bodies were returned to Yarlong for burial in tumuli in the Valley of the Kings, and they continued to look on it as their true homeland until the end of the monarchy in the ninth century.

# Sights

## YUMBU LAKANG

The castle of Yumbu Lakang is the oldest-known dwelling in Tibet, reputedly the home of the Yarlong kings. It stands 12 kilometres (7.5 miles) south of Tsedang, perched dramatically on a pinnacle above the valley. When the monarchy ended, the castle became a small monastery. Smashed to rubble in the 1960s, it has been rebuilt. Original stonework in the lower part dates back at least to the seventh century.

History and myth intermingle for the 700 years of the Yarlong kings before Songtsen Gampo (608–50 AD). Legend ascribes the building of Yumbu Lakang to Nyatri Tsenpo, the first of the heavenly kings, who is believed to have descended from the sky around 130 BC. It is more likely that the castle was built in the sixth century during the reign of Songtsen Gampo's great-grandfather.

A steep track goes up from the road to the castle's base. Here, one can circle the building clockwise and avoid a steep flight of steps, while getting a fine view of the valley and fields below, where agriculture first occurred in Tibet some 2,000 years ago. The way leads in through a primitive kitchen and upstairs to a terrace. The small chanting hall has been richly redecorated under the supervision of five resident monks. A gallery above has interesting murals. One tells the legend of Yumbu Lakang's founding, with Buddhist details added from a later period. Different scenes show King Nyatri Tsenpo's arrival from the sky. He is carried on the shoulders of yak herders to a white stupa (still standing across the valley) where he gives a sermon. Buddhist scriptures miraculously fall to earth. He founds a monastery on nearby Mt Shira (now destroyed), where a 'sky burial' can be seen in the foreground. Then, realizing that he must stay on earth, he builds Yumbu Lakang as a home, thereby teaching Tibetans how to build houses. An adjacent mural has tales about the female deity Tara.

## MINDROLING MONASTERY

Tibet's major Red Hat (Nyingmapa) monastery lies 54 kilometres (33 miles) west of Tsedang, a drive of one and a half hours. A small road turns south off the main road, 44 kilometres (27 miles) west of Tsedang at kilometre stone 147. The right-hand road at a fork in the first village leads into a side valley where the monastery stands.

Nyingmapa means 'Ancient Ones'. It is the oldest, most unreformed sect of Tibetan Buddhism, founded in the eighth century by the Indian saint-magician Padmasambhava. It retained many elements of the pre-Buddhist Bön faith. As other sects proliferated and gained influence, the Nyingmapas remained strictly anti-establishment, with no pretensions to political power. Their lamas were often married and

lived in very small groups as hermits, tantrists, yogis and sorcerers. They called themselves madmen and endeared themselves to the common people by their quizzical approach to life, their gibes at the excesses of the mighty, and their love of folklore and poetry. As madmen they sought access to the 'Treasury of the Mind', their source of inspiration and creativity. They scorned books and declared learning useless, yet they produced an extensive literature.

Mindroling, meaning 'Place of Perfect Emancipation', was founded in 1676 by Terdak Lingpa, whose ancestor was a famous Nyingmapa *terton*, 'discoverer of religious texts and treasures'. The teachings of this visionary had been carried on by his direct descendants for 300 years. Some of their doctrines were kept secret, especially their forms of meditation. Both the Second and Third dalai lamas are known to have studied these methods with Nyingmapa teachers. Terdak Lingpa became a tutor of the Great Fifth Dalai Lama, who may have influenced him to found Mindroling as an orderly, monastic teaching centre. When the Great Fifth made the Yellow Hat Sect supreme in Tibet by crushing rival sects, the Nyingmapas were ignored. Whether because it lacked wealth and posed no political threat, or because of the dalai lama's personal interest, Mindroling flourished.

Descendants of the *terton* became abbots of Mindroling, succeeding one another from father to son, not by way of reincarnation. One son of the abbot would become a monk, while another son, destined to become the abbot, was expected to marry and continue the line. If he died, the monk brother was obliged to marry his widow. This continued for over 20 generations; the present abbot lives in India.

Mindroling became the foremost monastery of the Nyingmapa Sect; it is now the only significant one left. Almost as important, however, was Dorje Drak Monastery near Gonggar, which was destroyed in the 1960s but is now rebuilt and functioning (see page 140).

Mindroling and the village below it are built of finely dressed stone. The monastery formerly had many buildings around its large courtyard, including a five-storey stupa. It housed over 300 monks. The Main Chanting Hall and an assembly hall still stand, and the past few years have brought a flurry of new building activity. A growing community of monks and novices looks after the site, which is among the most handsome and impressive in all Tibet.

The **Main Chanting Hall**, entered from the north, is dominated by a large statue of Terdak Lingpa, the founder, sitting in a glass case with fine, gilded woodwork. He is depicted in old age, with the white hair and beard of a patriarch, wearing the red hat of his sect. On the east side of the hall is a collection of copper stupas filled with writings. The heavy bases are original, although some of the tops were damaged and recently replaced. On the walls, volumes of scriptures are wrapped in red, not the prevalent yellow of the dalai lamas. Extensive *tsampa* and butter sculpture graces the

*Yumbu Lakang, south of Tsedang in the Yarlong region*

altar. A throne awaits the abbot's return from exile in India.

The **South Chapel** contains a giant statue of Sakyamuni holding a black bowl of clear water in front of a sculpted backdrop of mythical characters and beasts. Eight tall, androgynous figures represent bodhisattvas.

The Chanting Hall roof has two levels. On the lower is a chapel with a gilded Tara and over 100 small copper stupas and figures behind wire netting. Some of these are magnificent, with details that deserve careful study. On the upper level is a chapel with extraordinary murals, mostly originals, depicting all the important lamas ever to have lived here. All different, they display many personalities and degrees of magical power. The Sakyamuni in a glass case on the altar is said to be 300 years old.

## Valley of the Kings

In a valley 27 kilometres (16 miles) south of Tsedang are large mounds of earth resembling natural hills but believed to contain the tombs of Tibet's later kings. The road follows a river to the town of Chonggye (also spelt Qonggyai or Qiongjie) and enters the valley one kilometre (half a mile) beyond the bridge.

The biggest tumulus, on the right, is ascribed to King Songtsen Gampo (seventh century AD). Steps lead up the side to a charming little temple on top. The temple was rebuilt and its murals restored in 1983. Three monks care for it and tend the flowers and apple trees in its courtyard.

The temple is dedicated to Songtsen Gampo, who was declared by the Fifth Dalai

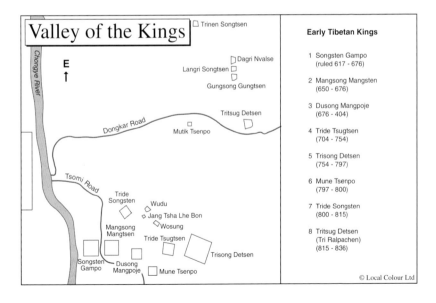

Lama to be an incarnation of Chenrezi, the bodhisattva of compassion, 1,000 years after his death. His statue is seated on a painted chest at the centre of the altar. Beside him, his Chinese wife, Wen Cheng, holds a Buddhist wheel of life, and his Nepalese wife, Tritsun, holds a crystal ball. Wise ministers stand on either side. Tönmi Sambhota, the philologist who created Tibetan writing, is on the right, holding a book. A chapel behind the altar has a large, crowned Maitreya flanked by two Sakya-munis. The mural on the right wall depicts an Indian sage and attendant deities contemporary with King Trisong Detsen (eighth century AD).

Some scholars doubt that Songstsen Gampo's body actually rests inside this tumulus, which has not been excavated, and suggest he was interred at the Jokhang in Lhasa. However, if the annals are to be credited, a rich, elaborate tomb lies below, with an internal configuration of symbolic importance. The king's body was reputed-ly placed in a silver coffin in a central, subterranean chamber, and nine smaller chambers were filled with vast treasures. (Nine and thirteen were sacred Bön num-bers.) Funeral rites included the sacrifice of men and horses, who were buried with the king. The tomb layout made it into a magical projection of the world, with the king's body at the centre holding the continuing prosperity of the kingdom.

Songtsen Gampo's reign marks the line between Tibetan mythology and recorded history. Very little exists to tell us about the kings who preceded him. The annals indicate that there were more than 30, in several lines of dynasties. Each one was said to have made discoveries and inventions that benefited the Tibetan people. Organ-ized agriculture, a system of law, bridge-building, irrigation, charcoal, Chinese science and military skills all made their appearance in Yarlong before the seventh century.

The first seven kings left no traces on earth, for they were not kings so much as gods exercising an earthly function. The king descended from the sky on a rainbow sky-rope to rule by day, returning to his heavenly home at night. As soon as his son learned to ride a horse, at the age of 13, he departed for good. This first royal line ended when the king arrogantly fought a duel without his magic weapons and accidentally cut his rainbow sky-rope. He was the first one to leave a corpse (which was put into a river), and thereafter the kings lived out their lives as humans. The early kings disposed of their dead in various ways, according to the practice of their dynasty. Royal remains were put in vessels and sarcophagi, in rivers, or were dismembered for sky burial. By Songtsen Gampo's time, burial in tombs beneath tumuli was an established custom.

The eight kings of the Tubo line, whose tumuli fill the Valley of the Kings, were all warriors. From their small base in Yarlong they kept up a series of huge military enterprises for almost 200 years. Military and civil administration were one and the same in Yarlong. Agriculture occupied the Tibetans for the summer season, and the

rest of the year was taken up with warfare. All of Tibet's neighbours suffered from internal disruptions, which made them easy prey. Each conquered territory produced new skills and methods, which Tibetans were quick to absorb. Skilful alliances furthered their success. Tibet under the Tubo kings became one of the mightiest powers of Central Asia.

Campaigns took Tibetans from the capital of China to Samarkand, where Arabs told them about far away Byzantium and Rome. (One scholar has even suggested that Gesar's name was a Tibetan version of Caesar.) When Tibet slid down from this pinnacle, the descent was swift. King Lang Darma turned the war machine against his own people in a furious effort to stamp out Buddhism. When his short reign ended with murder in 842, he had wiped out the monarchy and Tibet's role as a conquering power.

## TRANDRUK TEMPLE

Reconstruction of this ancient monastery took many years, and much has been lost, but visitors can still sense the quality and strength of the site. An entranceway and cluster of buildings stand in Trandruk (Changzhu) village, five kilometres (three miles) south of Tsedang on the road to Yumbu Lakang.

The temple, one of the first in Tibet, is thought to have been founded in the seventh century during the reign of Songtsen Gampo, perhaps by the great king himself. It was one of a group of strategically placed temples intended to subdue an earth-demoness who brought danger and destruction to the realm. The original temple was made of wood and thatch. In the 14th century it was rebuilt, enlarged and turned into a monastery. Further improvements were made by the Seventh Dalai Lama in the 17th century, at which time Tandruk supported 300 monks. The monastery contained numerous halls, including a Great Hall that was said to resemble the Jokhang. It was famous for its huge bell and sublime statuary. Although small, the monastery owned a disproportionate number of masterpieces of Buddhist art.

In the forecourt of the monastery can be seen the immense beams and massive pillars of the 14th-century entrance. One small temple stands in the inner courtyard. Inside is a banner embroidered with almost 30,000 pearls, representing Chenrezi in repose. The style is Indian, and it is undoubtedly very old, saved from a razed monastery in Nedong. Trandruk Temple is now the repository for a hodgepodge of saved religious objects gathered from various parts of Tibet.

Extensive renovations began in 1982. A new dormitory for the seven resident monks and another religious building are being constructed from scratch. The forecourt has great historical value and merits restoration, but the murals have been so badly obliterated that it is doubtful any contemporary restorer could approximate the originals.

*Rock paintings of the protective deity Yamantaka, Tsong Kapa and religious master*

## THE YARLONG TSANGPO RIVER

The Yarlong Tsangpo, Tibet's principal waterway, is the upper half of India's great Brahmaputra River. It is 2,900 kilometres (1,800 miles) long from its source in western Tibet to its mouth in Bangladesh. Tsangpo, appropriately, means 'mighty'. The Yarlong Tsangpo is the highest river in the world, with an average altitude of 4,000 metres (13,000 feet). It flows from west to east parallel to the Himalaya Mountains on their northern side.

Cascading from a high glacier, gathering snow water, the Yarlong Tsangpo enters a long, flat valley above Shigatse as a typical braided river winding among sandbanks. It flows through temperate, fertile central Tibet to Tsedang, where the river nurtured Tibet's first civilization. Along the 650 kilometres (400 miles) of its middle reaches, a wide, navigable channel, shifting with the seasons, is plied by river craft: passenger and cargo boats driven by converted tractor engines; oblong, wooden box-boats; and round coracles made of yak hide and willow boughs.

In eastern Tibet, the river hooks dramatically around the snow-capped massif of Namcha Barwa, 7,756 metres (25,447 feet) high, and turns south to India, where it is renamed Brahmaputra (Son of Brahma, the Creator). Here it turns west, crossing the plain of Assam for hundreds of miles, parallel to its course through Tibet but in the opposite direction and on

## RECHUNGPUK MONASTERY

This monastery is about 100 metres (yards) up on a ridge dividing the Yarlong and Chonggye valleys. It was built around a retreat cave used for meditation by Rechungpa, a famous disciple of Milarepa. Formerly large and impressive, it now has only a few small restored buildings amongst the ruins. It has a small community of fewer than a dozen monks and nuns. A young incarnate lama from Kham is the abbot, and its tradition draws from both Nyingma and Kagyu sources. Young people visiting from neighbouring villages often give it a cheerful teenage ambience.

## UPPER YARLONG VALLEY

The Yarlong Valley, extending 90 kilometres (60 miles) south from Tsedang, is an interesting and historic area to explore on foot, by bicycle (available in Tsedang) or by riding on walking-tractors. It has many friendly villages, and there is an intact monastery at Chedagong with two monks who have recently commenced restorations. The road rises steadily to a pass leading up to a high plateau. The beautiful and isolated snow peak to the right is **Yarla Shampo**, one of Tibet's sacred mountains the south side of the Himalayas. Its waters finally merge with those of the Ganges in a vast delta flowing south to the Bay of Bengal.

For a long time the Yarlong Tsangpo's source remained a mystery for Western geographers. An Indian named Kinthup, one of the intrepid surveyor-spies employed by the British in the 1800s (see page 197), first traced it to the sacred Kailash Range of western Tibet. In 1904–5, after Colonel Younghusband had forced Tibet into cordial relations with British India (see page 185), four British army surveyors recorded their journey up the river from Shigatse through formidable terrain and hardships to confirm its source in a huge glacier southeast of Mt Kailash and Lake Manasarovar.

Even more perplexing was its course through the eastern Himalayas, once people realized that the Yarlong Tsangpo and the Brahmaputra were one and the same river. They knew only that it entered the mountains on the north at 3,600 metres (12,000 feet) and that it dropped an astounding 3,350 metres (11,000 feet) before emerging in India on the south. Excited geographers predicted an immense, hidden waterfall. Explorers finished their work in 1924 but found no falls higher than nine metres (30 feet). Instead they discovered a series of incredible rapids and cascades, whose violent waters raced ten metres (yards) per second through towering cliffs and gorges, eroding the riverbed deeper and deeper into the limestone rock.

(6,594 metres or 21,634 feet). It is possible to circumambulate this mountain and return to the Yarlong Valley via a pass to the west.

The road running south from here crosses plateaus and valleys, leading eventually to Tsona (Cona) near the border with Bhutan. This interesting area is sensitive, due to the unresolved border conflict with India, and exploration is not possible at present except for the lucky and intrepid. The rewards of visiting this area are considerable.

## NEDONG CARPET FACTORY

This small, primitive factory, hidden behind mud-brick walls on the south side of Nedong, does all the preliminary work on the premises. Carding is done with wire hand-brushes, spinning with treadle spinning wheels and hand dyeing in large vats. It employs 56 workers, of whom 22 are weavers. The rugs are mostly one-by-two metre (three-by-six foot) size, to be sold in Tibet. Although most carry typically bright designs featuring flowers and dragons, here also can be found such rarities as the 700-year-old chequerboard design and an esoteric design of old Buddhist and

*Foot soldier of the Zimchongpa, a ceremonial force believed to be descended from the Mongols*

royal symbols in muted shades of beige and black. In the past the owners were normally unwilling to sell to passing individuals, but the factory now has a sales outlet where rugs can be bought .

## TSEDANG PRIMARY SCHOOL

Situated on the edge of Tsedang's old Tibetan quarter, this school has become a Chinese model for teaching national minority children.

It was established in 1982, the outgrowth of an agricultural commune school, when money became available to improve Tibetan schools. It has six grades in which Chinese and Tibetan children, in roughly equal numbers, study both languages while following an otherwise standard Chinese primary curriculum. Foreign tourists can visit the school by arrangement with CITS and see the classes in session.

## WALKS IN TSEDANG

There is not much to do in Tsedang when the sightseeing tours are over, but because it is at a relatively low altitude, walking is pleasant and easy.

The **river walk** begins on the main avenue north of the two tourist hotels. You soon come to the edge of the town, and a small sandy road continues north towards the Yarlong Tsangpo River between fields of barley and vegetables, ending after about two kilometres (a mile) at a small village. Paths lead beyond it through groves of willow trees to the water's edge. A stroll along the riverbank at sunset can restore the most jaded spirits. The round-trip hike is about six kilometres (four miles).

The **hill walk** leads to a tiny monastery hidden on the flank of Mt Gongbori. Walk north from the tourist hotels on the main avenue and turn right to Tsedang's old Tibetan quarter. (In many ways this is still a farm village in spite of its urban surroundings.) A dusty road leads uphill past the ruins of **Ngachö Monastery** to a point where a shrine with many prayer flags can be seen on the mountainside a few hundred metres (yards) ahead on the right. A well-worn path leads to a water-source where women and children gather with their water pots. A path leads past the shrine, which consists of a big pile of stones and a mass of prayer flags, then around a shoulder of the mountain to tiny **Sangga Zimche Nunnery**. An old lama, two monks and young nuns keep a little temple here that is not included on any sightseeing tour. There is a fine view over Tsedang. Local pilgrims seem proud to show off this holy place of their own. The pilgrim path continues for a short distance beyond the temple to a square, white shrine, then circles back to the old town. The round-trip hike is about four kilometres (2.5 miles).

## SAMYE MONASTERY

Tibet's first monastery was founded in 779 by Trisong Detsen, Tibet's 'Second Religious King' (see page 63), after he had invited prominent Buddhists to Tibet from India, the most famous of whom were Padmasambhava, the magician-saint (see page 64), and Santarakshita, his personal tutor. The two teachers helped him found Samye as a school for training Tibetan monks, modelling it after a monastery in Bihar, India.

Legend has it that Padmasambhava magically compelled Tibetan demons to haul stone and wood from the rivers and forests each night so men could build the monastery by day, and forced the Nagas, the water-serpent deities, to give up their gold to finance the operation.

GETTING THERE

Samye Monastery is located north of the Yarlong Tsangpo River, about 30 kilometres (18 miles) from Tsedang as the crow flies. A visit takes a full day. Visitors need a travel permit to Samye (obtainable from the Public Security bureaus in Lhasa or Tsedang), and Lhasa police treat it as an offence to buy a bus ticket to Samye ferry without one. Two popular treks lead to Samye from the Lhasa Valley (see page 160).

Visitors leave their bus or car at a riverside ferry mooring 36 kilometres (22 miles) west of Tsedang, near kilometer stone 155. There is a rudimentary 'boat-stop' hotel where one can get sweet tea and bad thukpa and sleep in a grimy bed if stuck. It can be hard to get an onward bus here, as they often roar past full up. Friendly Chinese army officers in jeeps sometimes pick up stranded people, something truck drivers can no longer do. The only other transport here is walking-tractors, which shuttle between villages and might get you a bit closer to Tsedang.

The crossing is on an open, flat-bottomed ferry propelled by a modified walking-tractor engine. A crossing costs Rmb10. You may share the boat with up to 50 villagers and pilgrims and a couple of cows and it may run aground on a few of the river's many shifting sandbanks. Crossing towards Samye, the boat lands a few kilometres upstream, taking about an hour and a half. The return journey downstream takes about an hour. At busy times of year, the boats run all day, but at quiet seasons they run only between 9 am and noon. In spring, the river plain is very exposed to dust-storms that roar straight along the open valley, so take a dust-mask and protect your camera. Except on dusty or overcast days, there is a wonderful limpid light along the river in its broad sweep of valley flanked by barren mountains.

Bird life on the river here is minimal, with occasional ducks or brown-headed seagulls, perhaps an ibis bill wader and, in the summer, martins darting around catching flies on the wing.

With the increasing flow of traffic to Samye and its district, the ferries are now met by a couple of trucks and tractors with trailers, which carry you across a rough

# STUPAS

One of the most ubiquitous structures throughout the Buddhist world is the stupa: a round dome or cylinder on a (usually) square base, with a shaft or spike emerging upwards. The stupa is as fundamental a symbol to Buddhists as the cross is to Christians.

Stupas probably evolved in India from prehistoric times as burial mounds for local rulers and heroes. Legend says that in the fifth century BC Sakyamuni, the historical Buddha, asked to have his ashes interred in a stupa. With the launching of the new religion, stupas became formalized objects of worship. King Ashoka of India (273–232 BC) built innumerable stupas as an act of piety and to gain religious merit.

In early Buddhist art, Sakyamuni was never portrayed in human form, since the state of Buddhahood was considered indescribable. Instead, a stupa became the Buddha's symbol, a reminder of his earthly existence and a place of devotion. Stupas were erected by pilgrims in places where the main events of his life took place. Stupas became the main cult objects in monasteries, where they were used to hold the mummified bodies or ashes of saints, like the tombs of the dalai lamas in the Potala, or to hold sacred objects, relics or scriptures. They were built to commemorate events, such as the founding of Drepung Monastery on Mt Gambo Utse, or to mark the place where a deity or a saint, such as Atisha, was said to have lived.

The shape of stupas was adapted to local architecture wherever they spread and came to include a huge variety of types. The slender pagodas of China and Japan evolved from earlier, squat stupas. Sizes could range from tiny, ritual altar stupas to the former West Gate of Lhasa (now gone), whose base arched over a main thoroughfare. Yet all kept the same basic components.

The different parts are associated with the elements: the base standing for earth, the dome for water and the shaft  for fire, topped by a half-moon for air and a sun for infinite space. The shaft is usually formed of 13 rings, which represent the 13 steps to enlightenment. Richly decorated stupa-tombs have a face of open grill-work on the dome if a mummified body lies inside. Stupas containing scriptures, charms or treasures are closed, but may have a niche for a statue.

*Chorten* is the Tibetan word for a stupa. It refers not only to recognizable stupas, but also to any sacred protuberance—a rock, a cairn or a pile of *mani* stones, to be worshipped by clockwise circumambulation, with the sacred object always on the pilgrim's right.

sandy desert for 45 minutes (not a nice walk), through a village in which willow baskets are made and past a cluster of five ancient chortens, into Samye. The fare is pro rata for your share of the vehicle, usually working out at Rmb5. For the return journey, trucks or tractors park at a yard near the monastery main gate and circle the monastery hooting to attract passengers.

The monastery is surrounded by a large village occupying an oasis of fields and willow and poplar trees, separated from the river by a rolling expanse of crescent sand dunes. The little sacred mountain, Hepori, rises across the fields to the east.

### ■ HISTORICAL BACKGROUND

The first Tibetan monk, a Yarlong aristocrat who had attended a Buddhist university in India, was ordained by Santarakshita and installed as the first abbot of Samye. Santarakshita then ordained seven more nobles, whom the king had selected for their intelligence to receive this honour. Would-be monks came from near and far to be trained by them. The king enacted new religious laws placing monks above the royal law. Samye's abbot, entitled head of the superiors, received more privileges than a minister of state. Certain landowning families of Yarlong were made subject to the monastery rather than the king and were obliged to provide the monks with food, income, butter, cloth, paper and ink, each according to his rank and degree. Anyone doing harm to a monk was severely punished—to the point where even a dirty look could mean having an eye put out.

In 791 King Trisong Detsen proclaimed Buddhism the official religion of Tibet, upon which two of his five queens and 300 other people promptly took religious vows and joined holy orders. Yet most of the aristocrats of Yarlong clung tenaciously to the old Bön faith. They hated the newly privileged class of Buddhist monks, which they saw as a mortal threat not only to the power of the nobility but also to the monarchy itself. History proved them entirely correct. King Trisong Detsen grappled continually with the nobles. When he demanded that one of them build a stupa at Samye as an act of piety, the reluctant lord made it black, the colour of Bön.

Two divergent streams of Buddhism clashed at Samye. Chinese influence was as strong as that of the Indians, Padmasambhava and Santarakshita. From 781 onwards, China sent two monks to Samye, replacing them every two years. Chinese Chan Buddhism, a forerunner of Zen, sought salvation through meditation and sudden insight, laying little store in ritual or good works. The Indians, on the other hand, embraced a moral code of good and bad deeds repayable in a future life, a slower route to salvation.

A great debate took place in the king's presence from 791 to 793. Two learned monks, one from China, the other from India, carried on a profound discourse, the text of which has been preserved. The Indian view triumphed and was adopted as the future course for Tibetan Buddhism to follow. Nonetheless, Chinese elements were incorporated into Lamaism.

Though the esoteric teachings of Tibetan Buddhism were always transmitted by word of mouth, in the context of a strong personal bond between teacher and pupil, many translations and catalogues of Buddhist texts were produced at Samye, and much scholarly writing was done during Trisong Detsen's time.

A difficult but fascinating Tibetan text on this period is the biography of Padmasambhava's consort, which is available in translation with copious notes and scholarly interpretations under the title *The Life of Yeshe Tsogyel* by Keith Dowman. It is based on *terma*, the texts hidden by Padmasambhava and rediscovered in later centuries.

### ■ LAYOUT

Samye was built between 775 and 787 at the site of a temple founded by Trisong Detsen's father. Offerings from chief ministers and Trisong Detsen's five queens helped to pay the costs. At the centre was the large, three-storeyed Great Hall, surmounted by gold roofs and enclosed within a protective cloister with elaborate gates at the cardinal points. Opposite the corners stood four big stupas built by individuals in different pagoda styles and coloured red, white, green and black. Many surrounding buildings and temples completed the monastery. The whole was originally enclosed by a zigzag wall that was destroyed by fire. It was replaced in the tenth century by a great circular wall 3.5 metres (12 feet) high and 2.5 kilometres (1.5 miles) in circumference. Nain Singh, the surveyor-spy for the British (see page 197), who stayed at Samye in the 1860s, gave an exact report of its physical features and its four large colleges. Photographs taken in the 1940s record its impressive layout, barely changed since the eighth century.

The **Great Hall** (Ütse) faces east. The surrounding square cloister, which houses the monks and novices, is entered by the east portal, which features two stone elephants and a giant bronze bell. Just inside is a huge prayer wheel under a canopy. The architecture of the Great Hall combined styles that expressed the borrowings and mergings typical of Tibetan Buddhism. The lower part was constructed in the Tibetan manner, with two roofs, by builders from Khotan, north of the Kunlun Mountains. The middle part was made in Chinese style with three roofs by Chinese carpenters. The upper part, also with three roofs, was built in Indian style by Indian craftsmen. Craftsmen and villagers have been rebuilding the third storey, destroyed in the Cultural Revolution, but the high golden roof may not be restored to its former glory for a long time.

The main **Chanting Hall** (dukhang) has altar statues of five ancient historical figures: from left to right, a foremost translator of scriptures into Tibetan; an Afghan

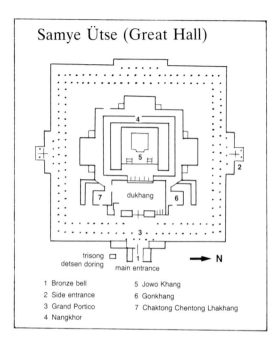

# Samye Ütse (Great Hall)

4

5

2

dukhang

7

6

3

trisong
detsen doring

main entrance

→ N

1 Bronze bell
2 Side entrance
3 Grand Portico
4 Nangkhor

5 Jowo Khang
6 Gonkhang
7 Chaktong Chentong Lhakhang

sage invited by the king to give guidance on Samye's construction; in the middle, with jewelled breastplate and popping eyes, an Indian exorcist (a colleague of Padmasambhava's) who rid the region of ghosts; King Trisong Detsen; and finally his ancestor, King Songtsen Gampo.

Butter and *tsampa* sculptures in glass cases, made at the Tibetan New Year, display excellent workmanship and show that this art form is still alive.

The **West Chapel** (Jowo Khang) has a very large central figure of Sakyamuni dating from the eighth century. Beneath the garments the figure is stone; only the recently destroyed head has been restored in clay. Pious Buddhists believe that the figure formed spontaneously out of rock from Mt Hepori.

The **North Chapel** (Gonkhang) is a dark chamber whose three demon deities are considered so frightening that their heads are hidden under white scarves. Samye Monastery belongs simultaneously to three sects of Buddhism—the orthodox Yellow Hat Sect and two of the unreformed Red Hat sects. The latter still retain strong elements of magic and demonology derived from the pre-Buddhist Bön faith, as is demonstrated here.

The **South Chapel** (Chaktong Chentong Lhakhang), with a separate entrance outside, has a memorable statue of Chenrezi with multiple heads and arms and 10,000 hands, in front of whom sits a fierce image of Padmasambhava (Guru Rinpoche).

Two upper levels of the Chanting Hall still contain some rare murals in spite of much damage. At the top, a pillared hall holds three statues, of which Padmasambhava (centre) and Sakyamuni (right) are familiar. The left-hand statue is said to have come from the temple founded by King Trisong Detsen's father on this site before Samye was built. The modern pattern on its lap-robe adds an unexpectedly light-hearted touch.

The **roof** offers a grand view over the village and countryside.

A red, rounded structure to the southwest is the base of Samye's destroyed red stupa, which was considerably taller than the monastery.

The **cloister** has living quarters for the monks on the upper tier. Below the gallery are remarkable murals, some original, some damaged, some restored. To the left of the portal on entering, beyond a row of prayer wheels, is a marvellously executed scheme of Samye Monastery as it was in the eighth century, complete with zigzag wall. Beyond is a depiction of Chimpuk Cave, an important tantric centre northeast of Samye and still a sacred destination for pilgrims.

### ■ ACCOMMODATION

There is a **guesthouse** south of the monastery run by two irritable ladies. If it is full, as it often is, see if the Chinese woman who runs the Happy Restaurant on the square can arrange a bed with a local family. The community is clearly not prepared for an influx of foreigners and pilgrims, and you may not find a bed at all. Accept that resources are limited, remain polite and keep your plans flexible. Adventurous souls can explore the villages a few kilometres (miles) upvalley to the north and seek invitations to stay.

Above Ningom Village, there are lovely walks into valleys full of small trees and shrubs, flowers and rare birds. This is the last stage of the two treks from Dagze Dzong and Ganden (see page 160).

Food in Samye is limited, so bring your own food and drink. Besides the Happy Restaurant, a dining hall in a yard to the north has *thukpa* and sweet tea.

## CHIMPUK CAVE

The cave, a four-hour walk northeast across the desert, is a tantric retreat centre. To get there, cross the fields to Hepori, the low mountain to the east. From the shrine at the top you can just see two little white spots on the face of a mountain to the northeast. The left spot is the hermitage chapel; to the right is a large chorten. A track runs north of Mt Hepori across barren desert, past two abandoned villages and a ruined temple. Take lots of water, as this area is completely dry. The track then climbs steeply through rocks and shrubs, past a sky-burial ground, to the caves and huts of the retreat centre.

You can camp here and meet the resident monks and nuns (now numbering over 50) and the many pilgrims. They cannot feed you. Bring food or brick-tea for them and gain merit.

(following pages) *Selling printed prayers and cloth prayer flags on the Barkhor, central Lhasa*

# Two Treks to Samye

Two major pilgrim paths run from the Lhasa Valley to Samye. These are popular trekking routes for experienced hikers.

## FROM DAGZE DZONG

This trek takes three days and crosses one high pass. Barring an emergency, there is no need to camp out.

Dagze Dzong, the starting point, is a ruined fort on a little hill on the south side of the Kyichu (Lhasa) River, about 30 kilometres (20 miles) upstream from Lhasa. The first day entails about five hours of easy walking. Head due south along a broad valley with fields, keeping a narrow rocky ridge to your left. After you pass a water-mill and a shrine, take the left fork of the valley, which rises, passing two villages and a small hydro-electric station beside the stream. After a long narrow section the valley broadens, and the village of Chenze spreads out across a plain. This is a good place to stay the night in a herder's cottage. Campers can walk an hour or two further.

The second day is a hard 11-hour walk over a pass, requiring an early start. Take the stream valley eastwards. You will pass two narrow stream gorges to the right. Look for where the path zigzags up and to the right to rejoin a second stream higher up. Climb up a steep section, then turn left, away from the stream and around the hill. The trail passes a cairn (rock pile) at the end of the hill and runs level into a glacial cirque (bowl-shaped hollow) with rocky crags and a marshy floor. (This place sometimes gets a lot of snow.) The path zigzags steeply up on the left between the crags and around a stony hill to the windswept Gokhar La Pass, nearly 5,000 metres (16,400 feet) high and marked by cairns and flags. Then there is a long descent southeast into a deep wooded valley with small trees, shrubs, flowers, birds and enough fuel and shelter to make camping out comfortable. The path here is well marked and unevenly paved with rocks. (Look out for Elwe's eared pheasant here, a large and rare bird with distinctive ear-like tufts of feathers.) The valley turns south past a mill and animal corrals. The village of Nyingo is at the apex of a sharp, rocky ridge over the confluence of two streams. The route from Ganden to Samye merges here, and this is a good place to stay.

The third day is an easy seven-hour walk down the valley. There is time for a side trip to the small, ruined Yamalung Monastery, on the side of the ridge two kilometres (a mile) north, on the west side of the east branch of the river (see page 162). The straightforward walk down to Samye passes a number of villages. Look for the shrine marking the birthplace of King Trisong Detsen at Dakmar and the ruins of many old

*Prayer flags and landscape at the Kamba La Pass, southwest of Lhasa*

habitations on the right side of the trail. The last few kilometres to Samye are slow and tiring, as the surface is soft sand.

## From Ganden Monastery

This trek takes perhaps four, usually five, days and crosses two high passes. Camping gear is essential, as you remain high up in exposed areas between the passes. There is a small guesthouse at Ganden, where some travellers may want to spend a day acclimatizing to the altitude.

The trail starts along the ridge above Ganden, from near the prayer flags and juniper incense hearths. It angles along the slope into the valley on the right (south) to the village of Hebu—so far an easy, short walk. This is the last village before you go high, and you can stay here. Yaks can be hired. West of Hebu, the trail turns up a side valley. After 20 minutes, there are some caves in the side of a rock outcrop on the left, but you have to climb a steep slope before you can see them. There is good water here, and you can camp.

The second day is a hard ascent up to Jokar La Pass, about 5,300 metres (17,400 feet) high. The pass is marked by cairns and prayer flags. After the pass, the trail angles left down to a small river. There is a ruined building near the water that gives some protection. A little further up, in a wide, high valley, is a small lake. A ruin stands nearby, 50 metres (yards) up. Camp here. The altitude is about 4,600 metres (15,000 feet).

From this point, day stages depend upon your walking speed and weather conditions. The trail is very indistinct—and disappears completely if there is snow—so look for nomads to ask directions. The valley branches near the lake. Take the right branch and make another long ascent to the second high pass, which is about 5,000 metres (16,400 feet). There is a lake and some streams near the pass. After the pass, the trail descends to a long, narrow river gorge. Heavy rain or melting snow can make this gorge impassable, and trekkers have been forced to turn back in summer. (You should carry extra food for contingencies such as this.)

Keep on the left side of the river. Lower, the valley broadens, and you cross on a wooden bridge a stream flowing from the left. This area has many shrubs and flowers and is good for camping.

Visible on the low but steep ridge on the right side of the river are the ruins of **Yamalung Monastery**, built around a meditation retreat cave used by Padmasambhava and his consort Yeshe Tsogyel. Two monks now live there. A little wooden bridge covered in prayer flags has been put across the river, and it is a steep scramble 150 metres (yards) up to the ruins.

Two kilometres (a mile) further down the valley, a second valley joins from the right, which is the route from Dagze Dzong. A stone bridge takes you over the river into Nyingo, a farm village and a good place to stay.

The final day is described under *From Dagze Dzong to Samye* (see page 160).

# Ambushed

*So we began our usual tasks: photographing, sighting, jotting down things in our note-books, examining the landscape through binoculars. . . . The binoculars revealed nothing, absolutely nothing to cause alarm.*

*I recollect that Liotard had to lie flat on his stomach to make his observations, as the wind was so violent.*

*Meanwhile, a few feet away, the caravan was waiting. The Tibetans had followed Liotard's example and lit their bamboo pipes; they were gossiping, with their hands on their horses' bridles. The horses never neighed once. There was nowhere for the yaks to graze on this dead earth, so they stood there motionless like statues. Our dog Roupie, crouched like a sphinx, was relaxing after her day's scamperings after the marmots. During the whole of our ten minutes on the pass she didn't once growl. She remained quiet, absolutely quiet.*

*At length we resumed our march. Just as I was plunging down the left slope of the valley, Liotard, laconic as ever, remarked:*

*'16,250 feet.'*

*He had just tapped the glass of his altimeter with his finger to set it going.*

*That was the last time I was to hear his voice.*

*The sky was marvellously blue and the rocks of the pass shone fawn-coloured in the sunlight. Down below us, at the foot of the valley, a little stream meandered across the yellowing grass-lands. My watch said 12.30.*

*Everything that followed is engraved on my memory in a rapid succession of pictures, a sort of uninterrupted film-sequence of violent scenes.*

*We had just started our descent. I was walking at a good speed down the faint track which ran midway along the slope of the hill. My horse's bridle weighed heavily on my arm, and I felt its muzzle pushing gently into the small of my back. Tchrachy was on horseback, a little to my left, his* rifle slung over his shoulder. I could hear him praying.

After a few steps I turned round to make sure that the caravan was following in good order. The ten yaks were barging about on the narrow ledge, knocking their loads together, panting and snorting. Behind them Yong Rine was cracking his whip, urging them along with shouts. Tze, placid as ever, was leading his horse by the bridle and paying no attention at all to his surroundings.

Liotard, on foot, brought up the rear, leading his white horse by the bridle. Handsome, serious and black-bearded like a stained-glass window saint, he wore that familiar expression on his face, cold and contemplative, sunk in his own thoughts. Like me, he was probably wondering about the country that lay ahead of us, picturing those far-distant mountains, contemplating the future.

How extraordinary that at that moment none of us, not one, should have had the faintest shadow of doubt or premonition!

And yet two of us were within a few minutes of death.

I had just seen Liotard for the last time.

.        .        .        .        .        .        .

A shot rang out on my left, a little behind me! It was so muffled that I would have thought it a long way off, had not a sound like the buzzing of a bee told me that a bullet had just grazed my ear.

For a split second I thought that the shot had been fired by one of our party. I turned round in astonishment. There, behind a rock, was a man with a gun levelled at me. The barrel was still smoking, and he had not yet had time to re-load. He was so close that I could see his dark eyes fixed on me.

So that was that! We'd been attacked. The first shot was the signal for a volley. Later on I was to discover that the bullet had pierced my jacket in two places.

For a moment I considered taking cover behind my horse. But the poor beast had been hit and started bucking. I let go of his bridle. He was probably fatally wounded.

In a flash I saw several more Tibetans ambushed behind rocks, forming a kind of redoubt. They were firing at us almost point-blank, and in a circle *of twenty feet radius had complete command of the narrow ledge where our caravan was assembled. They'd chosen their position well. They had us entirely covered and, to make their position still more secure, had waited for me to pass before starting the fight. The result was that Tchrachy and myself were cut off from the others both by their guns and by the frightened yaks who blocked the pass.*

*If I stayed three seconds longer on the track I should be riddled with bullets. There was nothing for it; I had to jump down into the valley at the risk of breaking my legs. So I hurled myself down on to some scraggy bushes which broke my fall, and at the same moment saw Tchrachy leap off his horse and seize hold of the sling of his rifle. The agonized expression on his face proved once and for all that there had been no treachery on the part of our men.*

*My hands were torn and bleeding. I rolled down a few feet and landed up against a boulder. Here I could take cover and return the enemy's fire. Lying on my stomach on the sloping ground I took my revolver out of its holster. I should have to shoot high and the peak of my pith helmet got in my way. For a moment I considered throwing it away, but then a confused thought occurred to me that it was a mistake to dispense with anything in a crisis like this, so I calmly fastened the strap under my chin and threw the cap on to the back of my neck.*

*I let off my first shots haphazardly. I was shooting from below, so I couldn't even see where my shots were going. I should have been extraordinarily lucky to have hit even one of those men, and I continued firing more from the principle than anything else, to show them that we meant to defend ourselves.*

*Now that I could see the situation as a whole, it was obvious that we were in a tight spot. Our attackers had the enormous advantage of position. The intensity of their fire proved that they were also superior in numbers. There were at least twenty of them, perhaps more, and I guessed them to be bristling with ammunition pouches like all bandits. We, for our part, were four armed men; we had two rifles and two revolvers between us and very little ammunition. It was useless to think of our ammunition cases; they were attached to our yaks' backs and therefore out of reach.*

*If only we had been all together! But I didn't even know where my* friends were. They must have taken cover somewhere so as to return the fire. And I could actually hear them shooting back; the reports from the European rifles were much sharper and the clean whistle of their bullets unmistakable.

They were shooting! They were alive! That was all that mattered for the moment. We were in a jam and our only hope was to unite and escape from this massacre.

Our attackers kept up their running fire. I could see their faces above me and the barrels of their guns resting on their hunting-forks. In the rarefied air of this site, higher than Mont Blanc, the noise of the reports was extraordinarily muffled. The bullets ricocheting round me sounded much louder than the actual discharge. Our enemies' powder couldn't be too good because the whizz of their bullets was weak and sizzling. I had the queer impression that it took them some time to reach their objective.

Even more remarkable than the sizzling bullets was the silence of the shooters. Since Liotard last spoke I hadn't heard a human voice. Our enemies hadn't made a sound, not even at the very first moment of the attack. No wild yelling to express their hatred and frenzy! They just went on mechanically shooting, loading and unloading their guns with the diligence of conscientious workmen. There was something pitiless about this silence. What could it mean? Usually Tibetans are more noisy in an affair of this kind. When they pounce upon a caravan they rely as much on their shouts as on their weapons to terrify their prey. Why were they so quiet to-day? Why were they not revelling in their war-cries? I was beginning to feel vaguely that this time there was more in it than mere plunder.

André Guibaut, Tibetan Venture, 1947

*André Guibaut, a native of Bordeaux, France, was a pilot, sailor and officer in the French merchant navy. Later, he studied at the Institute of Ethnology and went on an expedition to Tibet with his friend, Morris Liotard. It was on their second expedition, in 1940, that Liotard lost his life in a bandit attack. Their mission was primarily scientific; they planned to study the remote Ngolo-Setas tribe, map the source of the Tong (Tatu) and demarcate the basins of the Blue and Yellow rivers.*

# Shigatse

Shigatse, at an altitude of 3,900 metres (12,800 feet), is Tibet's second largest city, with a population of over 50,000. It is the administrative centre of a vast area, formerly called Tsang, that includes most of west-central Tibet. Historically, it often rivalled Lhasa, which controlled Ü, or east-central Tibet.

Shigatse stands near the confluence of the Yarlong Tsangpo and Nyangchu (Liancuo) rivers. The latter flows from southeast to northwest, watering a broad, beautiful valley 100 kilometres (60 miles) long, with Gyantse at one end and Shigatse at the other. It is one of Tibet's richest farming areas. Barley, rape seed, wheat, beans and many varieties of vegetables colour the valley with all shades of green in summer, and with bright yellow patches in June and July, when the rape flower is in bloom.

Shigatse was previously both a stronghold and a monastery city. Today, as with all sizeable Tibetan towns, an undistinguished, modern, Chinese section equals the old town in size. Shigatse forms a horseshoe around a rocky prominence that was formerly topped by an awesome fortress. At the western tip, beneath Mt Drolmari, lies Tashilhunpo Monastery, seat of the panchen lamas (see page 173) and one of Tibet's four greatest monasteries.

## Getting There

The **southern** route from Lhasa to Shigatse (300 kilometres or 188 miles) follows the old caravan trade route to India as far as Gyantse, then turns northwest along the Nyangchu River. It crosses two high passes. Twenty kilometres (12 miles) past the bridge over the Yarlong Tsangpo, the road becomes unpaved gravel. Summer rains can cause mudslides in the narrow, debris-littered upper gorge of the Nyangchu River. The bus from Lhasa to Shigatse leaves Lhasa at 8.00 to 8.30 am and takes ten hours; tickets go on sale two days beforehand. Early booking gets the most comfortable front seats. The journey takes at least six hours by four-wheel-drive vehicle.

The first pass, 82 kilometres (51 miles) from Lhasa, is the 4,794-metre (15,724-foot) Kamba La. This is the traditional boundary between the provinces of Ü and Tsang. The views are dramatic. To the north, down a long, barren valley, glistens the Yarlong Tsangpo River. To the south lies a finger of the oddly scorpion-shaped Yamdrok Yamtso, Tibet's third-largest lake. In bright sun it shines sapphire-blue, with bright green triangles of farmland on its shores under looming, treeless peaks. The second pass, 163 kilometres (101 miles) from Lhasa, is the Karo La, altitude

(preceding pages) *Yaks in a valley near Shigatse*

5,045 metres (16,551 feet). It offers no sudden views and can be noticed only by its stone cairn and clusters of prayer flags. Just beyond, on the right, a glacier approaches the road, but a half-hour scramble is needed to reach it. Other glaciers dot the mountaintops on both sides. Following the upper Nyangchu River through rocky hills, the road emerges in a narrow valley with mud-brick telephone poles marching along it like little fat men. At Gyantse, the landscape opens into a fertile plain that leads straight to Shigatse.

The **river route** is the most direct way from Lhasa to Shigatse. One initially wonders why it took until 1992 to open the paved road along this most obvious route westward. But the topography soon answers the question; great stretches of road had to be carved out of the Yarlong Tsangpo gorge's near-vertical walls. The trip to Shigatse takes about five hours in a jeep and avoids the high passes that mark the other two routes.

About an hour west of Nyemo it is possible to turn south away from the river and journey to Gyantse. This route has much of cultural interest; old agricultural settlements, traditional bridges, beehive-shaped granaries, peat mounds for fuel. It passes through **Rinpung**, centre of a region whose princes ruled Tibet for 130 years (1435–1565), where the remains of a striking fortress overlook the town and its monastery.

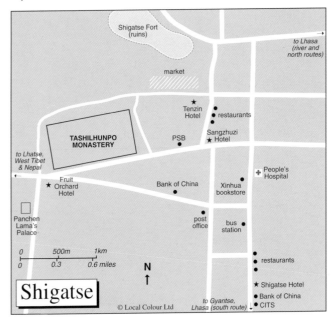

# THE PANCHEN LAMAS

The panchen lamas, abbots of Tashilhunpo Monastery, came into existence in the 17th century when the Fifth Dalai Lama gave this title to his beloved and learned tutor. *Panchen* means 'great scholar'. So-called hidden texts were then discovered that proved he was a reincarnation of Amitabha, the Buddha of infinite light, and traced the incarnations back two centuries to one of the first abbots of Tashilhunpo. He thus counted not as the first but as the Fourth Panchen Lama. In a similar fashion, the Great Fifth had already been established as an incarnation of Tibet's patron deity, Chenrezi, the bodhisattva of compassion. From the 17th century on, the panchen and dalai lamas initiated one another as divine leaders, and the older one served as tutor to the younger. When a panchen lama died, a search began at once for the infant boy who was believed to be his new incarnation, just like the dalai lamas (see page 84).

Some Tibetans consider the panchen lamas even holier than the dalai lamas. They were thought to be less tainted by worldly affairs because they had no secular authority. Foreigners named them tashi lamas (misappropriating the first syllables of Tashilhunpo) and created a myth that they were wise, all-knowing holy men. In fact, they mixed in politics, sometimes rivalled the dalai lamas and conducted independent foreign policies, which foreign powers tried to exploit. There have been ten panchen lamas.

The First, Second and Third panchen lamas were all learned scholars and successive abbots of Tashilhunpo who upheld the Yellow Hat Sect.

The Fourth (1569–1662) was the learned tutor of the Fifth Dalai Lama, who honoured him with divine status and the title of panchen.

The Fifth (1663–1737) lived through the mixed-up succession to the Sixth Dalai Lama. In 1728 the Chinese emperor, hoping to divide Tibet, offered him sovereignty over all of western Tibet, but he did not accept it.

The Sixth (1738–80) was distinguished by his writings and interest in the world. He befriended George Bogle (see page 197). The gold he naively sent as a gift to the governor of India whetted Britain's interest in Tibet. He also travelled to China, but in Peking he caught smallpox and died.

The Seventh (1781–1854) was protected by China from Nepalese raids.

The Eighth (1854–82) died before he got caught up in foreign affairs.

The Ninth (1883–1937) had severe conflicts with the Thirteenth Dalai

Lama. Both the Chinese and the British tried to woo him. Fearing revenge from the Dalai Lama for his support of China, he fled and died in exile.

The Tenth (b 1938) was born in China and not confirmed as a genuine incarnation until age 11. His close but stormy relations with Tibet's new Chinese administrators resulted in his virtual disappearance for many years after 1961. He held honorific positions (he was a vice-chairman of the NPC) and worked in Beijing. He returned to Tibet twice in the early 1980s briefly to visit Tashilhunpo; he stayed at length in Lhasa to attend *Monlam*, the Great Prayer Festival, in early 1986, and came again in 1987 to Lhasa and Tashilhunpo. He promoted cultural and development programmes in Tibet, and maintained offices in Beijing, Lhasa and Shigatse. He died in early 1989 of a heart attack whilst visiting Shigatse.

The Eleventh incarnation was found in 1995, although there is disagreement about the true identity of the successor.

The Yum La is the one significant pass between Rinpung and Gyantse. After ascending a dramatic, craggy valley the view from the top reveals central Tibet's vast landscape.

An alternative, less-travelled **northern route** loops west from Lhasa along the edge of the great northern plateau. The 340-kilometre (210-mile) route takes about seven hours. An unpaved road branches west from Yangbajing, 87 kilometres (54 miles) from Lhasa, and proceeds across three high passes. First, the Shuge La, 5,350 metres (17,552 feet), gives a view of snowcapped mountains and grazing yak herds. The next two, the Dunggu La, 4,960 metres (16,273 feet), and the Gangdisi La, 4,100 metres (13,451 feet), would be easy to miss except for piles of stones and prayer flags as the road begins its descent through wild valleys, known mainly to nomads, toward the Yarlong Tsangpo River.

A tug-drawn barge ferries vehicles across the river at Daktsukhar, 80 kilometres (50 miles) from Shigatse. There are two Bön monasteries near here. **Menri** is to the north and **Yungdrungling** is three kilometres (two miles) to the east.

The road from Daktsukhar follows the south bank upstream to Shigatse.

# Historical Background

Shigatse, the capital of Tsang, took part for centuries in struggles to control Tibet with rivalries between the regions of Ü (Lhasa) and Tsang, and between the reformed Yellow Hat and old Red Hat sects. Tibet had stagnated for 200 years after its last king, Lang Darma (see page 66) tried to stamp out Buddhism. Then, in 1042, Atisha arrived from India, and his Tibetan disciples set off a surge of intellectual and religious activity. Old monasteries were revived, and hundreds of new ones started in all the settled areas. Battles for power were soon raging, because Tibet still had no central government to control them.

In Tsang, Buddhist monks and priests of the old Bön religion attacked each other with words and sorcery. The three big noble families of the region joined the fray. These lords, with huge wealth in land holdings, claimed divine ancestry like the former kings. They now founded important monasteries such as Sakya (see page 205) and Shalu (see page 182). They made sure that members of their families became monks and abbots, then began jockeying for wider control by making foreign alliances, notably with the Mongols. In 1206, Genghis Khan's hordes threatened central Tibet. Tibet's nobles offered submission without a fight, and certain monasteries profited from having a foreign patron, especially Sakya, in the centre of Tsang, which received both gifts and an invitation to send Buddhist missionaries to Mongolia. Kublai Khan, future emperor of China, chose Sakya's abbot to be his tutor in 1254 and as a reward gave Sakya sovereignty over all Tibet. There was much friction and strife under Sakya's rule. Within a century, Mongol power waned, Sakya declined, and infighting among sects and monasteries once more became the rule in Tibet.

In the 15th century, Tsong Khapa reformed Tibetan Buddhism. His new Yellow Hat Sect dominated Ü through the three great monasteries of Lhasa (Ganden, Drepung and Sera). But in spite of the establishment of a fourth important Yellow Hat monastery at Shigatse (Tashilhunpo), Tsang remained firmly in the hands of the Red Hats. In addition, the lords of Tsang became implacable enemies of the Yellow Hats, and new wars erupted.

The Fifth Dalai Lama ended all this in the 17th century by emulating Sakya 400 years earlier: he obtained a mighty Mongol patron. With a Mongol army he finally defeated Tsang and ended Red Hat hopes of power. From then on the dalai lama controlled all of Tibet and the panchen lama acted as his spiritual right hand in Tsang.

Today, visitors to Shigatse can still see the different layers of history, from Yellow Hat Tashilhunpo Monastery back to Red Hat Shalu Monastery. Also, counter-clockwise swastikas (see page 138) can sometimes be observed on floors or walls, evidence that the ancient Bön religion lives on to the present time.

(following pages) *Tashilhunpo Monastery, Shigatse*

# Sights

## TASHILHUNPO MONASTERY

Tashilhunpo, meaning Heap of Glory, was the seat of the panchen lamas. It lies at the foot of Drolmari, or Tara's Mountain, on the west side of Shigatse and is today one of Tibet's most active monasteries.

It was founded in 1447 by Tsong Khapa's youngest disciple, who was his nephew and the main organizer of the Yellow Hat sect. The early abbots, who posthumously were named the First, Second and Third panchen lamas, were learned scholars who often had to flee to the province of Ü from their fierce Red Hat opponents in Tsang.

The enlargement of Tashilhunpo took place mostly under the Fourth, Fifth and Sixth panchen lamas, after the Yellow Hat Sect had been firmly established as Tibet's official religion. But it still had troubles. When the broadminded Sixth Panchen Lama died of smallpox in Peking, his brother, the treasurer of Tashilhunpo, stole his entire huge fortune. He refused to distribute it to the monastery or share it with his other brothers, and he thereafter became the governor of Tsang. Another brother, who lived in Nepal, led an army of Gurkha warriors to Shigatse in 1791, where they sacked and looted Tashilhunpo. The Chinese drove out the Nepalese and at the same time strengthened their influence over Tibet.

Tashilhunpo had over 4,000 monks and was organized like Lhasa's great monasteries. It had four tantric colleges, each with its own abbot. After the death of a panchen lama, these four abbots led the search for his infant reincarnation, and one of them always acted as the prime minister of Tsang, under the control of the dalai lama in Lhasa.

Tashilhunpo was disbanded as a monastery by the Chinese army in 1960, while the Tenth Panchen Lama was absent. Less physical damage was inflicted than on many other sites, and a handful of caretaker monks was allowed to remain. Today there are nearly 800 monks.

### ■ LAYOUT

The most remarkable object on the monastery grounds is an enormous Thangka Wall nine storeys high, which stands like a huge drive-in movie screen, clearly visible from the city. This structure is used most of the year for storing three gigantic banners bearing images of the Buddha, which are displayed on the wall for only three days a year during summer festivities.

The monastery itself, facing south, is one of the most spectacular in Tibet, its salmon-rose main buildings set off by the ecclesiastical red-brown of the parapets and clear black-and-white trim. The buildings form a horizontal line: the gigantic Maitreya Chapel on the west, the Panchen Lama's Palace (containing the stupa-tomb of the Fourth) in the middle, and on the east a cluster of buildings around a large courtyard known as the Kelsang Temple.

A path runs north from the main gate between white stone buildings and courtyards that house smaller chanting halls, the Debating Garden, dormitories and workshops. Pilgrims coming to Tashilhunpo generally bring bags of *tsampa* as offerings, rather than yak butter as in Lhasa.

The **Maitreya Chapel** (Jamba Chyenmu), on the west side, is the tallest building of the monastery. It was erected in 1914 by the Ninth Panchen Lama to house a gigantic statue of the Maitreya Buddha, 26.2 metres (86 feet) high. The statue sits on a splendid lotus throne in the European posture with its hands in the symbolic teaching pose. A single finger is 1.2 metres (almost four feet) long. The statue contains 279 kilograms (614 pounds) of gold and 150,000 kilograms (330,000 pounds) of copper and brass moulded on a wooden frame by Tibetan and Nepalese craftsmen. A clockwise walk around the back shows how this was done with metal sheets. Murals on either side of the door show a more active, antic style than any to be seen in Lhasa.

A lane leads east to the **Panchen Lama's Palace** (Gudong), entered by a door in its east side. Within, a narrow courtyard gives access to a temple containing the Fourth Panchen Lama's tomb. The temple vestibule has very large inscriptions at either end praising the Fourth Panchen Lama. Inside, the silver and gold stupa-tomb rivals any in the Potala for the splendour of its workmanship and jewels. Measuring 11 metres (36 feet) in height, it contains 85 kilograms (187 pounds) of gold and countless semi-precious stones. On the left is a statue in a wooden enclosure representing Amitabha, the Buddha of infinite light, whom the panchen lamas are thought to embody. An upper level has long chapels with embroidered silk thangkas that relate the lives and events surrounding all the panchen lamas. Most were made in Hangzhou, in the east of China, during the 1920s. Unfortunately, the

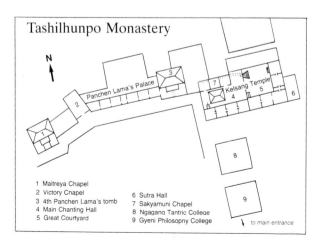

Tashilhunpo Monastery

N

Panchen Lama's Palace

Kelsang Temple

1 Maitreya Chapel
2 Victory Chapel
3 4th Panchen Lama's tomb
4 Main Chanting Hall
5 Great Courtyard
6 Sutra Hall
7 Sakyamuni Chapel
8 Ngagang Tantric College
9 Gyeni Philosopny College

to main entrance

*Gold roofs and eaves with the emblem of the Kalachakra in relief, Tashilhunpo Monastery*

living quarters of the panchen lama are no longer open to the public. The rooms are more modest and human than any in the Potala.

To the left of the Fourth Panchen Lama's stupa-tomb is a large room whose extensive murals depict the Jataka tales, stories of the Buddha's previous lives. This room has taken on great importance because it now houses the relics of the 10th Panchen Lama, who died near here on 14 January 1989. The lama's body has been preserved by a salting process, and he gazes out of a glass box, face and hands gilded, to the astonishment and adoration of pilgrims.

Outside is a huge six-storey structure that will eventually house the 10th Panchen Lama. Its construction, still underway, has taken years and the building is certain to be a fantastically opulent final resting place for the lama.

The flagstoned **Great Courtyard** of the Kelsang Temple to the east has walls covered by 1,000 repeated Sakyamunis, their hands in five symbolic poses (*mudras*). On the west side, the **Main Chanting Hall** contains the panchen lamas' throne and two connected chapels. The left-hand one is devoted to an elaborately ensconced Sakyamuni with eight bodhisattvas robed in brocade. The right-hand one is dedicated to Tara (see page 65), the goddess who sanctifies the mountain above, and whose image can be found throughout the monastery. A White Tara occupies the centre of the altar, with a Green Tara on either side.

The gallery surrounding the courtyard leads to chapels on the east housing hundreds of tiny Buddha statues. A **Sutra Hall** behind them is the repository of some 10,000 hand-carved wooden blocks used for printing the Buddhist scriptures. Tourists can buy the coloured prayer flags and Tibetan lunar calendars printed here.

The **roof** has several chapels. On the north side, above the chapels of the Chant-ing Hall, is the funerary stupa of the First Dalai Lama (Tsong Khapa's nephew, who founded Tashilhunpo), the only one not entombed in Lhasa. On the east side is a small chamber of horrors chapel. Painted demons, considered now to be defenders of Buddhism, betray their origins as the terrifying gods of the old animist Bön faith, who only later were absorbed by Buddhism. On the south side is a charming Tara chapel.

Less frequently visited is the small chanting hall of **Ngagang Tantric College** on the west side of the main north-south path, upstairs from a small courtyard. Here a morning chanting ceremony with musical instruments sometimes takes place. Pil-grims may circumambulate the hall, but tourists, especially photographers, should be sensitive to the religious atmosphere. Directly below the Panchen Lama's Palace, east of the main path, is the **Gyeni Philosophy College** and the **Debating Garden** with many fine trees. The roof of the chanting hall has a bizarre chapel on the north side, where two very tall guardians are formed from its structural columns by the use of masks and ancient armour. Outside are some extraordinary animal murals that seem to have emerged from folklore and animism. Open 9 am–5.30 pm, closed for lunch 12.30–3.30 pm.

## Pilgrim Walk

An interesting three-kilometre (two-mile) walk leads back to the city by way of the giant Thangka Wall, the ruins of Shigatse's citadel or *dzong* and an open-air Tibetan market. It is important to do the walk returning from Tashilhunpo (not starting from Shigatse) to maintain a clockwise direction and avoid offending pilgrims on the path.

A sandy road parallel to the west wall of Tashilhunpo quickly becomes a well-worn path leading up behind the mona-stery, past prayer wheels and shrines, to the foot of the Thangka Wall, which cannot, however, be entered. Many paths crisscross Tara's Mountain above, up to the sacred, flag-festooned peak. The path divides at the Thangka Wall, one branch descending beside the east wall to make a circle around the monastery, the other continuing level along the flank of the mountain towards Shigatse. After passing an array of carved and painted rocks it emerges below the rocky prominence that dominates the city. Here a hiker can either

*Exterior view of the Gudong Palace, Tashilhunpo Monastery*

climb up to the ruins or take a right-hand route down to the market.

The dzong, totally destroyed in 1961, was once a small Potala covering the whole hilltop, with up-sweeping white walls that seemed to grow from the crags. It had a central Red Palace and turret-like fortifications at the outer ends. The formidable structure was seen as both a homage and a challenge to the power of Lhasa embodied in the real Potala. Only the foundations remain, but the site offers a magnificent view over Shigatse and its surrounding valleys.

The market below, just south of the dzong, consists of an organized street with neat, covered stalls, where Tibetan artifacts, jewellery, cloth, leather, copperware, and other items are for sale. Visitors may find shopping here easier than on the Barkhor in Lhasa. Prices are all open to bargaining.

## SHALU MONASTERY

This small monastery lies 22 kilometres (14 miles) south of Shigatse. For centuries it was renowned as a centre of scholarly learning and psychic training, and its mural paintings were considered the most ancient and beautiful in Tibet. Shalu still had 100 monks in this century, and its reputation lasted up to its destruction in the 1960s. A small part of it, housing a few superior murals, is still standing. A dozen or so monks and novices are in residence.

Shalu was founded in 1040 near a flourishing, long-vanished market town. It was the first of the major monasteries built by noble families of Tsang during Tibet's great revival of Buddhism. Shalu's monks kept in close touch with Sakya Monastery, which was founded soon afterwards and was bigger and politically more powerful.

In 1329 an earthquake demolished Shalu. The Mongol emperor of China ordered local lords to rebuild it in 1333. The new style was Mongolian, featuring massive, in-ward-sloping walls around a main courtyard, strong woodwork and glazed roof tiles from Qinghai that have a Chinese flavour.

The man in charge of Shalu at the time of the earthquake was Buton (1290–1364), its enormously energetic 11th abbot. He is remembered not only as a capable administrator, but also as a prodigious scholar and Tibet's most celebrated historian. He catalogued all the Buddhist scriptures—4,569 religious and philosophical works—and put them into a logical, usable order. He wrote countless commentaries of his own and produced new translations of many religious texts. In addition, he wrote his famous *History of Buddhism in India and Tibet,* to which scholars still refer. Buton's activity naturally attracted other intellectuals to Shalu. Although the monastery was only intended for 500 monks, up to 3,000 would assemble there for lectures.

After Buton's time, Shalu became an important centre of esoteric studies and psychic training. The avowed purpose of lamas who cultivated paranormal abilities was not to become magicians or miracle-workers but to attain philosophical enlightenment—a realization, in the Buddhist tradition, that all earthly phenomena are mere creations of the mind. Nonetheless, after many years of training in intense concentration (often sealed up in caves in total darkness), the adepts were said to have performed extraordinary feats. The commonest, called *tumo*, was a monk's ability deliberately to raise his body temperature to a level where he could live at frigid temperatures wearing only the lightest of clothing. Long-distance runners, called *lung-gompas*, learned to cross Tibet's vast spaces with superhuman leaps while in a trance state. These served as messengers. Some masters were able to transmigrate their human consciousness into the bodies of birds, animals or even dead people. Others could become invisible at will by learning how to leave no impression upon the memories of the people they encountered. Most Tibetans firmly believe that such feats actually took place almost routinely. These practices are described at length by Alexandra David-Neel in *With Mystics and Magicians in Tibet* and by Lama Anagarika Govinda in *The Way of the White Clouds*. The monastery stands in a small valley facing east. It is mostly destroyed; only the outer wall, the main building (its roof damaged) and a few adjacent tumble-down structures remain.

The few surviving murals on the wall outside the chapel follow an iconographic scheme developed by Buton himself. To the right of the doorway is a primer of monastic discipline. At the top, Buton and two disciples are enveloped in clouds. Below, precise rules are laid out for the monks on what to wear, where to place their robes, when to bathe—in short, how to behave under all circumstances. Eight monks demonstrate how they must sleep and meditate perched in trees when travelling away from the monastery. The mural on the left is an allegory in which an elephant, representing a human soul, evolves through many steps and earthly trials to Nirvana.

Inside are several intricate mandalas (see page 114). Three exquisite examples are on the south wall behind the altar, each three metres (ten feet) in diameter and still in a good state of preservation. All the others, as well as the painted, coffered ceiling, have suffered various degrees of damage from forced neglect and rain entering through the roof. Mandalas were a speciality of Shalu. Formerly, the designs were also created out of coloured sand, but these were never kept for longer than a year.

The only other chapel open to visitors is on the west side of the roof. Remnants of former mandala murals are concealed by over 100 thangkas, most of which were embroidered in Hangzhou early in this century. A fine thangka hanging over a small altar that stands alone was painted several decades ago by Shalu's present head monk. The large upper-storey porch over the wrecked chanting hall was the apartment of Buton and subsequent abbots, but this cannot be visited.

## NARTHANG MONASTERY

These mud-brick ruins lie 15 kilometres (nine miles) west of Shigatse beside the main road. Founded in 1153 by one of Atisha's disciples, Narthang was the fourth great monastery of Tsang, along with Shalu, Sakya and Tashilhunpo. Like Sakya, it was a big, square, walled compound in the Mongolian style. Parts of the high fortress walls still stand. Narthang was first famous for its scriptural teaching and monastic discipline. After the 14th century it gained great eminence as the oldest of Tibet's three great printing centres (the others being the Potala and Derge, in eastern Tibet). The Fifth Panchen Lama took Narthang under the control of Tashilhunpo, and it continued printing the Buddhist scriptures, the *Kanjur* and *Tenjur,* up until 1959. A few of the ancient woodblocks and early editions might have survived in the collection at Tashilhunpo.

Narthang's five main buildings and large chanting hall were razed to the ground in 1966. They had contained priceless 14th-century murals, probably painted by the artists of Shalu. Today, only the foundations can be discerned, though small chapels have sprung up and a village has grown around the old site. It is worthwhile stopping here for a short visit despite the ruination.

## SUMMER PALACE

The Panchen Lama's Summer Palace, built in 1950, lies one kilometre (half a mile) south of Tashilhunpo Monastery at the end of a straight road. It is not open to the public. A grand portal graces the high enclosing wall on the east side. Around the back of the property the wall gives way to a fence, from where two inner walled compounds can be seen. The large yellow mansion is the residence. The white compound houses the kitchens, servants' quarters, etc. The grounds have some fine trees but are otherwise totally neglected. It is in no way comparable to the Norbulingka summer palace in Lhasa.

## SHIGATSE GOLD, SILVER AND COPPER CRAFTS FACTORY

This primitive silver-working factory on the southern edge of Shigatse was set up in 1965. Ornamental cups, bowls, ewers and votive butter lamps are hand-made by master craftsmen and workers, many of whom are young apprentices. They work primarily with hammers and small charcoal fires with bellows of hide. Gold and copperware vessels are also produced here, but no jewellery.

## CORACLE RIDE

The traditional Tibetan boat for ferrying or fishing is an oval-shaped coracle made of willow branches and yak hide. It is virtually unsinkable and can be carried upstream on the back of one strong man. A coracle ride on the Yarlong Tsangpo River north of Shigatse, through a beautiful stretch known as the Dongkar Valley, is an experience full of freshness and excitement. Thirty-three kilometres (20 miles) from Shigatse, near the river, lies Dongkar Monastery, where barley is milled for the vast appetite of Tashilhunpo's 800 monks.

# BRITAIN INVADES TIBET

Unlikely as it seems, Gyantse briefly became a household name in England in 1904, when through a series of bungles Britain invaded Tibet. In 1902, sudden unfounded rumours claimed that China had offered mineral rights and other concessions in Tibet to the tsar of Russia. The British Empire reeled, and India's alarmed viceroy sent a young diplomat named Francis Younghusband to the Tibetan border to find out the truth. The Tibetans, who had long since sealed themselves off from the world, were so suspicious of foreigners that they refused to talk to the British diplomatic mission.

Seeing this as a snub, London authorized Younghusband to march in with British troops as far as Gyantse, show the flag and force the lamas into an English-style agreement opening up trade between Tibet and India. Younghusband was given the instant rank of colonel, four artillery pieces and 1,000 soldiers under a bone-headed brigadier-general. This small army entered Tibet's Chumbi Valley in the December snow of 1903, accompanied by 1,450 coolies, 7,000 mules, 3,451 yaks, six camels and several foreign correspondents from London newspapers. The troops were served turkey and plum pudding for Christmas, though the frozen champagne was undrinkable. Then the cold, hunger, altitude and illness brought misery and deaths.

Tibetan troops, armed only with muzzle-loaded muskets and magic charms against foreign bullets, gathered south of Gyantse. Younghusband, anxious to avoid bloodshed, made a bold, informal visit by night, alone, to the amiable Tibetan general to explain his mission. But angry lamas, who made policy, demanded immediate British withdrawal. The British proceeded. When the two armies met, shooting began by mistake. In a four minute massacre, 700 Tibetans were left dead or dying, and the living walked slowly from the battlefield in sorrow and disbelief. Their bafflement only increased when a British army field hospital tried to save the wounded and gave treatment to any Tibetan who asked for it.

The British captured the fortress at Gyantse, and the Tibetans were decimated in one-sided battles. London sent an ultimatum to Lhasa. There was no reply. In August 1904, Younghusband marched into Lhasa, only to find that the Thirteenth Dalai Lama had fled to Mongolia. He forced a treaty on the regent, giving Britain exclusive privileges, and withdrew. Britain established a flourishing trade mission at Gyantse, and the next time Tibet was invaded (by China in 1910) the Dalai Lama fled to India as a guest of the English.

Francis Younghusband, on his last night in Lhasa, had a deep religious experience that changed his life. He resigned and from then on devoted himself with great ability to humanitarian works.

(following pages) *Dancers and actors perform musical dramas known as Ache Lhamo*

# An Unfortunate Incident

*On March 31, after we had given fair warning to the Tibetans, the advance was made. Light snow lay on the ground. The cold was even now intense. News that the Tibetans were still in position has reached us, and the crucial moment which was to decide upon peace or war was now approaching.*

*We moved along as rapidly as possible at those high altitudes and encumbered with heavy clothing. A short way out we were met by a messenger from the Tibetan General, urging us to go back to India. I told the messenger to gallop back at once and tell the Lhasa General that we were on our way to Gyantse, and we were going as far as Guru, ten miles distant that day. I said that we did not want to fight, and would not unless we were opposed, but that road must be left clear for us, and the Tibetans must withdraw from their positions across it. Farther on, as we advanced across an almost level gravely plain, we came in sight of the Tibetan position in a series of sangars on a ridge. At 1,000 yards' distance we halted, and awaited the arrival of the Tibetans for our last palaver. They rode up briskly with a little cavalcade and we all dismounted, set out rugs and coats on the ground, and sat down for the final discussion. I reiterated the same the same old statement—that we had no wish or intention of fighting if we were not opposed, but that we must advance to Gyantse. If they did not obstruct our progress or did not attack us, we would not attack them. But advance we must, for we had found it impossible to negotiate anywhere else. They replied with the request—or, indeed, almost order— that we must go back to Yatung, and they would negotiate there. They said these were their instructions from Lhasa. They also did not wish to fight, but they had orders to send us back to Yatung.*

*There was no possible reasoning with such people. They had such overweening confidence in their Lama's powers. How could anyone dare resist the orders of the Great Lama? Surely lightening would descend from heaven or the earth open up and destroy anyone who had such temerity! I pointed out our troops, now ready deployed for action. I said that we had* tried for fourteen years inside our frontier to settle matters. I urged that for eight months now I had patiently tried to negotiate, but no one with authority came to see me, my letters were returned, and even messages were refused. I had therefore received the commands of the Emperor to advance to Gyantse, in the hope that perhaps there responsible negotiators would meet us. Anyhow, the time for further parlaying here was gone. The moment for advance had arrived. I would give them a quarter of an hour after their return to their lines within which to make up their minds. After that interval General Macdonald would advance, and if the Tibetans had not already left their positions blocking our line of advance, he would expel them by force.

... The General and their following returned to their camp. The quarter of an hour elapsed. And now the great moment arrived. But I wished still to give them just one last chance, in the hope that at the eleventh hour, and at the fifty-ninth minute of the eleventh hour, they might change their minds. I therefore asked General Macdonald to order his men not to fire upon the Tibetans until the Tibetans first fired on them. In making this request I well knew the responsibility I was incurring. We were but a handful of men—about 100 Englishmen and 1,200 Indians—in the face of superior number of Tibetans, in the heart of the country, 15,000 feet above the sea, and separated from India by two high passes; and the advantage our troops possessed from arms of precision I took from them.

It was the last and final effort to carry out our object without the shedding of blood. The troops responded with admirable discipline to the call. They steadily advance across the plain and up the hillside to the Tibetan lines, expecting at any moment that from behind the sangars a destructive volley might be opened upon them before they could fire a shot. Some of them aftewards, and very naturally, told me that they hoped they would never again be put in so awkward a position. But I trust their discipline will at any rate show to those in England who so decried this day's action, and spoke about our 'massacring unarmed Tibetans'—that men on the remotest confines of the Empire can and do exercise moderation and restraint in the discharge of their duty, and do not always act with that wantoness and reckless cruelty with which they are so often credited at home.

> . . . The Tibetans on their side showed great indecision. They also had apparently received orders not not to fire first; and the whole affair seemed likely to end in comedy rather than in the tragedy which actually followed. The Tibetans first ran into their sangars and then ran out again. Gradually our troops crept up and round the flanks. They arrived eventually face to face with the Tibetans, as will be seen in the accompanying photograph by Lieutenant Bailey, and things were almost at an impasse till the Tibetans slowly yielded to the admonitions of our troops, and allowed themselves to be shouldered out of their position and be 'moved on', as London policemen would disperse a crowd from Trafalgar Square.
>
> At this point the two Lhasa Majors who had met me previously in the day rode out again, and told me that the Tibetans had been ordered not to fire, and begged me to stop the troops from advancing. I replied that we must continue the advance, and could not allow any troops to remain on the road. There was a post actually on the road, with a wall newly and deliberately built across it, and it was obvious that if we were ever to get to Gyantse the Tibetans behind that wall must be removed. Yet I thought the affair was practically over. The Tibetans were streaming away from their position along the ridge, and had even begun to leave their post on the road. Then a change came. The Lhasa General, or possibly the monks, recalled the men to their post, and an officer reported to General Macdonald that, though surrounded by our troops, they refused to retreat: they were not fighting, but they would not leave the wall they had built across the road.
>
> General Macdonald and I had a consultation together, and agreed that in these circumstances the only thing to do was to disarm them and let them go. We rode together to the spot, and found the Tibetans huddled together like a flock of sheep behind the wall. Our infantry were in position on the hillside only 200 yards above them on the one side; on the other our Maxims and guns were trained upon them at not 200 yards' distance. Our mounted infantry were in readiness in the plain only a quarter of a mile away. Our sepoys were actually standing up to the wall, with their rifles pointing over at the Tibetans within a few feet of them. And the Lhasa General himself with his staff was on our side of the wall, in among our sepoys.

He had, of course, completely lost his head. Though in command of some thousands of armed men, and though I had given him ample warning of our intention to advance, he was totally unprepared for action when our advance was made. He had brought his men back into an absurd position; his action when he had got them back was simply childish. I sent Captain O'Connor to announce to him that General Macdonald and I had decided that his men must be disarmed, but he remained sullen and did nothing; and when, after a pause, the disarmament was actually commenced, he threw himself upon a sepoy, drew a revolver, and shot the sepoy in the jaw.

Not, as I think, with any deliberate intention, but from sheer inanity, the signal had now been given. Other Tibetan shots immediately followed. Simultaneously volleys from our own troops rang out; the guns and Maxims commenced to fire. Tibetan swordsmen made a rush upon any within reach, and the plucky and enterprising Edmund Chandler, the very able correspondent of the Daily Mail, received more than a dozen wounds, while Major Wallace Dunlop, one of the best officers in the force, was severely handled. For just one single instant the Tibetans, by a concerted and concentrated rush, might have broken our thin line, and have carried the Mission and the military staff. But that instant passed in a flash. Before a few seconds were over, rifles and gun were dealing the deadliest destruction on them in their huddled masses. The Lhasa General himself was killed at the start, and in a few minutes the whole affair was over. The plain was strewn with dead Tibetans, and our troops instinctively and without direct orders ceased firing—though, in fact, they had only fired thirteen rounds per man.

*Francis Younghusband*, India and Tibet, *1910*

*Sir Francis Younghusband was born in India and joined the British army at the age of 19. He was an explorer as well as a soldier and crossed Asia from Beijing to Yarkand to India. He is credited with the discovery of the Aghil Mountains. He was knighted for leading the British expendition to Lhasa, which resulted in the Anglo-Tibetan Treaty of 1904. This book is an attempt to justify the action of the British. Later he became a mystic and founded the World Conference of Faiths.*

# Gyantse

Gyantse, altitude 3,950 metres (12,960 feet), is about 210 kilometres (130 miles) from Lhasa and 95 kilometres (60 miles) from Shigatse. It was once Tibet's third most important city, lying at the head of the Nyangchu Valley, astride the main routes from India and Nepal to Lhasa. In former times it was a fort, the centre of Tibet's wool trade and a gateway to the outside world. In recent years, other places in Tibet have grown more quickly, and in comparison it is now a fairly small town.

A high, rocky ridge topped by a ruined fortress runs through the middle of Gyantse, dividing it into two parts. On the west are a large monastery complex and part of the original city with a main market street. A newly built avenue leads around the outer edge right to the monastery. On the east is another section of the old town, including a rug factory and the principal approach to the citadel above. A few Chinese work units form a suburban ring around the Tibetan town.

Gyantse is a lovely place, with its friendly and relaxed small-town air. Visits to the monastery, exploring the town and the surrounding fields and villages, climbing the fort, and just watching and meeting the people can fill several days. Crossing the lowest part of the small rocky ridge to the right of the monastery brings you into a concealed Tibetan residential area, with streets of beautiful old houses.

## Getting There

Today, with the completion of the river route westward from Lhasa, most visitors to Gyantse arrive from Shigatse, a mere two hours away by car. This section passes through the beautiful agricultural valley of the Nyangchu River. The most interesting way to reach Gyantse is by the river route (see page 171) from Lhasa, then turning southwest to Rinpung, an old aristrocratic centre, and then over the Yum La Pass, which affords one of Central Tibet's great dramatic views. There is a major crossroads at the southeast edge of Gyantse. Here the southern route from Lhasa (see page 170) runs straight ahead into town, and the right-hand turn leads into the suburbs. The left-hand road southwards leads either to Shigatse and Nepal or to Yadong and India.

## Historical Background

For centuries, yak caravans loaded with bags of sheep and yak wool made their way from the northern plateau to Gyantse. Throughout Tibet's history, wool has been its

*Crown and finials atop the Gyantse Kumbum stupa*

chief export. Gyantse's traditional caravan trade routes to Nepal and China were abruptly superseded by a new one to India early in this century, when Britain forced a trade agreement on Tibet (see page 185). After 1959, Tibet's trade was rerouted through Lhasa, and Gyantse lost importance.

Gyantse was a prominent trading centre by the 15th century. Its lords married with other noble clans of Tsang and founded Palkhor Chöde Monastery in a natural bowl of Gyantse's high, rocky spine. Its cosmopolitan character was reflected in a Nepalese-style stupa, the Kumbum, erected in 1427, and in the Chinese-style fortified wall protecting the whole monastic complex. Gyantse also lay in the way of invasions from the south. Its citadel, *dzong,* and mini Great Wall withstood attacks by Nepalese Gurkhas, Sikhs and Ladakhis. Only when modern weapons overpowered Tibet's medieval army did Gyantse fall to a foreign power—the British in 1904.

# Sights

## THE KUMBUM

This spectacular stupa temple, whose name means 'Place of a Thousand Images', was the centrepiece of Palkhor Chöde Monastery and the pride of Gyantse. A new road on the west edge of Gyantse leads straight to it.

The great pagoda has a massive base consisting of four tiers of interlocking, multi-faceted chapels. Above, a tall cylindrical section corresponds to the more common dome of most stupas and contains four large chapels. Over this rises a shaft with all-seeing eyes on its four sides in typical Nepalese style, plus a gilded tower with 13 rings, a parasol of filigreed metal and, at the top, a series of gold finials.

The Kumbum is the finest example of 15th-century Newari art extant in the world. The Newar people of Nepal's Kathmandu Valley, especially their fresco painters, were honoured and much sought after as artists in Tibet.

On the lowest floor, four lofty chapels with restorations of indifferent quality mark the cardinal points. Sixteen smaller chapels, squeezed between them at sharp angles, provide many examples of the superior Newari art. Each of these chapels contains one dominant sculptured figure and elaborate, thematic murals. Those dedicated to sublime deities like Tara are beautiful. Others are awesome. A few display cruelty and terror. Pilgrims progress through them all, ascending clockwise through the different levels of the stupa to the top in a symbolic journey upwards to Nirvana.

## PALKHOR CHÖDE MONASTERY

The monastery is behind Gyantse's mountain ridge on the west. Only four buildings remain: the Kumbum; the three-storey Main Chanting Hall; a dormitory for monks;

*The white stepped storeys of the Gyantse Kumbum*

and the Thangka Wall upon which giant Buddha banners were displayed once a year.

Palkhor was founded in 1365 and housed about 1,000 monks, prospering from its fertile lands and good location for trade. It suffered much damage in recent times. Current restoration is poor, but some original art remains in the Chanting Hall and some fine bodhisattva statuary exists in the North and West chapels. At the lower roof level, the walls of one chapel are lined with lacquered statues of seated saints showing a marked Indian influence. On the top roof level, the North Chapel has a superb collection of 15 mandala murals, all three metres (ten feet) in diameter.

West of the front porch, on the ground floor, is the Protector Chapel, a weird chamber of horrors whose main deities are almost totally hidden by countless scarves of offering. The principal protector is Guru Gonpo of the Sakya school.

A pack of Gyantse's dogs often lurks around the monastery gate and courtyard. They are especially active around dawn and a while after, when the morning light makes this area especially beautiful. Approach cautiously if alone, carrying a stick or stones, or wait to accompany a group of pilgrims into the monastery courtyard.

## GYANTSE COUNTY RUG FACTORY
This Tibetan rug factory on the east side of Gyantse continues a long tradition of Tsang rug making. Carding, spinning and dyeing of wool are done on the premises. Modern technology extends to treadle spinning wheels and electric finishing scissors.

## THE DZONG
Gyantse's great fortress was shelled, stormed, and partly destroyed by the British in 1904 (see page 185). Subsequent damage in the 1960s left it in ruins. A path leads from opposite the Gyantse Hotel, through a village, to the south foot of the rocky crag. To get the key, knock on the yard door of the cottage immediately to the right of where the path starts to ascend towards the main portal. Protected by cliffs and ramparts, the fortress contains a small monastery halfway up on the west side, various ruined garrison quarters, and at the top a cluster of elegantly placed apartments and a chorten. The view over the town at your feet and a panorama of countryside, with crows and buzzards soaring overhead, well rewards the scramble to the top.

## YADONG
Five kilometres (three miles) south of Gyantse, a road branching to the left leads for 213 kilometres (132 miles) to Yadong, near the Indian border. This beautifully situated Himalayan town has a mild climate and marvellous mountain views and forests. It boasts a fine, wooden, Sikkimese-style monastery, 11 kilometres (seven miles) south on the border. Yadong is the gateway to Sikkim, Bhutan and India. Informal discussions are underway to open the border for trade and, eventually, tourism.

# Explorers, Characters and Cranks

Tibet exerted a magnetic pull upon Western travellers for over 100 years largely because it was forbidden. Intrepid, foolhardy, serious and determined, they tried to reach Lhasa by every conceivable means—and most failed. They were spies, missionaries, scholars, geographers, mystics, soldiers, cranks, and their true stories put fiction to shame.

Tibet was not always forbidden to foreigners. The first Europeans to arrive were Portuguese missionaries in 1624. They were amiably received by the Tibetans and allowed to build a church. The next century brought more Jesuits and Capuchins from Europe, who met opposition from Tibet's lamas and were finally expelled in 1745. However, the hard feelings were not directed against foreigners as such. In 1774, George Bogle, an Englishman, came to Shigatse to investigate trade for the British East India Company. He not only befriended the Panchen Lama but also ended up marrying a Tibetan and introducing the first potatoes into Tibet.

Tension mounted in the 19th century. The British Empire was encroaching north from India into the Himalayas and Afghanistan. The Russian Empire of the tsars was expanding south into Central Asia. Each power suspected that the other had designs on Tibet, about which almost nothing was known. China, which claimed Tibet as a protectorate, fanned Tibet's fears that foreigners threatened its gold-fields and religion. Tibet's answer was to clamp shut its borders, except to China. Mutilation, torture and death awaited any Tibetan who even unwittingly gave assistance to a foreigner.

In 1865, the British started secretly mapping Tibet. Indian surveyor-spies disguised as pilgrims or traders counted their strides on rosaries clear across Tibet and took readings at night. Nain Singh, the most famous, measured the longitude, latitude and altitude of Lhasa, and traced the Yarlong Tsangpo River far westward without being discovered.

Seven years later, Nicholas Przewalski, a great Russian explorer and colonel in the tsar's army, entered Tibet from the north. He gathered much scientific information, but in three tries, he never reached Lhasa. In spite of his Cossack escort and his reputation among simple Tibetans as a wizard, the terrain and offical stubbornness defeated him.

From then on until the end of the century many tried their luck for many reasons—to write a bestseller, explore the unknown, become famous, fulfil a dream. Tales of incredible hardship, ferocious weather, bandits and intransigent monk-officials accompanied all those who returned.

The first American to try the trek to Lhasa was William Rockhill, a young diplomat in Peking, in 1889. Disguised as a Mongolian, speaking Tibetan and Chinese, he failed because his guides deserted him in the vast uninhabited wasteland. Two years later he tried again and was repelled only 177 kilometres (110 miles) from Lhasa. But he brought back much knowledge.

In 1892, Annie Taylor, a English missionary, became the first European woman to approach Lhasa. She came within three days' march of it. Armed only with indomitable faith and fearlessness, she survived bandits, betrayal, illness and exposure. When finally caught, she out-talked her Tibetan judge and saved her life.

In 1895, Mr St George Littledale, an English gentleman and veteran of two previous Central Asian explorations, set out for Lhasa with his wife, nephew and little dog, Tanny. The small band braved blizzards; servants deserted; pack animals died. Fearing detection, they travelled by night. They were finally stopped by 500 armed Tibetans only 80 kilometres (50 miles) from Lhasa, and neither a proffered bribe nor Mrs Littledale's assertion that she was Queen Victoria's sister could save them from expulsion. But the Royal Geographical Society awarded Mr Littledale its gold medal, and Tanny was made an honorary fellow with a silver collar.

The 20th century opened with violence. British India was frustrated by murky relations with Tibet and afraid that the strategic land might bestow its favours on Russia. In 1904, a military expedition led by Colonel Francis Younghusband (see page 185) forced its way to Lhasa, leaving hundreds of Tibetan soldiers dead. After imposing a treaty, Younghusband withdrew. The British wanted Tibet to remain closed to all foreigners but themselves. (Sir Charles Bell, the political officer for Tibet, became a profound scholar of Tibetology and a close friend and adviser to the Thirteenth Dalai Lama.)

Nevertheless, others came. Sven Hedin, a peerless Swedish explorer, defied the British and continued his decade-long work of quietly mapping western and southern Tibet. Alexandra David-Neel, a French Buddhist scholar and mystic, reached Shigatse, where she was ordained by the Panchen Lama. Later, aged 53 and disguised as a beggar, she became the first European woman to reach Lhasa. Giuseppe Tucci, an Italian archaeologist, began a 20-year study of Tibet in 1927, travelling thousands of miles on foot, to produce some of the definitive books on Tibetan religion and culture.

At the start of World War II, two Austrian mountaineers in the Himalayas became prisoners-of-war in British India. Heinrich Harrer and his companion escaped into Tibet and miraculously reached Lhasa, where Harrer eventually served as the young Dalai Lama's tutor. His book, *Seven Years in Tibet*, written after the war, aroused great interest in Tibet. The Dalai Lama shrewdly invited well-known American commentators, Lowell Thomas and Lowell Thomas Jr, to visit Tibet in 1949. As he hoped, their films created worldwide sympathy and goodwill towards his exotic land.

After 1951, the Chinese invited hand-picked foreign journalists to report favourably about the changes going on, but with minimal effect. Now Tibet is open to all foreigners and their tales and photographs, more than anything else, will keep the world well informed about Tibet.

*Lake Yamdrok Yamtso, the Scorpion Lake, on the southern route to Gyantse*

# A Narrow Escape

As though we suspected nothing we went on a short way in the same direction, talking rapidly to one another. The two men were now on either side of us while the boy walked behind. Stealing a glance to right and left we estimated our chances, if it came to a fight. The two men wore double sheepskin cloaks, as robbers do, to protect them against knife-thrusts, and long swords were stuck in their belts. Their faces had an expresion of lamb-like innocence.

Something had to happen. Aufschnaiter thought we ought to first change our direction, so as not to walk blindly into a trap. No sooner said than done. Still speaking, we abruptly turned away.

The Khampas stopped for a moment in surprise; but in a moment rejoined us and barred our way, asking us, in none too friendly tones, where we were going. 'To fetch the dog,' we answered curtly. Our manner of speaking seemed to intimidate them. They saw that we were prepared to go to any lengths, so they let us go and after staring after us for a while they hurriedly went on their way, probably to inform their accomplices.

... Next morning we worked out our new travel-plan. There was nothing for it but to take the hard road which led through uninhabited country. We bought more meat from the nomads, as we should probably be a week before seeing a soul.

To avoid going back to Labrang Trova we took a short cut entailing a laborious and steep ascent but leading, as we hoped, to the route we meant to follow. Halfway up the steep slope we turned to look at the view and saw, to our horror, two men following us in the distance. No doubt they were Khampas. They had probably visited the nomads and been told which direction we had taken.

What were we to do? We said nothing, but later confessed to one another that we had silently made up our minds to sell our lives as dearly as possible. We tried as first to speed up our pace, but we could not go faster than our yak, who seemed to us to be moving at a snail's pace. We kept on looking back, but could not be sure whether our pursuers were coming up on us or not. We fully realised how heavily handicapped we were by our lack of arms. We only had tent-poles and stones to defend ourselves with against their sharp swords. To have a chance we must depend on our wits.... So we marched on for an hour which seemed endless, panting with exertion and constantly turning round. Then we saw that the men had sat down. We hurried on towards the top of the ridge, looking as we went which would, if need be, serve as good fighting ground. The two men got up, seemed to be taking council together and then we saw them turn round and go back. We breathed again and drove our yak on so that we might soon be out of sight over the far side of the mountain.

When we reached the crest of the ridge we understood why our two pursuers had preferred to turn back. Before us lay the loneliest landscape I had ever seen. A sea of snowy mountain heights streched onwards endlessly. In the far distance were the Transhimalayas and like a gap in a row of teeth was the pass which we calculated would lead us to the road we aimed at. First put on the map by Sven Hedin, this pass—the Selala—leads to Shigatse. Being uncertain whether the Khampas had really given up the pursuit, we went on marching even after nightfall. Luckily the moon was high and, with the snow, gave us plenty of light. We could even see the distant ranges.

I shall never forget that night march. I have never been through an experience which placed such a strain on the body and the spirit. Our escape from the Khampas was due to the desolation of the region, the nature of which brought us new obstacles to surmount. It was a good thing I had long ago thrown away my thermometer. Here it would certainly have marked -30 degrees as that was the lowest it could record. But that was certainly more than the reality. Sven Hedin registered -40 degrees hereabout at this season of the year.

We loped on for hours over the virgin snow, and as we went our minds travelled afar on their own journeys. I was tormented by visions of a warm, comfortable room, delicious food and steaming hot drinks. Curiously *enough, it was the evocation of a commonplace buffet at Graz, known to me in my student days, which nearly drove me crazy. Aufschnaiter's thoughts lay in another direction. He harboured dark plans of revenge against the robbers and swore to come back with a magazine of arms. Woe to all the Khampas!*

*At last we broke off our march, unloaded our yak and crawled under cover. We had taken out our bag of tsampa and some raw meat as we were ravenously hungry, but as soon as we put a spoonful of dry meal into our mouths the metal stuck to our lips and would not come away. We had to tear it loose, amid curses and oaths. With appetites blunted by this painful experience we huddled up together under our blankets and fell, despite the piercing cold, into the leaden sleep of exhaustion.*

*Next day we toiled on painfully, trudging along in the footprints of our gallant yak and hardly looking up. In the afternoon we suddenly thought we were seeing the fata morgana; for, far away on the horizon, yet very clearly outlined, appeared three caravans of yaks moving through the snowy scene. They were moving very slowly forward; and then they seemed to come to a stop—but did not vanish. So it was no mirage. The sight gave us new courage. We summoned up all our strengh, drove our yak on, and after three hours' march reached the spot where the caravans were laagered. There were some fifteen persons in the caravan—men and women—and when we arrived their tents were already pitched. They were astonished to see us, but greeted us kindly and brought us to get warm by the fire. We found out that they were returning from a combined pilgrimage and trading voyage to Mount Kailash to their homes by Lake Namtso. They had been warned by the district officials about the brigands and so had chosen to follow this difficult route in order to avoid the region infested by the Khampas. They were bringing home fifty yaks and a couple of hundred sheep. The rest of the herds had been bartered for goods and they would have been a rich prize for the robbers. This was why the three groups had joined together and they now invited us to come along with them. Reinforcements could be useful, if they met the Khampas.*

*What a pleasure it was to be once more sitting by a fire and ladling down hot soup. We felt this meeting had been ordained by providence. We did not forget our brave Armin, for we knew how much we owed him, and asked the caravan leader to load our baggage on one of their free yaks, for which we would pay a day's hire. So our beast was able to enjoy a little rest.*

*Day after day we wandered on with the caravans and pitched our little mountaineer's tent alongside theirs. We suffered very much from the difficulty of pitching our tent during the hurricanes that often blew in these regions. Unlike the heavy yak-hair tents which could resist the wind, our light canvas hut would not stand up in rough weather and we sometimes had to bivouac in the open air. We swore if we ever again came on an expedition to Tibet we should have with us three yaks, a driver, a nomad's tent and a rifle!*

Heinrich Harrer, Seven Years in Tibet,
Translated by Rupert Hart-Davis, 1953

*Austrian-born Harrer, a professional mountaineer, was on his way to climb Everest when the expedition members were rounded up in India by the British and incarcerated in a POW camp. He plotted his escape and, together with his companion Aufschneiter, made a miraculous journey around Tibet's outer perimeter through the world's most inhospitable terrain. Harrer and Aufschneiter managed to stay in Lhasa, where Harrer became tutor to the young Dalai Lama.*

# Shigatse to Nepal

The overland route from Lhasa to Nepal leads through Shigatse to Zhangmu (also called Kasa) on the border of Nepal. Via Gyantse, this is a journey of 830 kilometres (520 miles). Travellers intending to continue from Zhangmu to Kathmandu do not need to have a Nepalese visa; visas can be obtained after crossing the frontier at the small border town of Kodari. The cost is US$15 for a 15-day visa.

Travel in the reverse direction, from Nepal into Tibet, has been subject to an array of contradictory regulations over the past years. It is easy (and expensive) to join a group tour, but individual tourists with a valid Chinese visa run some risk of being turned back at Zhangmu. It is wise to get the latest information from travel agents in Kathmandu or from travellers who have recently been in Tibet.

In general, however, it is more comfortable to take this trip leaving Tibet, when fully acclimatized, than entering it, because of the extreme changes in altitude along the route. The trip from Lhasa to Shigatse is described on page 170. This section starts at Shigatse and proceeds southwest to Nepal.

## Getting There

It is difficult to pick up transportation in Shigatse, so the whole trip to Zhangmu should be arranged in Lhasa. Individuals usually gather a group to hire a landcruiser together. Hitch-hiking the latter parts of this route on long distance trucks is no longer possible due to strict controls on truck drivers carrying foreigners.

The distance from Shigatse to Zhangmu is 530 kilometres (330 miles). It can be driven in one hard day in a four-wheel-drive vehicle. Other possibilities are spending a night in New Tinggri (Shegar) roughly halfway, where adequate accommodation is available, or roughing it in a smaller place.

The route crosses two major passes between Shigatse and New Tinggri. The Tsuo La, 113 kilometres (70 miles) from Shigatse, is 4,500 metres (14,760 feet) high and has a rugged, highland view. The Jia Tsuo La, 235 kilometres (147 miles) from Shigatse on open uplands, has a sign giving its height as 5,220 metres (17,122 feet), but reliable maps indicate it is a bit higher, at 5,252 metres (17,226 feet). Beyond Tinggri, the Lalung Leh Pass, 441 kilometres (275 miles) from Shigatse, has an altitude of 5,214 metres (17,102 feet) and commands an incomparable view of the Himalayas in all their snowbound glory. From here the road descends rapidly for another 90 kilometres (56 miles), dropping 3,000 metres (almost 10,000 feet) in two hours, down to the pine forests of Zhangmu.

# Sakya Monastery

This important old monastery, whose name means 'Tawny Soil', governed the whole of Tibet in the 13th century, after the downfall of the kings. Its medieval Mongolian architecture is quite unlike that of monasteries in Lhasa or Yarlong. It is worth taking the time for a side trip off the main road to see it (three hours for the round trip and a visit).

## GETTING THERE

The turn-off to Sakya is on the left, immediately after crossing the Sakya River bridge, 128 kilometres (80 miles) west of Shigatse—15 kilometres (nine miles) from the top of the Tsuo La Pass. A rough road leads down a long, dry valley for 26 kilometres (16 miles) to Sakya village. The forbidding, fortress-like monastery can be seen from a distance, looking like a single grey and red block with one horizontal white stripe.

## HISTORICAL BACKGROUND

The monastery stood in two parts, built at different times, on either side of the river. The first was founded in 1071 by a powerful noble family of Tsang. Its buildings, incorporating a cave, were piled against the mountainside across a river in typical Tibetan style. The abbots were strong administrators, and, since the succession passed from paternal uncle to nephew, power stayed in the hands of the founding family. Soon, the monastery controlled so much of Tsang Province that the abbot needed assistance from a civil and military governor, quaintly entitled the 'great hermit'. Much scholarship was carried on, as Sakya owned a large trove of Buddhist texts, all that were left after the demise of Indian Buddhism. A separate sect of Tibetan Buddhism, named Sakyapa (see page 156), took form here.

One abbot, Sakya Pandit, was such an outstanding scholar and debater that his fame reached Mongolia. In 1244, the son of Genghis Khan sent for him to be his teacher. In return, he granted the monastery provisional rulership over central Tibet. Sakya Pandit took along his nine-year-old nephew, Phakpa, who was later to become Sakya's greatest abbot and the lifelong spiritual guide of Kublai Khan, the emperor of China. Such was the influence of Sakya Monastery.

Sakya reached its heyday in the second half of the 13th century, when it was showered with gifts and privileges and given control over all Tibet by Kublai Khan. In 1268, a new, more magnificent monastery was built across the river from the old one in purely Mongolian style. For almost a century Sakya remained the secular and religious centre of Tibet.

After Kublai Khan's death, Mongolian power waned. The Mongols abandoned

Buddhism (to be later reconverted by the Third Dalai Lama), and Sakya was overthrown by rival monasteries. Tashilhunpo, founded by the Yellow Hat Sect in 1447, took over as the religious centre of Tsang.

The first monastery (known as the Northern Monastery), already in disrepair by the 15th century, was demolished by the Chinese after 1959. Today, however, across the narrow valley, beyond the small river, are the new, jumbled, tightly packed residences of villagers and monks. The colours grey and white predominate to create a handsome effect. Chapels and stupas dot the hillsides—in 1986 nothing stood here but ruins.

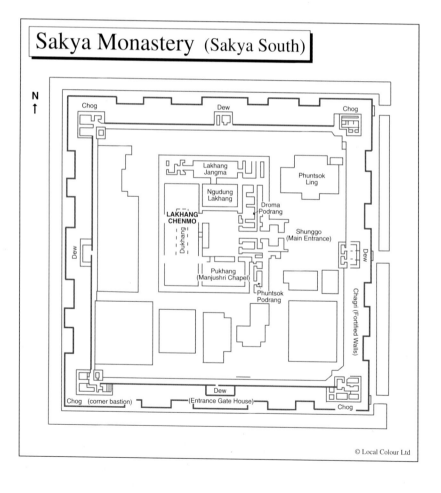

Sakya Monastery (Sakya South)

# ■ LAYOUT

Four buildings of the 13th-century Southern Monastery remain, protected by massive, windowless, fortress walls with corner towers—a typical Mongolian feature. Narthang Monastery (see page 184) and, after being devastated by an earthquake, Shalu (see page 182) were built along the same lines as Sakya. The grey and murky maroon hue of the outer wall appears drab, but these two colours are favoured throughout the region, painted in stripes on village walls, and the colours have a peculiarly powerful aesthetic impact.

Enter the monastery through the east gateway, which leads to a huge open courtyard. The first room to see is on the left, up a steep flight of stairs, after reaching the inner courtyard through an enclosed walkway. This is the Phuntsok Podrang, which has stupas that honour the relics of former Sakya lamas, and a giant image of Kunga Nyingpo as a venerable old man. He was a master scholar of Sakya's great period, equal in learning to Sakya Pandit. He organized a systematic teaching of the *tantras*, and is always portrayed as aged with white hair.

The next chapel, on the inner courtyard's south side, is the Pukhang, or Manjushri Chapel. An enclosed mandala is the centrepiece, backed by two main images, a Jowo Sakyamuni to the left and Manjushri, the bodhisattva of wisdom, to the right. It is said that Sakya Pandit created these statues. Multiple volumes that make up the *Kanjur* and *Tenjur* are here, as are thousands of small statues.

The **Main Chanting Hall**, or Lakhang Chenmo, is wider than it is deep, with columns made from whole tree trunks. Daylight entering from high windows illuminates a fine frieze of Buddhas, saints, guardians and Mongolian hierarchs, embellished by lion decorations, near the ceiling above the altar. Everything in the room is big and gilded brass figures placed high on the pillars and walls increase the sense of space.

The two primary human figures, side by side, are Sakya Pandit and Jungu Choje. Sakya Pandit wears a red hat. A statue of Kunga Nyingpo is raised and to the right of these two. In front of the altar are some of Sakya's treasures—artifacts of silver, porcelain, ivory and shell. Jewelled stupas holding the ashes of the founders also indicate its former wealth. The resplendent Chanting Hall is among the finest, most impressive in all Tibet. Take time to look carefully and investigate the many objects—ancient, refined, outlandish, beautiful, weird.

The **North Hall**, or Ngudung Lakhang, contains seven large stupas and four lesser ones, the reliquaries of the Throne Holders of the Sakya sect. Restored murals show the family of five Buddhas, a giant portrait of Kunga Nyingpo and big, bold mandalas. It is rare to see a portrait mural of these dimensions in Tibet. A mandala of coloured sand is kept permanently in a corner of the hall. An inner chapel houses six large white stupas containing the remains of Sakya's early abbots.

The final room to visit is the Droma Podrang, up a flight of stairs at the northeast corner of the inner courtyard. Here are excellent murals and a statue of Padmasambhava (Guru Rinpoche). Five stupas of fine construction also stand in this worthy chapel.

# New Tinggri (Shegar)

New Tinggri lies in a side valley north of the main road, 280 kilometres (175 miles) from Shigatse.

After leaving the Sakya bridge, the next important settlement is **Lhatse**, a county seat and truck stop at the junction with the road to western Tibet and Kashgar. At the west end of town stands Chomze Gompa, a Sakyapa monastery. Lhatse has a number of Chinese and Tibetan restaurants and two cheap hotels along the main street.

Taking the southernmost fork at the junction west of Lhatse, you soon find yourself crossing uninhabited country. Wildlife can sometimes be seen, such as musk hare, antelope, gazelle and a variety of birds, including wild geese. The road enters a long, rocky gorge and emerges on a desert plateau almost too high for grass to grow; only a thin layer of peat covers the barren soil. The Jia Tsuo La Pass would be imperceptible but for its rock piles and prayer flags.

Descending towards New Tinggri, the white range of the Himalayas is seen in the distance. New Tinggri is not visible from the road. You must go right, up a small valley. If you reach a security checkpost barring the main route, an unmistakable landmark, you have gone too far by several kilometres. All vehicles are required to stop at the checkpost, and everyone must show their travel documents before being allowed to continue onward to Nepal.

New Tinggri formerly had a fortress perched on the cliffs above and a monastery known as Shining Crystal. Now the town is composed of an old Tibetan quarter and a larger Chinese section, where the hotel is located. Above the old village, part of the fortress wall with its tall towers marches up the mountainside from a reconstructed chapel to a bare pinnacle where the bastion's foundations remain.

# Rongbuk

Formerly the site of the highest monastery in the world, at 5,030 metres (16,500 feet), Rongbuk is now known as the starting point for climbing expeditions up Mt Everest. A fairly new road to Rongbuk turns south 11 kilometres (seven miles) west of the security checkpost. The old road, in poor condition, goes south from Tinggri

(Tinggri West) 48 kilometres (30 miles) further west. Both roads are sometimes broken by floods during the summer rainy season.

The stony valley of the Rongbuk River rises gradually, with Mt Everest filling the southern horizon. The ruined monastery at the head of the valley was formerly a supremely sacred pilgrimage site housing over 100 monks. The first English mountaineers reported that wild animals, such as antelope, blue sheep and the Tibetan wild ass, were abundant in the valley—and tame, because they had never been harmed. The monks tried to discourage Everest's climbers during the 1920s and 1930s, fearing the spirits of the mountain would kill them. Mural paintings depict their imagined fate at the hands of angry gods, demons and snow leopards.

The monastery was destroyed during the Cultural Revolution and became a dumping ground for mountaineering expeditions. The base camp of Mt Everest is six kilometres (four miles) further up the slope, where the track beyond the monastery ends.

## Trek to Everest Base Camp

Most hikers who go to the base camp area begin walking from the main Shigatse–Nepal highway, 11 kilometres (seven miles) west of the checkpost, itself several kilometres beyond the turn-off to New Tinggri (Shegar). Two hundred metres (yards) past kilometre stone 5144 is a small bridge, and just after this a dirt road leading off to the left. This is the beginning of the trek. The first village, Che, is reached after an hour's walk. From here it is possible to see the road winding its way ahead to the 5,200-metre (17,000-foot) Pang La Pass. By staying to the right side of the valley it is possible to take a short cut, saving precious energy during the ascent.

Following are approximate distances and times between stages:

| | | |
|---|---|---|
| Km 5144–Che | 4 km (2.5 miles) | 1 hour |
| Che–Peruchi | 31 km (19 miles) | 9 hours |
| Peruchi–Ja-pe (Jarba) | 17 km (10.5 miles) | 6 hours |
| Ja-pe–Che Dzong | 6 km (4 miles) | 2 hours |
| Che Dzong–Rongbuk | 20 km (12.5 miles) | 7 hours |
| Rongbuk–Base Camp | 10 km (6 miles) | 3 hours |

The trek is taxing. If you are not fit and well acclimatized, do not attempt it. Plan on four days of walking to reach base camp from the main highway, although it can be done more quickly. Above all, attempt this trek only if you are well equipped and able to bring enough food to remain self-sufficient for eight to ten days.

A second, less well-known route to the base camp begins at Tinggri (Tinggri

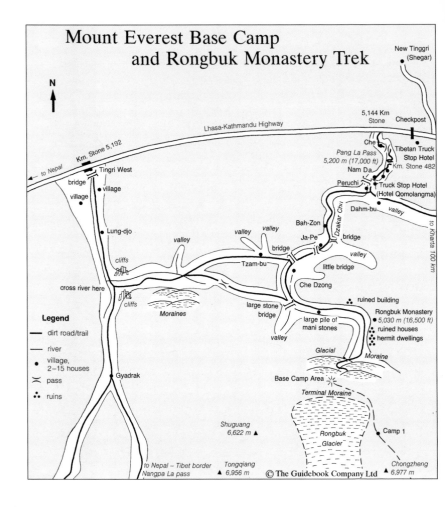

## Mount Everest Base Camp and Rongbuk Monastery Trek

West), marked by kilometre stone 5192. It is a more difficult walk but has several advantages: fewer foreigners, more wildlife, greener valleys and a greater likelihood of finding and hiring yaks for transport. A good plan might be to enter the Mt Everest region from Tinggri West and leave via the Rongbuk Valley back to kilometre stone 5144. Unneeded equipment can be stored at New Tinggri or the checkpost.

After Tinggri West, the only places where it is possible to stay with Tibetan families are Lung-djo and Tzam-bu. The route is marked here and there with stone animal enclosures, which can be used for shelter, and the occasional nomad camp. Winds can be fierce, and temperatures extremely cold. Flooding in the late spring makes crossing rivers dangerous. Use bridges if at all possible. Yaks capable of carrying two heavy backpacks can occasionally be hired at Lung-djo.

# Tinggri (Tinggri West)

The small community, with a couple of small guesthouses and restaurants on the north side of the main road, 60 kilometres (37 miles) west of the checkpost. From here there is a spectacular view in clear weather to the peaks of Everest, Lhotse and Makalu, the highest knot of mountains in the world.

Tinggri used to be an important trading post where Sherpas from Nepal exchanged rice, grain and iron for Tibetan wool and salt. It gives its name to the broad upland basin, more than 4,200 metres (14,000 feet) high, known as the Tinggri Plain, at this point over 30 kilometres (20 miles) wide. Shallow, fast-running rivers of snow water make its grassy meadowland ideal for grazing.

# Nyalam

This little town of stone and cement buildings and tin roofs is perched on a mountainside 33 kilometres (21 miles) from Zhangmu, at 3,750 metres (12,300 feet). Two rivers meet here at the head of a precipitous gorge. Caravan traders from Nepal used to call it the Gates of Hell, because the trail between Nyalam and the Nepalese border was so dangerous to negotiate. Though it is barely an hour's drive from Zhangmu, bad weather or landslides can force travellers to wait here for several days.

If you have a little spare time (contingency time) or want one more taste of Tibetan scenery, there are several possibilities: a visit to Milarepa's Cave; an easy trek along a track westwards to Xixabangma Base Camp (for which vehicles can also be hired in Nyalam), followed by harder trekking up into the mountains; and some tempting ridges for experienced hikers and climbers. People on their way into Tibet and reacting badly to altitude might consider a few days of extra acclimatization at Zhangmu or Nyalam before they move on.

From Tinggri, the road loops around an impenetrable mass of Himalayan rock before it turns south. The Tinggri Plain becomes a windswept desert, with snowy peaks on all horizons. As the valley narrows, the road climbs ever higher to a wasteland of dry, gravelly hills. The only bright colour here is the green line of a stream winding down a shallow valley and the blue sky above. All else is tan, with the white heads of the Himalayas rising dramatically over the southern horizon.

North of Lalung Leh Pass is an army camp called Gutsuo, which should be avoided, though some respectable tour companies in Kathmandu advertise it as an overnight stop. Not only is it unhealthy to stay overnight at such high altitude if not yet acclimatized, but the soldiers often refuse to provide hot drinking water and overcharge for minimal and inadequate services (Rmb15 per bed, and often not enough quilts to go round). There have even been instances of drunken and abusive behaviour.

The Lalung Leh Pass is defined by two scarcely noticeable high points, with a steep valley between them. It marks the edge of the wasteland and gives a breath-taking view of a whole range of the snowclad Himalayas. From here the road plunges through a crack in the mountains into a totally different climate. The effect of South Asia's monsoon could hardly be demonstrated more clearly than in the three-hour descent from the Lalung Leh Pass to Zhangmu.

Warm monsoon winds laden with moisture blow over India from the Bay of Bengal every June or July to start the wet season. Rising to cross the Himalayas, the air cools and drops torrential rain on the southern slopes, which are consequently covered with forests or jungle. Scarcely a drop falls on the northern face, however, where lifeless gravel desert stretches down from the snowline.

Beyond the pass, the road follows a rapidly falling river right through the Himalayas in a series of gorges, hugging the mountainside. Patches of barley edge the river wherever the ground is flat. Low, flowering shrubs start to appear among the rocks, then leafy plants, and finally tall wildflowers.

# Milarepa's Cave

A cave where Milarepa spent many years of his life is ten kilometres (six miles) north of Nyalam, between the main road and the river at a tiny village called Zhonggang. A path leads from the roadside through the village and down the hillside, where a small monastery has recently been rebuilt on a terrace overlooking the river. The hermit's cave is entered from its vestibule. Pilgrims' offerings of decorated stones along the path—and sweet-smelling herbs and wild flowers growing all around—make this a spot of great peace and beauty.

The cave, which is quite small with a low, rock ceiling, is kept as a shrine by caretaker monks. A statue of Milarepa in a glass case shows him happily listening to his own singing, but he has been uncharacteristically dressed in warm clothing. The monastery, consisting of a small chanting hall and vestibule, is named Pelgyeling, as is a monastery in Nepal consecrated to Milarepa.

A monastery had existed at the site of this cave since the 17th century to take care of pilgrims, but it was totally destroyed in 1966. Its chapel was rebuilt in the mid-1980s with the help of Nepalese craftsmen.

# The Gates of Hell

The road south of Nyalam accompanies a rushing river through a gorge enclosed by high cliffs. The road is sometimes high above the river, sometimes close to the water. Scrub pine bushes appear near the upper end of the gorge, and the riverbed is filled with mossy boulders. Trees grow thicker and taller as the road descends. Waterfalls cascade down the cliffs through green grottoes of fern and moss. The sight of so much lush greenery seems unbelievable after the bleakness of the high desert. Towering pine trees have formed a real forest by the time Zhangmu's roofs appear on the mountainside below.

From Nyalam to Zhangmu is only 33 kilometres (21 miles)—about an hour's drive—but the road can be damaged at any time of year. During the heavy monsoon rains between June and October, it is broken in numerous places by rockfalls and mudslides, and the mess can take weeks to clear up. During the monsoon, parts of the walk are quite dangerous, especially the massive rockfall that obliterated the northern end of Zhangmu town, covering it in a slippery scree of huge boulders. During the monsoon, travellers sometimes have to run the 300 metres (yards) across the danger zone, listening for warning whistle-blasts from watchmen posted on the towering cliffs above. Work to stabilize the slope may take years to complete.

Neither Zhangmu nor Nyalam has long-distance communications facilities, so travellers cannot change onward air reservations from Kathmandu if they are stranded here. Allow time for delays.

If you have to walk through and need transport, you can hire a local farmer with *dzos* as pack animals, which cost about half as much as porters. Nepalese porters can be seen up to Nyalam, but they work only for Nepalese traders on this section.

An early start is essential for the long walk down from Nyalam. If you arrive after dark, you will have to stay at a teahouse in the bazaar beyond the north end of town. If the rockfall is active, animals cannot be taken across it and you need to find porters willing to risk it. (At least four porters lost their lives here in 1987.) Steep slippery paths wind down through the trees as far as possible from falling rocks, then cross the rockfall past demolished buildings to the lower side of the town.

# Zhangmu (Kasa)

Zhangmu is considerably bigger than Nyalam. It snakes down a steep mountainside on both sides of the road above the Sun Kosi River, in sight of the Nepalese border.

# Song of the Peacock

In the Buddhist tradition the peacock symbolizes the bodhisattva's practice of utilizing poisons on the path. This is the basic principle of tantric practice. It involves the deliberate use of negative emotions and conditions to accelerate mental development, like the peacock, who is said to eat poisonous plants to improve its plumage. Such practice is difficult and dangerous; the protection inherent in the mind truly aimed at enlightenment is necessary before this should be attempted. Mila's gesture of neutralizing the priest's afflictions by consuming his poisons is an extension of this peacock-bodhisattva analogy. This story also appears in a slightly different version in Mila's autobiography.

Milarepa was generally disliked by all the Bön priests of Nya Nang and Drin. One of these evil-minded priests mixed a poison powder into a bowlful of yoghurt and gave it to a leper woman, telling her, 'Offer this to Jetsun.' The priest paid her a turquoise gem in return for this favor.

When she offered the yoghurt, Jetsun said, 'I will drink this so that you may earn the turquoise. Because you did not know it was poisoned, you will not suffer any harmful consequences.' He washed the bowl out and gave it back saying, 'I cannot offer the remainder to you.' †

'Why is that?' asked Shengom Repa. Mila replied with this song:

> I bow to my royal doctor, my lama
> Who revealed his three supreme dimensions
> By curing the sick torment of the three poisons
> With the medicine of the three vehicles.
>
> Like the peacock,
> I spread the wings of method and wisdom
> From a state of natural realization.
> A crest of radiant self-illumination
> Adorns the head of supreme gnosis
> Which rests on the long neck of the ever-present void.

*My golden beak shines with good qualities*
*My two bright eyes see both realities. ††*
*A variety of colors in my long tail feathers*
*Symbolizes the five gnoses, which*
*Provide benefit to all,*
*And my two feet are the knowledge*
*Of what to accept and what to reject.*

*Consuming the virulent poison in an offering*
*Tainted by the three afflictive poisons,*
*This peacock of the actual state*
*Relieves the afflictions of the donor.*
*May he be freed from the darkness of the three poisons.*

*Tell that Bön priest*
*'Though you may not like it,*
*I will be staying on this earth a while longer.'*

*In tears, the leper woman beat her breast. Jetsun told her, 'You had no bad intention, so you will incur no consequence at all. Do not cry.' At that he became slightly sick, but was cured through the care of his disciples.*

Lama Kunga and Brian Cutillo, Miraculous Journey—New Stories and Songs by Milarepa, 1986

† *This refers to the custom of returning the last portion of a food offering to the giver.*

†† *The superficial and absolute levels of reality.*

*The stories and songs of the Tibetan poet-yogi Milarepa have been handed down from storyteller to storyteller for 10 centuries. They have lost none of their spontaneity and their penetrating insight and vivid imagery have widened and heightened the perceptions of all those who hear them.*

# Milarepa

Of all the religious masters and strange characters that have appeared in Tibet's history, Milarepa is the people's favourite. He was a combination of poet, eccentric, hermit, magician and saint, avocations that were much appreciated by Tibetans. An extraordinary, exuberant man, Milarepa left a legacy of many thousands of songs and poems, and a biography written by his chief disciple. In some ways his life resembled that of St Francis of Assissi—a sinner in youth who repented, devoted his maturity to selfless works and ended his life as a beloved, revered saint. Mila was his family name. Repa means cotton-clad, as once he had become a hermit he never wore more than a cotton cloth, despite the bitter cold.

He was born in 1040 to a family of comfortable means. His father died when he was seven. By Tibetan custom, the widow, her son and daughter and all the family property were entrusted to the father's brother until Milarepa came of age. This faithless uncle took the property for himself and forced the family to be his servants. Milarepa's mother possessed one asset—a plot of land in her own name, which she now sold to pay for a special education for her son. She sent Milarepa to learn black magic from a sorcerer, so that he could wreak revenge on the uncle.

Milarepa succeeded brilliantly at his studies. He brought about the death of his uncle's oldest son (and several other people) by collapsing the roof of a house on to his cousin's wedding party. He also destroyed the uncle's crops with hailstones. Thus defeated, the uncle returned the patrimony. But Milarepa was overcome with remorse. He renounced worldly goods and went looking for a teacher who could lead him to the light.

He went to Marpa (1012–96), a fearsome, contradictory tantric master who was violent and wordly yet a remarkable scholar and teacher. Marpa refused to take him, as he could not pay, so Milarepa offered his own person, body and soul, and entered a long, cruel apprenticeship designed to purge him of his sins, endlessly building and tearing down a tower. Satisfied at last, Marpa taught him, initiated him and sent him to a life of contemplation, rather than scholarship like his other disciples. He earned Milarepa's lifelong devotion, as many of the songs show.

Milarepa lived as an extreme ascetic. He ate nothing but nettles until his hair turned green, singing his joyful songs of praise and wisdom. He developed great occult powers and clairvoyance, which he used, allegorically, in contests of magic to convince the Bön priest of Buddhism's superiority, or to perform his countless acts of kindness. Milarepa lived to the age of 83, a wise, inspired, compassionate madman who captured the hearts of all Tibetans. His images usually portray him smiling ecstatically, with his hand raised to his ear as he sings.

*Khagangma, sitting carpet for special occasions, c. 1900–1920.*
*The general introduction of Tibetan rugs to the rest of the world occurred with the exodus of the*
*Dalai Lama and 80,000 of his followers from Chinese-occupied Tibet in 1959. Although the*
*carpets that the refugees brought with them to India and Nepal occasioned the awareness of the*
*Tibetan carpet as an art form, sadly it also marked the end of traditional rug weaving in Tibet. The*
*craft survives, but the post-1959 product is far less imaginative and more commercial.*
*Tibetan rugs appeared in all manner of guises. From nomad tents to monasteries, rugs were used*
*for sitting and sleeping. Khaden rugs for sleeping usually lay on elevated platforms, sometimes in*
*matching pairs. Khagangma were the smaller sitting mats offered to special visitors. Rugs that*
*adorned temples included pillar rugs (kathum), long thin runners (tsokden), drum covers, back*
*rests (thigyarbya) and cushions. Rugs were also used as good luck tokens at weddings.*
*Photo courtesy of Altfield Gallery, text by Antonia Tozer.*

The road makes several hairpin turns back and forth through the town. From its upper end to its lower is about four kilometres (2.5 miles) by road, but steps connect its different levels more directly for hardy people on foot. The average altitude is 2,300 metres (7,550 feet).

## Exit Procedures

Nepalese rupees, known as *nibi* in Chinese, circulate freely in Zhangmu. Rmb1 equals approximately 8 rupees. A branch of the Bank of China is located high above the Zhangmu Hotel. A post office can be found at the street level above the bank.

The Chinese border post, for passport control and customs, is next to the Zhangmu Hotel at the road barrier. The actual border is the Friendship Bridge over the Sun Kosi River, several kilometres further down the mountain.

## From Zhangmu to Kathmandu

The Chinese-built Friendship Bridge at Kodari lies far below Zhangmu. The road down is often damaged in the summer rainy season, in which case travellers must descend on foot for five kilometres (three miles). Shortcuts between road levels are steep. It is easy to hire porters to carry baggage—the standard rate is 80–100 rupees per load as far as the Nepalese customs house on the far side of the river.

Nepal is 2 hours 15 minutes behind China standard time and 3 hours 15 minutes behind from April to November.

# Western Tibet

Just beyond the town of Lhatse the main road from Shigatse to Nepal divides. The left branch carries on in a southwesterly direction towards Tinggri and the border town of Zhangmu. Two other branches provide routes to western Tibet, known as Ngari, or Ali in Chinese. The few outsiders who travel this way all have one destination in mind, the area of Mt Kailash and Lake Manasarovar. The so-called southern route to Kailash is the fastest, taking four days from Shigatse, though the road is subject to flooding and delays in the summer. The north route is considerably longer (800 kilometres, 500 miles) and crosses a large stretch of Tibet's great northern plateau, the Changtang, much of it above 4,500 metres (14,750 feet).

For thousands of years the Kailash area, from where the Indus, Sutlej, Ganges and Yarlong Tsangpo (Brahmaputra) rivers originate, has been held sacred by Hindus, Buddhists, Jains and followers of Bön, Tibet's indigenous religion. Even today, pilgrims carry out devotional circumambulations here, having converged on Mt Kailash by pilgrim paths from all over Tibet.

In their descriptions of this numinous mountain, Hindus declare it to be Siva's throne. Siva, one of three primary gods in Hinduism, sits in eternal paradise, the long strands of his matted hair falling and flowing all about him. The holy Ganges River is said to emanate from one of these strands.

Buddhist cosmography identifies Kailash with the mighty Mt Sumeru, the central peak of the world. Holy Lake Manasarovar, the mother-principle, represents Buddhist transcendent consciousness. The father-mountain itself represents the means to enlightenment. Jains identify the Kailash area with the place of their first saint's spiritual liberation. As a Bön centre, Mt Kailash has enjoyed great popularity in the folk religion of Tibet. It is the soul of the country and assures perpetuity and protection for all the Tibetan people.

Physically, too, the area is outstanding. At 6,714 metres (22,027 feet), Mt Kailash is one of the highest mountains in western Tibet. Lake Manasarovar is generally recognized to be the highest body of fresh water in the world.

The main local town is Burang (Taklakot), 110 kilometres (70 miles) south of Mt Kailash. There is a tourist office here. The administrative centre of the Ngari (Ali) District is the town of Shiquanhe, 250 kilometres (155 miles) west of Mt Kailash on the road to Kashgar, in Xinjiang.

Western Tibet holds two sites of significant art historical and archaeological interest. These are **Töling** and **Tsaparang**, the main centres of the Kingdom of Guge. Guge established itself after the period of confusion in Central Tibet when the Yarlong Dynasty failed and Buddhism suffered persecution. Its greatest flowering took place in the 11th and 12th centuries. Atisha, who played such an important role in the revival of Buddhism, stayed at Töling for three years (1042–45), teaching and writing.

The crumbling monastic cities lie two days by jeep from Shiquanhe. Travel on the main road southeast towards Mt Kailash to Ba'er. Then turn right and continue for another 180 kilometres (112 miles) to Zada (Töling); this is the place to stay for exploring the art and architecture of Töling and Tsaparang and the high, vast landscapes all around.

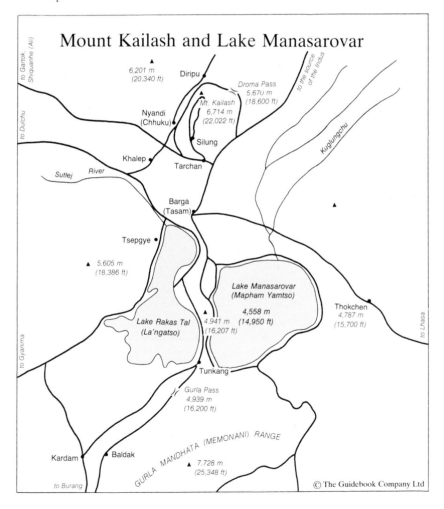

# Mount Kailash and Lake Manasarovar

to Gartok,
Shiquanhe (Ali)

to Dulchu

6,201 m
(20,340 ft)

Diripu

to the source
of the Indus

Droma Pass
5,670 m
(18,600 ft)

Mt. Kailash
6,714 m
(22,022 ft)

Nyandi
(Chhuku)

Kuglungchu

Silung

Khalep

Tarchan

Sutlej    River

Barga
(Tasam)

Tsepgye

5,605 m
(18,386 ft)

Lake Manasarovar
(Mapham Yamtso)

4,558 m
(14,950 ft)

Thokchen
4,787 m
(15,700 ft)

to Lhasa

Lake Rakas Tal
(La'ngatso)

4,941 m
(16,207 ft)

to Gyanima

Tunkang

Gurla Pass
4,939 m
(16,200 ft)

GURLA MANDHATA (MEMONANI) RANGE

Kardam

Baldak

7,728 m
(25,348 ft)

to Burang

© The Guidebook Company Ltd

(following pages) *Rugged nomads of the high plateau*

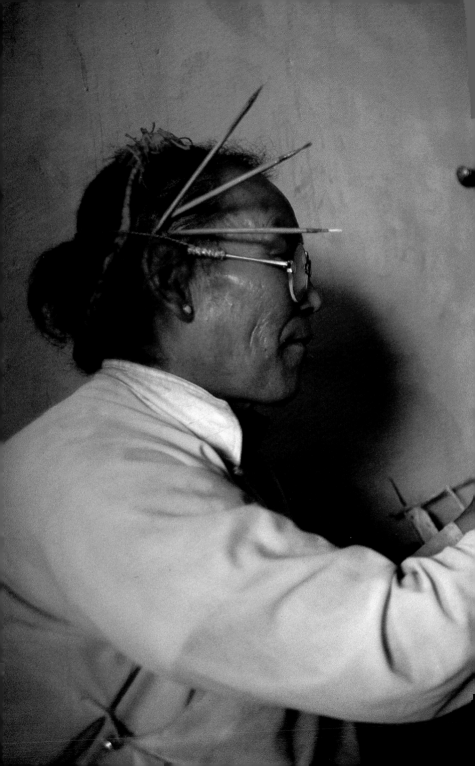

# Major Tibetan Festivals

The annual cycle of ceremonies and festivals in Lhasa before the Chinese takeover was a magnificent round of pomp and gaiety that combined the Tibetans' love of formality and spectacle with devotions, pilgrimages, renewal of friendships, eating and drinking. Hugh Richardson's *Ceremonies of the Lhasa Year*, Serindia Publications, London, recounts in detail 41 specific ceremonies that marked the annual lunar calendar.

| Lunar Month | Day | Festival |
| --- | --- | --- |
| 1st month | 1–7 | New Year Festival. Special ceremonies performed by the Dalai Lama and preparations for the Great Prayer. |
| | 4–25 | Great Prayer Festival (Monlam), begun by Tsong Khapa. Hordes of pilgrims at Lhasa's Jokhang, carnivals, horse racing, archery. |
| | 15 | Festival of the Great Miracle. Fires on roof-tops and lamps in windows commemorate the Buddha's miracle at Sravasti. |
| | 26 | The Gallop Behind the Fort. |
| 2nd month | 19 | The Great Assembly of Worship. |
| | 29 | The Demon-Ransom King. Festival to drive out evil and expel scapegoat. |
| | 30 | The Golden Procession of the    Assembly of Worship. Monks encircle Lhasa and giant banners hung on the Potala's south face. |
| 4th month | 3 | The Great Procession. Vast, colourful ceremony during which the Dalai Lama moves from the Potala to the Norbulingka for six months. |
| | 15 | Full Moon Day of the Saga Constellation. Celebration of the Buddha's enlightenment and entry to nirvana. |
| 5th month | 5 | The Birthday Festival. |

| | 8 | The Comparison of the Gods at Nechung. Gathering at Nechung Monastery of numerous oracles in a state of trance. |
|---|---|---|
| | 15 | The Universal Incense-offering. |
| 6th month | 4 | Fourth of the Sixth Month. Feast of Buddha's first sermon. Pilgrims climb holy mountain. |
| | 29 | Start of the Curd Feast. |
| | 30 | The Curd Feast at Sera and Drepung monasteries. Hanging of giant banners. |
| 7th month | 1–5 | The Curd Feast at Lhasa. |
| | 1–15 | The Circumambulation of the Fields. Ceremonies to ensure good crops. |
| 8th month | | The Bathing Festival. Ritual bathing in rivers; picnics. |
| 9th month | 22 | The Divine Descent. Celebration of the Buddha's descent from heaven after preaching to his mother. Pilgrims to monasteries. |
| 10th month | | Procession to the Potala. |
| | 25 | The Offerings on the Twenty-fifth Day at Ganden. Memorial festival of Tsong Khapa's death. Lamps, fires. |
| 11th month | 4–5 | The Conjunction of Nine Evils. On this most inauspicious day shops close and people do not travel. |
| 12th month | 29 | The Votive Offering of the Twenty-ninth Day. Culmination of the Old Year. Day-long pageantry and ritual dances at the Potala's Inner Courtyard. |

The Tibetan lunar calendar lags approximately four to six weeks behind the solar calendar. For example, the Tibetan First Month usually falls in February, the Fifth Month in June or early July and the Eight Month in September.

# Recommended Reading

## General History, Religion and Culture

Bell, Charles. *The Religion of Tibet*. Oxford University Press, 1931. Sir Charles Bell may be said to be the most important of the early Western writers on Tibet. His friendship with many high Tibetans, including the Thirteenth Dalai Lama, and his understanding of Tibetan history put his writings in a special class. This title, a wide-ranging work on Tibet and its religion, was written after Bell's year-long stay in Lhasa.

David-Neel, Alexandra. *Magic and Mystery in Tibet*. Dover, 1971. Madame David-Neel, the first European woman to reach Lhasa, wrote prodigiously about Tibet and her travels there. *Magic and Mystery in Tibet*, with chapters such as 'Dealing With Ghosts' and 'Demons and Psychic Sports', is a lively and wonderful telling of Tibetan life and her direct experiences there over two decades.

Snellgrove, David and Richardson, Hugh. *A Cultural History of Tibet*. Prajna Press, 1980. This comprehensive work is perhaps the best single volume to introduce serious students to Tibet. It covers all aspects of life, religion and history and has been recognized for its thoroughness since publication in 1968. The difficult transliteration system of Tibetan names and terms should not deter readers.

Stein, R A. *Tibetan Civilization*. Stanford University Press, 1972. Another one-volume presentation of the Tibetan world, Stein's book is recommended for its readability and clear presentation of Tibet's history and social institutions.

Thubten Jigme Norbu and Turnbull, Colin. *Tibet, Its History, Religion and People*. Penguin Books, 1983. The Dalai Lama's brother and the famous anthropologist have colaborated to produce a valuable book on the land and people of Tibet. It gives a practical understanding to aspects of Tibetan culture.

Tucci, Giuseppe. *The Religions of Tibet*. Routledge & Kegan Paul, 1980. The great Italian scholar poured a lifetime of research into this dense volume.

Waddell, L Austine. *Buddhism and Lamaism of Tibet*. Educational Enterprise Ltd, 1985. This old classic, first published in 1894, is still useful for its wealth of detail and useful information. It has over 180 plates and illustrations. The Victorian commentary and occasional misrepresentations of Tibetan religion should be recognized and understood.

# Religion

Conze, Edward. *A Short History of Buddhism*. George Allen & Unwin, 1982. Conze's little 132-page gem wastes no space and fits in an amazing amount of information. The evolution of Buddhist philosophy and the link between different schools of thought and practice are its strengths.

Dowman, Keith. *Pilgrim's Guide: The Power Places of Central Tibet*. Routledge & Kegan Paul, 1987. Dowman's book, based on a traditional Tibetan guide for pilgrims, is useful for travellers who want to visit multiple, out-of-the-way religious sites and understand the significance of what they see.

Evans-Wentz, W Y. *The Tibetan Book of the Dead*. Oxford University Press, 1957. Descriptions and guidance for the post-death experience are the themes of this famous Buddhist book. Descriptions are often bizarre and unfamiliar to Western readers, but the work, known as the *Bardo Thodol*, has been an invaluable text for Tibetans for centuries.

Evans-Wentz, W Y. *Tibet's Great Yogi Milarepa*. Oxford University Press, 1969. This autobiography by the 11th-century sage, beloved by Tibetans of all religious schools, is a marvelous document that recounts his turning from evil to a life of great devotion and accomplishment, as poet, saint, magician and hermit.

Govinda, Lama Anagarika. *The Way of the White Clouds*. Rider, 1966. An evocative and rewarding story of the author's remarkable journey to West Tibet in 1948.

Tucci, Giuseppe. *The Theory and Practice of the Mandala*. This technical and sometimes difficult book is worth the effort to understand the power and symbolic meaning of mandalas, which Tucci describes as 'psycho-cosmograms'.

# Art

Gordon, Antoinette K. *The Iconography of Tibetan Lamaism*. C E Tuttle Company,

1959. This book gives a descriptive outline of the principal deities in the Tibetan pantheon, tracing the main features and symbols that are used to denote each one. The work is systematic, easy to use and contains over 180 illustrations, photographs and reproductions of thangkas.

Pal, Pratapaditya. *Art of Tibet*. Los Angeles County Museum of Art, 1983. A large-format book that presents outstanding examples of Tibetan art from the museum's collection. The introduction and detailed treatment of each entry are excellent.

Tarthang Tulku. *Sacred Art of Tibet*. Dharma Publishing, 1974. This catalogue of 36 select pieces of art, sculpture and painting, is sensitively written. Essays treat the development of Tibetan art and the role of sacred art.

Tucci, Giuseppe. *Transhimalaya*. Nagel Publishers, 1973.
Tucci presents here a summing up of the archaeology and prehistory of Tibet, with ample illustrations, and a full discussion of the historical genesis of Tibetan art. It is a valuable resource for understanding the full range of art on the Tibetan Plateau.

# Natural History

Cameron, Ian. *Mountains of the Gods*. Century, 1984. A good introduction to the Himalayas, their geography, discovery and exploration.

Vaurie, Charles. *Tibet and Its Birds*. H F & G Witherby Ltd, 1972. The long chapters on Geography and Natural Regions of Tibet and History and Ornithological Exploration are the finest written on the subjects. The second half of the book is for specialists; it contains, among other things, a systematic list and description of 505 bird species.

# Travel

Allen, Charles. *A Mountain in Tibet*. Futura, 1983. Subtitled *The Search for Mount Kailash and the Sources of the Great Rivers of India*, the book is a rousing telling of early exploration in Tibet. It is well researched.

Byron, Robert. *First Russia, Then Tibet*. Penguin, 1985. This classic of travel writing, first published in 1933, shows the author's sophisticated and wry insight into alien civilizations. He succeeded in travelling to Gyantse, largely out of curiosity and a sense of the fun of it all.

Fleming, Peter. *Bayonets to Lhasa*. Oxford, 1961. In 1904 a small British army led by Francis Younghusband invaded Tibet and occupied Lhasa, thus effectively opening the country. The story of Britain's motives and ultimate action is the subject of this exciting, well-written book.

Harrer, Heinrich. *Seven Years in Tibet*. E P Dutton, 1954. Harrer's account of escape from a British P O W camp in India and incredible journey of survival on foot to Lhasa is only the first part of this book, one of the classics of travel and adventure writing. The greater part tells of his years in the Tibetan capital and the revealing elements of day-to-day life.

Hopkirk, Peter. *Tresspassers on the Roof of the World*. Oxford, 1982. Hopkirk's book is a carefully researched and cleverly presented account of the West's infatuation with Tibet and the men and women who penetrated the high plateau with the aim of reaching the forbidden goal of Lhasa. The pace is fast and the stories bizarre and wonderful.

Miller, Luree. *On Top of the World: Five Women Explorers in Tibet*. Mountaineers Books, 1972. Presented here are five determined, often eccentric, always courageous women who went against the grain of the times to fulfill their dreams of exploration, equality for women and spiritual discovery.

# Tibet Since 1950

Avedon, John F. *In Exile From the Land of Snows*. Michael Joseph, 1984. In ten years this book has become a minor classic and is constantly referred to as the best single source for understanding Tibet's plight since 1950. It has a clear style and a mass of details. The many interviews with Tibetans make it invaluable.

Chan, Victor. *Tibet Handbook—a Pilgrimage Guide*. Moon Publications, 1993. Victor Chan spent half a decade walking in Tibet and has produced a monumental work of 1,100 pages and over 200 maps and diagrams. Trekkers, travellers, historians and people interested in Tibetan art will find this tome a most valuable resource.

# Health

Hackett, Peter H. *Mountain Sickness—Prevention, Recognition and Treatment.* The American Alpine Club, 1980. This small handbook is a complete reference for all matters relating to altitude sickness and is thus pertinent to all people planning a trip to Tibet.

# Practical Information

## Hotels

LHASA

Hotels in Lhasa range in size and quality from the new, modern Holiday Inn to very simple Tibetan inns. Prices range accordingly, but there is appropriate accommodation for all budgets. Apart from the hotels where CITS puts its guests, visitors to Lhasa must be prepared for a lack of plumbing, untrained staff and various inconveniences.

**Holiday Inn** (Lhasa Fandian)
No 1 Minzu Lu, tel (86) (891) 6324509, fax 6335796, tlx 68010 HILSA CN, cable 7391
The best hotel in town, near the Norbulingka in the western suburbs, is managed by Holiday Inn Asia Pacific. The 1,100-bed hotel has 468 guestrooms and suites (singles, twin and triple), all with private bath. Facilities include a coffee shop, Chinese restaurant, banquet rooms, lobby bar and shops, massage, disco, shuttle bus and vehicle hire. Economy rooms Rmb600, Superior Rmb992, Suites from Rmb1,470 (single rooms cost the same as doubles).

**Tibet Hotel** (Xi Zang Binguan)
221 Beijing Xi Lu, tel 6336784 / 6334966, fax 6336787, telex 68013 TGSTH CN
This neo-Tibetan-style, 188-bed hotel has singles and twins, all with private bathrooms. Though less grand than the Holiday Inn, by Tibetan standards it is still an upmarket facility. The hotel operates under Tibetan regional management, and its main purpose is to accommodate top officials on tour and foreigners. Rmb460 single/twin.

**Tibet Royal Hotel**
Chingdol Dong Lu
A new hotel, located to the southwest of the Jokhang near the river. Good facilities include business centre, health club and a pleasant bar and Chinese restaurant. 30 rooms; doubles cost Rmb480.

**Ying Qiao Hotel**
Lingkuo Bei Lu
Another new hotel, offers single rooms for Rmb180 and doubles for Rmb160-220. Opposite the Telecommunications Centre, near the PSB.

**Genguan Hotel**
83 Beijing Dong Lu
Situated between the Banak Shol and Kirey hotels in a very ugly building. Doubles with attached bathroom cost Rmb230, with no bathroom Rmb120.

**Yak Hotel** (Ya Lushe)
Beijing Dong Lu
Has ascended in popularity with budget travellers. Good location and ambience. Dorm beds Rmb25, singles Rmb60, doubles Rmb75–110.

---

* The international telephone code for China is 86; for Tibet follow this with 891

**Hotel Banak Shöl** (Balang Xue Lushe)
Beijing Dong Lu, tel 6323829.
This Tibetan-style hotel in the middle of
Old Lhasa is built around a courtyard
and is a favourite with young travellers.
Singles from Rmb40, doubles Rmb70,
dorm beds available for Rmb25. There is
also a newer wing with comfortable doubles for Rmb170.

**Snowland Hotel** (Xuecheng Luguan)
Zang Xi Yuan Lu, tel 6323687.
This privately operated Tibetan hotel enjoys an excellent location just around the
corner from the Jokhang. Very good restaurant. A popular place. Single rooms
cost Rmb40, doubles Rmb50. Beds are
Rmb25 in three-bed rooms.

**Kirey Hotel** (Jiri Binguan)
Beijing Dong Lu
A little closer to the Jokhang than the Banak Shol, this is another travellers'
hangout with a good restaurant. Dorm
beds cost Rmb25 in 3- or 4-bed rooms,
doubles Rmb60. Newer double rooms
with attached bath are Rmb100.

**Suns Hotel** (Riguang Binguan)
27 Linqu Lu, tel 6331124 / 6322853,
fax 6335675, telex 68016 TRCLS CN
A good mid-range place, this 150-bed hotel has 70 rooms with attached baths and
solar-heated water. The restaurant serves
breakfast for Rmb20 and lunch and dinner for Rmb30. The Lhasa Travel Agency
office is here, and vehicles are available
for hire. Doubles cost Rmb300, suites
Rmb700.

**Himalaya Hotel**
6 Lingkuo Dong Lu, tel 6322293 /
6323775 / 6334082, fax 6334855
Near the university and river in the
southeast part of town. Rather run-down
but with good facilities. Doubles cost
Rmb275.

## GONGGAR
**Gonggar Hotel**
New, kitsch Chinese hotel, situated at
the northwest corner of the main T-junction. Double rooms cost Rmb80. Terrible
plumbing. There are several good
Sichuanese restaurants along the street
leading to the airport entrance.

**Tashi's Guesthouse**
Basic Tibetan accommodation on the
south side of the main road from Lhasa.
Rmb15 per bed.

## TSEDANG
**Tsedang Hotel** (Zedang Fandian) This
500-bed hotel was planned and financed
from Guangzhou and is the area's newest
and best. It is on Tsedang's main avenue,
on the south side of town. Rooms are
nearly all doubles, with Western-style
bathrooms and solar-heated water. It has
a bar and three restaurants boasting Chinese chefs. The hotel has a fleet of 20 vehicles for sightseeing and day trips. Bicycles can be hired from CITS here for
Rmb20 per day. Double rooms cost
Rmb420.

**Tsedang Guesthouse** (Zedang Zhen
Zhaodaisuo) Close to the Tsedang Hotel,

this guesthouse is much simpler. Beer and tinned food are available at a hotel store downstairs. One of its two dining-rooms offers a fixed Chinese menu. The other provides cheap, simple fare. Doubles cost Rmb160.

## SHIGATSE
**Shigatse Hotel** (Rikaze Fandian)
13 Jiefang Zhong Lu
Perhaps the best hotel in Tibet outside of Lhasa (which isn't saying much), this large establishment caters mainly to tour groups. Handy for the Bank of China, but otherwise poorly situated at the southern end of town. A single room costs Rmb390, standard doubles are Rmb420. CITS is located here.

**Fruit Orchard Hotel**
Located opposite Tashilhunpo Monastery. Standard, badly-run Chinese concrete hotel. Rmb20 per bed in three-bed rooms. Has plumbing problems.

**Tenzin Hotel**
Small Tibetan guesthouse opposite the market below the old fort. A friendly place with good service. It has eight clean rooms; Rmb25–40 per bed.

**Sangzhuzi Hotel**
Well located in the centre of town. Basic accommodation at Rmb12 per bed.

## GYANTSE
**Gyantse Hotel** (Jiangzi Fandian) This large establishment is left (south) of the main crossroads when coming from Lhasa. With more than 100 rooms and new additions seemingly added every year, it is the primary hotel for tourists in Gyantse. It serves reasonably good food in large portions in a cavernous dining room. Singles and doubles cost Rmb380.

**Gyantse Guesthouse**
Basic Chinese hotel, with poor service. Rmb20 per bed in three-bed rooms with attached bathroom.

**Truck stop guesthouse**
Extremely basic. Rmb10 per bed in dorms.

## SAKYA
**Tibetan Guesthouse**
Near the northwest corner of Sakya Monastery. Rmb 15 per bed.

**Sakya Xian Guesthouse**
Around a courtyard near the monastery's northeast corner, beyond the market street. Rmb 15 per bed.

## NEW TINGGRI (SHEGAR)
**Mt Everest Hotel**
This relatively new hotel now takes in most of the tourist traffic coming and going between Shigatse and the Nepal border. Four-bed rooms for Rmb20 per bed; reasonable restaurant.

**Shegar Hotel**
Located outside of the town and somewhat overpriced at Rmb250 per double.

Just to the east of the monastery is an

extremely rudimentary **guesthouse** in a courtyard. Its kitchen does not operate on a regular basis. There are a couple of little shops in the street to the right, but anyone planning to stay a day or two should bring food and drink.

## TINGGRI

There are three guesthouses here: the Everest View and Himalaya are on the north side of the main road and are both very basic. A bed in a 6-bed room costs Rmb12. There is a small restaurant in the Himalaya Hotel, and two or three Chinese restaurants across the street. The third guesthouse (Rmb15) is located in the main part of the village a few hundred metres to the south of the road behind the hill.

## NYALAM

**Snowland Hotel**
Reasonably comfortable rooms in a Tibetan building. Some double rooms for Rmb40, other beds in 4-bed rooms for Rmb25.

**Government Guesthouse**
Opposite from the Snowland. Dingy place, with beds for Rmb15.

**Ngawang's Guesthouse** This little back-street hotel is the best place to stay in Nyalam and is quiet and clean. It is on the road leading west through the old Tibetan trading village towards a little gompa (now residential accommodation). Rmb20 per bed.

## ZHANGMU (KASA)

**Zhangmu Hotel** (Zhangmu Binguan)
At the lower end of town near the customs post. Has 40 double rooms for foreigners. Uninspired service. Double rooms with attached bathroom cost Rmb200. Triples are also available. Reasonable restaurant. CITS is located here.

**Himalaya Lodge**
Popular with backpackers, this small guesthouse has friendly service. Rmb20 per bed in double rooms.

**Reception Office Guesthouse**
Chinese hotel located in the middle section of Zhangmu. Ugly and draughty, but offers great views from the south-facing balcony. Rmb30 per bed in double rooms.

# Restaurants

## LHASA

Small restaurants—mostly clustered around the Banak Shöl, Kirey and Yak hotels, in the main street running down from the Holiday Inn, and along the main street between the Cultural Palace and the Barkhor—are opening and closing and changing cooks and addresses all the time. Ask around to see who had a good meal recently and find out where they got it.

**Tashi 2 Restaurant**
Located within the compound of the Kirey Hotel, this small, popular restau-

rant has a limited, though good, menu that satisfies the largely foreign clientele. The family that runs it is Tibetan, as is most of the cuisine. Prices are cheap.

### Snowland Restaurant
This large, clean restaurant offers quality Chinese and Western fare with plenty of vegetables. Beer is available; prices are reasonable.

### Kailash Restaurant
Inside the Banak Shöl compound. Pleasant, friendly service and good food.

### Holiday Inn (Lhasa Fandian)
No 1 Minzu Lu. The restaurants here are well worth trying because of the priority given to this hotel for all foodstuffs. Western, Tibetan and Chinese food.

### Barkhor Café
Enjoys fine views of the Jokhang, Potala and mountains. Open 10 am–8 pm daily. Tibetan, Chinese and Western food.

Half a dozen Moslem restaurants can be found in Old Lhasa's Moslem quarter, such as the **Qinghai**, on a wide street near the mosque. Elsewhere are the **Qingzhen Chuncheng** on the Barkhor and the **Halal Restaurant** on Xingfu Dong Lu.

A seemingly endless strip of restaurants runs from the Holiday Inn eastwards. They are almost all managed by Sichuanese; good food can be found, including spring rolls and fresh vegetables. Expect to pay Rmb30–40 per person for a full meal.

## SHIGATSE
There are a number of good Sichuanese places on the street running north from the Sangzhuzi Hotel.

## GYANTSE
The range of food in Gyantse is limited. However, the kitchen at the **Gyantse Hotel** is good. A pleasant little Tibetan restaurant called **Zdem Dzo** is not far from the Hotel in the main street and has excellent *momos* (meat dumplings) safely cooked in a pressure cooker.

The clutch of restaurants in a shanty town of new Chinese immigrants around the crossroads guarantees indigestion. Because shops in Gyantse are small and poorly stocked, it is recommended to bring food and drinks from Lhasa or Shigatse.

# Travel Agencies

## LHASA
**China International Travel Service (CITS) / Tibet Tourist Corporation**
208 Beijing Xi Lu (opposite Holiday Inn)
tel 6336626 / 6332980
fax 6335277 / 6332980
telex 68009 ZM LASCN / 68018 TTC CN

**Tibet International Sports Travel (TIST)**
Himalaya Hotel
6 Lingkuo Dong Lu
tel 6323775 / 6322293 / 6334082
fax 6334855
telex 68019 TIST CN

**Tibet Tsedang CITS**
Room 1120, Holiday Inn
1 Minzu Lu
tel 6334324 / 6332221
fax 6332346

**Chinese Youth Travel Service (CYTS)**
Room 1106, Holiday Inn
1 Minzu Lu
tel 6324173
fax 6335588
(also has a branch opposite the Yak
Hotel on Beijing Dong Lu)

**Lhasa Travel Agency**
Suns Hotel (formerly Sunlight Hotel)
27 Linqu Lu
tel 6323196
fax 6335675
telex 68016 TRCLS CN

**Golden Bridge Travel**
13 Minzu Lu
tel 6323828
fax 6325832
telex 68002 GBTL CN

## Budget Lhasa Travel Agents
Many of these have appeared recently. It
is difficult to recommend any of these
especially, as the quality of the trip can
depend on which particular guide you
happen to be assigned—and some guides
are definitely better than others. Tibet
Potala Folk Travel Service near the Kirey
Hotel (with another branch inside the Yak
Hotel) and Nyingchi Travel, opposite the
Snowland Hotel, are both popular, as is
Tibet Traffic Travel a short distance east

of the Yak Hotel. All offer competitive
prices.

## Chengdu
**China International Travel Service**
(BOU), 180 Renmin Nan Lu, tel 29653,
25914, tlx 60154

**CAAC**
31 Bei Xin Jie, tel 3087, 3038

## Kathmandu
**Yeti Travel**
PO Box 76, Durbar Marg, tel 221754,
221739, tlx 2204

**Adventure Travel Nepal**
PO Box 242, Durbar Marg, tel 221379,
222706, tlx 2216

**Yak & Yeti (Nepal Travel Agency)**
PO Box 1501, Ram Shah Path,
tel 413188, 412899, tlx 2277

**Himalayan Encounters**
PO Box 2769, Thamel, tel 417426, fax
417133

# Hospitals

## Lhasa
**People's Hospital (Renmin Yiyuan)**, tel
6322200 (emergency), 6322177 This
hospital, on Linkuo Bei Lu northeast of
the Potala, is the biggest and best in Lhasa. The emergency ward, on the left as
you go in the main entrance, is open 24
hours. There are departments specialized

in, for example, infectious diseases, dentistry and breathing and altitude problems.

**Mendzekhang Tibetan Hospital**, tel 6324211 (emergency), 6323244, Yuthok Lu, east of the Jokhang square.
This hospital uses traditional Tibetan treatment and some Western methods. Examination includes pulse diagnosis. Tibetan medicines use herbs and minerals primarily.

**Military Hospital Dental Clinic**, Beijing Xi Lu, near Holiday Inn
This new, well-equipped facility is recommended over the dentistry department at the Renmin Hospital, because of the latter's 'if in doubt, yank it out' approach. There are excellent dental facilities at West China Medical University in Chengdu and in Kathmandu.

**Bank of China**, Main Branch
Linkuo Xi Lu, west of the Potala

**Bank of China**
Beijing Dong Lu, next to Kirey Hotel

**Telecommunications Office**
Linkuo Dong Lu, at southwest point of roundabout opposite the Ying Qiao Hotel.

**Post Office**
Beijing Zhong Lu, near the Potala

CHENGDU
**United States Consulate**
Room 135, West Wing, Jinjiang Hotel, tel 51421, tlx 60128

KATHMANDU
**Chinese Embassy**
Baluwatar, tel 412589

# Other Useful Addresses

LHASA
**Public Security Bureau (PSB)**
Linkuo Bei Lu, just east of Sera Lu

**Civil Aviation Administration of China**
(CAAC, Zhongguo Minhang) Niang Re Lu, on the left when coming from Beijing Dong Lu

**Lhasa Bus Station**
Jin Zhu Zhong Lu, south of the Norbulingka

Practical information, such as telephone numbers, opening hours and hotel and restaurant prices, is notoriously subject to being outdated by changes or inflation. The author welcomes corrections and suggestions from guidebook users; please write to Local Colour Ltd, G/F 2 Lower Kai Yuen Lane, North Point, Hong Kong

# Tibetan Language Guide

*by Milan M Melvin*

The following list of Tibetan words and phrases, though all too brief, is sufficient for you to acquire the basic necessities and, depending on your inclination, to get out of or into trouble. Tibetans are wonderful, fun-loving people and even this small sample of their language can launch you into some unforgettable relationships.

## PRONUNCIATION

The vowel *a* must be pronounced like the *a* in *father*—soft and long, unless it appears as *ay*, in which case it is pronounced as in *say* or *day*. Note that words beginning with either b or p, d or t and g or k are pronounced halfway between the normal pronounciation of these consonant pairs (eg, b or p), and they are aspirated, like words starting with an h. A slash through a letter indicates the neutral vowel sound *uh*.

## WORD ORDER

Simple Tibetan sentences are constructed as follows:

| Subject | Object | Verb |
|---------|--------|------|
| I | mountains | going |
| *Nga* | *kang ree la* | *dro ge ray* |

The verb is always last.

## VERB TENSES

Tibetan verbs are composed of two parts: the root, which carries the meaning of the verb, and the ending, which indicates the tense (past, present or future). The simplest and most common verb form, consisting of the root plus the ending *-ge ray*, can be used for the present and future tenses. The root is strongly accented in speech. In order to form the past tense, substitute the ending *-song*.

> *nyo ge ray* means, loosely, 'buying, going to buy'
> *nyo song* means 'bought'

Only the verb roots are given in this glossary; remember to add the appropriate endings.

## PRONOUNS

| | | | |
|---|---|---|---|
| I | *nga* | we | *nga-tso* |
| you (singular) | *kherang* | you (plural) | *kirang-tso* |
| he, she, it | *korang/ko, morang, dee* | they | *korong-tso* |
| | | this | *deela, dee* |

| | |
|---|---|
| my, mine | nge, ngay, nga rang ghee |
| your, yours (singular) | kherang ghee |
| his, hers, its | korang ghee, mo rang ghee, dei |
| our, ours | ngarang-tso yee |
| your, yours (plural) | kirang-tso yee |
| their, theirs | korang-tso yee |

## RELATIONS

| | |
|---|---|
| man, husband | kyoga |
| woman, wife | keimen |
| child | poo goo |
| father | pa ba, pa la |
| mother | ah ma |
| relative | poonjah |
| boy | bu |
| girl | bu mo |
| older brother | cholag |
| older sister | ah jee la |
| younger brother/sister | ogma |
| name | ming la |

## TIME

| | |
|---|---|
| minute | ka ma |
| hour | chutso |
| morning | sho kay |
| afternoon | nyeen goon |
| day | nhee ma, shak ma |
| week | dun tak |
| month | da wa |
| year | lo |
| day before yesterday | ke nyee ma |
| yesterday | ke sang |
| last night | dang gong |
| today | taa ring |
| tomorrow | sang nyee, sang |

| | |
|---|---|
| day after tomorrow | nang nyee |
| always | tak par |
| now | tanda, ta ta |

## NUMBERS

| | |
|---|---|
| one | cheek |
| two | nhee |
| three | soom |
| four | shee |
| five | nga |
| six | trook |
| seven | doon |
| eight | gaye |
| nine | goo |
| ten | tchoo |
| eleven | tchoo cheek |
| twelve | tchoo nhee |
| thirteen | tchoo soom |
| fourteen | tchoo shee |
| fifteen | tchoo nga |
| sixteen | tchoo trook |
| seventeen | tchoo doon |
| eighteen | tchup gaye |
| nineteen | tchur goo |
| twenty | nhee shoo tamba |
| twenty-one | nhee shoo tsa cheek |
| twenty-two | nhee shoo tsa nhee |
| twenty-three | nhee shoo tsa soom |
| twenty-four | nhee shoo tsa shee |
| twenty-five | nhee shoo tsa nga |
| twenty-six | nhee shoo tsa trook |
| twenty-seven | nhee shoo tsa doon |
| twenty-eight | nhee shoo tsa gaye |
| twenty-nine | nhee shoo tsa goo |
| thirty | soom tchoo tamba |
| forty | sheep joo tamba |
| fifty | ngup tchoo tamba |
| sixty | trook tchoo tamba |
| seventy | doon tchoo tamba |

| | | | |
|---|---|---|---|
| eighty | *kyah joo tamba* | candle | *yangla* |
| ninety | *koop tchoo tamba* | cave | *trak phuk* |
| one hundred | *gyah tamba* | cigarette | *thamag* |
| two hundred | *ngee gyah* | cooking pot | *hai yoom, rak sang* |
| three hundred | *soom gyah* | cup | *shalkar* |
| | | dog | *kee, kyee* |

## FOOD

| | | | |
|---|---|---|---|
| barley | *droo, nay* | donkey | *poon goo* |
| beef | *lang sha* | fire | *may* |
| breakfast | *shokja* | house | *kang ba* |
| butter | *mar* | hill | *ree* |
| cheese | *choo ra* | kerosene | *sa noom* |
| chicken meat | *cha sha* | kettle | *khuti* |
| chilli peppers | *mar tsa* | knife | *tee, tree* |
| corn | *droo* | lake | *tso* |
| dinner | *kong dak ka lak* | matches | *tsak ta* |
| egg | *go nga* | medicine | *men* |
| flour | *to sheep, pak pay* | pill | *ree poo* |
| food | *kalak* | moon | *da wa* |
| fruit | *shing dong* | mountain | *ghang ree* |
| lunch | *nyeen goong ka lak* | mountain-pass | *la* |
| meat | *sha* | rain | *char pa* |
| milk | *o ma* | river | *tsang po, chu* |
| onion | *tsong* | rock | *do* |
| potato | *sho ko* | room | *kang mee* |
| rice | *dray* | snow | *kang,ka* |
| roasted barley flour | *tsampa* | spoon | *tur ma, too ma* |
| sugar | *chee ma ka ra* | star | *kar ma* |
| tea | *jah* | stomach | *tro ko* |
| vegetables | *ngup tsay, tsay* | sun | *nyee ma* |
| wheat | *tro, dro* | thread | *koo ba* |
| | | Tibet | *Pø* |

## OTHER NOUNS

| | | | |
|---|---|---|---|
| | | Tibetan language | *Pø khee* |
| bag | *noe fey* | Tibetan people | *Pø ba* |
| blanket | *nyal che* | trail | *lam ga* |
| book (common) | *deb* | umbrella | *nyee doo* |
| book (religious) | *pay zya* | water | *tchoo, chu* |
| boots | *som ba, lham* | Westerner | *nupchokpa* |
| bridge | *sam ba* | wind | *loong* |
| | | big wind | *bo chem bo* |

| | |
|---|---|
| wood | *shing* |

## VERBS

| | |
|---|---|
| arrive | *lep* |
| bring | *kay sho* |
| buy | *nyo* |
| carry | *care* |
| (to feel) cold | *khyak* |
| come | *yong* |
| cook | *ka lak so* |
| drink | *toong* |
| eat | *shay sa* |
| forget | *jay, chay* |
| get up | *lang* |
| give | *tay, nan* |
| go | *dro, do* |
| (to be) hungry | *tro ko tok* |
| learn | *lap* |
| look | *meek ta* |
| make, fix | *so* |
| see | *ton* |
| sell | *tsong* |
| (to be) sick | *na* |
| sit, stay | *day, shook* |
| teach | *lap* |
| wait | *goo* |
| work | *le ka jhay* |

## ADJECTIVES

| | |
|---|---|
| bad | *duk jah* |
| beautiful | *nying jhe po* |
| big | *chem bo* |
| cold | *trang mo* |
| different | *kye per, cheek be ma ray* |
| empty | *tong ba* |
| expensive | *gong chem bo* |
| few | *tet see tet see* |
| full | *gang* |

| | |
|---|---|
| good | *yak po* |
| heavy | *jee po, jee ba tsa po* |
| hot | *tsa bo* |
| light | *yang bo, yang* |
| lost | *lak song* |
| much, many | *mang bo* |
| same | *nang shing* |
| small | *choon choon* |
| strong | *shyook chem bo* |
| thirsty | *ka kam* |
| weak | *shook choon choon* |

## ADVERBS

| | |
|---|---|
| down | *ma la* |
| far | *ta ring bo* |
| here | *deh roo* |
| left | *yon ba* |
| near | *nye bo* |
| quickly | *gyok po, gyok po* |
| really | *ngo ne* |
| there | *pa roo, pa ge* |
| right | *yay ba* |
| slow | *ka lee* |
| up | *ya la* |
| very | *she ta, she tai* |

## MISCELLANEOUS

| | |
|---|---|
| again | *yangya* |
| and | *tang, ta* |
| how much, how many | *gha tzo* |
| maybe | *cheek chay na* |
| other, another | *shen da, yem ba* |
| sometimes | *tsam tsam* |
| where from | *ka ne* |
| what | *ka ray* |
| where to | *ka ba, ka par, ka roo* |
| who | *soo* |

why                     *ka ray chay nay*

## PHRASES

hello, greetings        *tashi delek*
enough, stop            *deek song*
finished                *tsar song, deek song*
right, really, yes      *ray, la ray*
I do not understand     *ha ko ma song*
I understand, I know    *ha ko gee doo, ha ko song*
very important          *kay chembo, ne ka chem bo*
what is this called?    *dee ming la ka ray ser ge ray? dee ka ra ray?*
how much is (this)?     *(dee la) gong ka tzø ray?*
it doesn't matter       *kay kay chee ge*

                        *ma ray, ghay yo ma ray*
be careful              *sap sap*
slowly                  *ka lee ka lee*
I am hungry             *nga tro ko to kee doo*
are/is there any (onions)   *(tsong) doo-ay, (tsong) doog-ay?*
please bring (onions)   *(tsong) kay sho ah*
okay, thanks            *la so, tukjay cheh*
goodnight               *sim ja nang ro*
how far is (Lhasa)?     *(Lhasa la) gyan lø yø ray?*
how are you?            *khyorang depo yin pe?*
how are you? (polite form)   *kherang kusuk depo yin pe?*
I am fine               *Nga depo yin, la yin*

# Index